TWO OLD FOOLS FAIR DINKUM

NEW YORK TIMES BESTSELLING AUTHOR

OLD FOOLS SERIES
BOOK 7

VICTORIA TWEAD

Ant Press
Large Print
Edition

Copyright © 2025 Victoria Twead

Formatted and published by Ant Press - www.antpress.org

ISBN Ebook edition: 978-1-922476-95-1

ISBN Paperback edition: 978-1-922476-70-8

ISBN Hardback edition: 978-1-922476-71-5

ISBN Large Print edition: 978-1-922476-72-2

ISBN Hardback Large Print edition: 978-1-922476-73-9

Digital edition available from Amazon.

LARGE PRINT EDITION

All rights reserved.

Please note that this book, aside from the recipes, is the original creation of the author. The author wrote and compiled it entirely without the use of any artificial intelligence.

USE OF THIS BOOK FOR AI TRAINING:

Without in any way limiting the author's and publisher's exclusive rights under copyright, any use of this publication to "train" generative artificial intelligence (AI) technologies to generate text is expressly prohibited. The author reserves all rights to license uses of this work for generative AI training and development of machine learning language models.

No part of this book may be reproduced in any form or by any electronic or mechanical means, including information storage and retrieval systems, without written permission from the author, except for the use of brief quotations in a book review.

THE OLD FOOLS SERIES

Chickens, Mules and Two Old Fools is the 7th book in the *Old Fools* series by New York Times and Wall Street Journal bestselling author, Victoria Twead.

Two Old Fools
Chickens, Mules and Two Old Fools
Two Old Fools ~ Olé!
Two Old Fools on a Camel
Two Old Fools in Spain Again
Two Old Fools in Turmoil
Two Old Fools Down Under
Two Old Fools, Fair Dinkum
Two Old Fools Find their Tribe

Prequels
One Young Fool in Dorset
One Young Fool in South Africa

FREE PHOTO BOOK
TO BROWSE OR DOWNLOAD

For photographs and additional unpublished material to accompany this book, browse or download the

Free Photo Book
from
www.victoriatwead.com/free-stuff

For Joe

*Greatly loved, greatly missed.
11th July, 1951 - 28th May, 2024*

CONTENTS

1. PLAYING POSSUM	1
Rhonda's Chocolate Weet-Bix Slice	17
2. ALIENS AND A CONTORTIONIST	19
Barbecued Sweet Potatoes	34
3. VERY FRIENDLY	36
Easter Bunny Tails	50
4. MEXICAN BROTHERS AND A HOLIDAY	52
Mexican Street Corn	63
5. BIKES	65
Pan-Fried Asparagus	78
6. HOUNDINI	80
German Butterkuchen	92
7. PAINFUL ARMS AND LEGS	94
Christmas Tree Waffles	104
8. COMING HOME	106
Queensland Vintage Upside-Down Cake	121
9. SKIP	124
Homemade Parrot Treats	135
10. DOGS, BIG AND SMALL	137
Paula's Nonna's Frittata	152
11. VISITORS FROM OVERSEAS	154
Hummingbird	169

12. TERRIBLE NIGHT, PERFECT DAY	171
Easy Lemon Spritzer	185
13. A NICE SMILE	187
White Chocolate Snowflakes	198
14. PRANKS	200
Pipis in Ginger and Sweet Chilli Sauce	213
15. SHEILA	215
Welsh Rarebit	228
16. MAIDEN VOYAGE	230
A Zombie Hand for Halloween	247
17. KARMA	249
Beer-Battered Deep Fried Fish	262
18. TRIPS	264
Sausages with Onion and Apple	276
19. DRAMAS	278
Mexican Beef Pizza	291
20. MORE DRAMAS	294
Sunset Cookies	308
21. GADGETS	310
Super-Quick Air Fryer Hot Dogs	323
22. DOGS, DOGS, DOGS	325
Homemade Grain-Free Doggy Dinner	339
23. FIRE	341
Fiery Red Pepper Potatoes	355
24. THREE TO TEN DAYS	357
Fire-Roasted Cherry Tomato Salsa	373
25. RAINDROPS AND SPIDERS	375

Apple Snack Cake	385
26. CHRISTMAS BEETLES AND COWS	388
Lattice Apple Pie	398
27. SHEEP	400
Slow-Cooked Roast Leg of Lamb	413
28. PLAGUES	415
Spooky Spider Devilled Eggs	427
29. Epilogue	429
A request …	433
A gift to my readers …	435
So what happened next?	437
The Old Fools memoirs series	442
Dear Fran, Love Dulcie	447
The Sixpenny Cross series	449
The Stillwater Murders by Victoria Twead	451
The Bone Garden by Victoria Twead	455
About the Author	459
Contacts and Links	461
Victoria's Bookstore	463
More Ant Press Memoirs	464

1
PLAYING POSSUM

"Vicky! Percy is back in the garden. He's looking through the window, waiting."

"Is he? Good thing I went shopping today. I'll get him an apple."

I adore Australia, especially the abundant, extraordinary wildlife and kaleidoscope of birds that share our lives. Carpet snakes love to live in loft spaces, big, blue-tongued lizards bask in our gardens, and some of us are lucky enough to enjoy twilight visits from possums, like Percy. Joe and I loved them all.

Oh, apart from the spiders. Yes, everyone knows spiders do a grand job, but try as I might, I can't love spiders. Every Australian has a spider story, and many of us have possum stories, too.

"Oh, you don't find possums *cute*, do you?" I've been asked by Facebook friends from the US.

Well, actually, I do.

There are some interesting differences between North American possums and Australian possums. Although both are marsupials, Australian possums are more closely related to kangaroos and koalas. North American possums are typically bigger with a rat-like tail, while Australian possums are smaller and have a bushy tail.

Australian possums are highly adaptable and thrive in urban environments above our heads, happily climbing buildings and running along fences. North American possums 'play possum'; Australian possums don't.

Well, only rarely.

My friend Tammy told me this possum story, and it is just too good to keep to myself. Her friend, who I'll call Gina, took a deep breath and related the sorry tale.

"It was a really hot day, and I decided to sit out in the shade on the deck," Gina began. "I was just settling down when I saw something odd. A possum. It was just lying there, on its back, dead."

"Where? On the deck?" asked Tammy.

"Yes. Well, actually, on the damp soil in the big

plant pot where I'd just planted a beautiful camelia."

"You are kidding! What did you do?"

"Well, I called my husband, of course. 'Jim,' I called, 'come quickly, there's a dead possum in our camelia.'"

Jim hurried out and the pair peered at the possum.

"I wonder what it died of," said Gina. "And why in our plant pot?"

"I don't really want to pick it up," Jim said. "We don't know how long it's been there and it might be riddled with maggots. I'll grab the pot and carry it through the house and deal with it out in the back garden."

The pot was big and heavy, but he circled his arms around it, braced his knees and began to stagger through the house with it. The leaves of the shrub rattled with every step he took.

Just as he crossed the tiled area near their dining table, in front of the TV, something most unexpected happened.

The possum sat up.

For a split second, human and possum stared at each other, eyeball to eyeball.

Jim's jaw dropped. The possum shrieked and exploded out of the plant pot. Jim gasped and lost his grip on the pot, which smashed on the tiled floor, spreading earthenware shards, soil and foliage far and wide.

"It was asleep!" squeaked the horror-struck Gina. "Quick! Chase it out!"

The terrified possum was now wide awake and running across the dining table. It leapt onto the back of the couch and then sprang to the mantlepiece, pausing to stare at the couple over its shoulder.

"Quick!" yelled Gina.

Jim galloped through the wet soil and lunged for the possum. He missed it entirely, tripped over the rug and slammed down onto the coffee table, smashing the glass and sending a vase and its contents flying.

"#@%," yelled Jim, picking himself up and lunging again. His shoes crunched on glass and crushed chrysanthemums as he headed towards the mantlepiece.

But this marsupial was feisty. It shot along the mantlepiece, dislodging ornaments and family photographs that crashed to the floor.

"You #@&% little #@%," yelled Jim.

The door to the garden was wide open and beckoning, but the possum wasn't ready to depart. Like a trapeze artist, it sprang across to the door jamb, climbed to the top and considered the room before leaping to a tall bookcase. There, it disappeared behind the top-row titles for a few seconds.

Gina slapped the side of the bookcase, hoping to flush it out. That worked. The possum rocketed out, and the chase was back on. Gina tried to shoo it towards the door, but it leapt onto the breakfast bar where Gina had set out a tray of freshly baked chocolate-iced slices to set.

"No!" roared Gina and hurled a cushion.

The cushion missed its target but knocked over a salt cellar. The possum stopped in its tracks.

Suddenly, it caught sight of the open door. An escape into the outside world and possum normality. It skipped over the baking tray, leaving pawprints in the chocolate icing and jumped to the floor before shooting out of the door to freedom.

Jim and Gina gaped at the carnage. Glass, crushed flowers, muddy footprints, leaves and ornaments littered the floor. The broken coffee table lay in a puddle of water.

"Look at the mess…" breathed Gina.

Another door opened, framing their teenage son.

"I heard shouting," he said. "Is everything okay?"

Then his eyes swept the wrecked room,

lingered on the soil, the smashed vase, the ruined blooms, the broken coffee table, and finishing at the cushion, spilt salt, and chocolate mess on the counter.

"*Oh boy!*" he said, admiration in his voice. "That must have been some argument you guys had! Have you made it up now?"

A possum named Percy roamed our garden, too, but thankfully, he behaved far better than Gina and Jim's possum. I was grateful to Percy because he entertained Joe in the evenings. He hung from the rafters of our pergola by his tail, looking in through the window, waiting for an apple to be handed to him. Not much made Joe smile in those dark days, but Percy's big, brown, liquid eyes and cheekiness did.

PLAYING POSSUM

Percy the possum

Even though Joe fought bravely, you'll remember that he nearly lost his life at the end of 2016. But to everybody's astonishment, including his own, he didn't die.

Healing was slow, but gradually, Joe gained strength and was discharged from the hospital to come home. I inherited the terrifying task of nursing him. Thank goodness, those fear-filled days when he kept tapping on death's door gradually became distant, fading memories.

Eventually, one happy day, I called the company that supplied his oxygen concentrator and portable oxygen tanks. The home oxygen concentrator Joe had did a wonderful job of taking in ordinary air, removing the nitrogen and supplying him with oxygen-enriched air to breathe.

"How can I help you?" asked the nice lady.

"Thank you for your assistance over these past months," I said, "but my husband won't be needing his oxygen concentrator any more."

"Oh, I'm so sorry to hear your sad news," said the lady politely. "Condolences. I'm sorry for your loss."

"No, Joe's breathing is getting stronger. He can manage without it!"

There was a slight pause, and when she spoke again I could hear the smile in the lady's voice.

"Well! That's wonderful news! I'll update your account and arrange for the machine to be collected. I have to say, I don't get news like that very often in this job! Thank you for making my day."

At first, Joe barely left the house, but slowly his confidence grew. When I took Lola out for a run on the oval, he came, too. I parked the car so that he could sit and enjoy the vast blue sky. The bush was alive with wildlife. We heard the territorial laugh of kookaburras and he watched them drop like stones from the high fence to snap up unsuspecting bugs. Eagles often wheeled overhead in lazy circles. Sulphur-crested cockatoos grazed in the grass alongside pink and grey galahs.

Lola, our spoodle, or 'cockapoo', as cocker spaniel/poodle crosses are known in the UK, has always had a tennis ball obsession. Offered a ball, a treat or a pat, she chose the ball every time. So we all enjoyed our frequent visits to the oval. Lola and I made friends with other dogs and dog owners while Joe watched us and the wildlife from the car.

Days passed, and he felt strong enough to leave the car and lean on the railings, watching.

"I think it's time you joined me shopping," I said one day. "It'll do you good. A change of scenery."

"I can't walk around the shops!"

"No, but you can ride."

"A wheelchair? We're not getting one of those."

"Nope, they offer those motorised cars at the mall. Free, too. You just have to book it in advance."

"Invalid carriages?"

"Well, yes, but they're just electric cars, really. Even the racing cars in Formula One are electric nowadays."

The combination of our builder, Fred, and his construction team diving in and out of our house doing finishing-off jobs and my relentless nagging finally wore him down. He agreed.

I learnt an interesting lesson that shopping day.

I clearly hadn't thought the process through properly. I parked the car, walked into the mall and approached the desk. Signing for the little red, shiny car didn't take long, and I was handed the key.

Now what?

It was too far for Joe to walk to collect the invalid carriage, so I had to drive it myself. Reluctantly, I climbed in. It had a steering wheel, a brake and two speeds: Painfully Slow and Excruciatingly Slow. I set off. The journey out to the car park and to our car was very short, but it felt like a hundred miles.

Plenty of people milled about, and most of them silently swerved away, avoiding eye contact at all costs. I felt invisible.

Just two people *did* speak to me. One was a man carrying a yellow shopping bag who stopped to let me through the automatic doors.

"Thank you," I muttered, stopping myself from explaining that I wasn't really disabled.

"You're welcome!" he bellowed.

At the pedestrian crossing, I stopped beside a lady who looked down at me.

"Nice day, isn't it?" she shouted as we both waited for a car to pass. That would have been normal except that she *shouted* it.

That day, I concluded that if you are driving an

invalid carriage, people assume you must also be deaf.

I arrived at our parked car, stopped and jumped out of the little red car. I hadn't enjoyed the experience at all, and it humbled me. When I felt eyes watching me, I turned my head and recognised the man with the yellow shopping bag who had stepped back to let me through the automatic doors. Judging by his surprised expression, he'd watched me leap out of the invalid car, not hampered by any disability whatsoever.

"I'm not disabled, I was just…" I started.

But he'd already made up his mind that I was a disreputable fraud and was probably cheating the government and getting undeserved handouts. With a look of disgust, he swung away. I never finished my sentence.

Sometimes, the family came to visit, which was always a tonic. Granddaughter Winter had become a fast crawler and was into everything. At that age, she constantly put things into her mouth and needed watching all the time.

Her big sister, Indy, was growing tall like her

daddy, Cam. The two little girls couldn't have been more different. Indy had curly, blonde hair, and Winter was a brunette with hair as straight as a yard of pump water, as my mother-in-law would have said.

February is the height of summer, but Australia never ceases to deliver surprises, whatever the season. Cam, Karly, Indy and Winter spent the day with us and the weather was perfect. However, soon after they left, huge, strange-coloured clouds banked overhead.

"The sky looks really odd," said Joe, returning to the house.

"Quick!" shouted a voice.

I swung round to see two boys dashing across the street towards me.

"Get blankets!" shouted the other boy.

In the house opposite us lived a delightful Tongan family. Two of the children, the oldest teenage boys, wore bicycle helmets. They reached me, panting.

"Cover your car!"

I stared at them for a split second before diving into the house to grab blankets.

"What on earth…" began Joe, but the Tongan brothers' urgency had fired me into action. No time to explain.

With the boys' help, I threw the blankets over the car. Just in time.

At first, I heard single metallic clangs like bullets hitting signposts. Then faster, faster, closer together, hailstones beating a tattoo on the hot metal roof of the pergola.

Now I understood why the boys were wearing helmets. The ice pellets bounced, sending up steam and spray, the deafening roar forcing us to shout above the clatter. The ground turned white with ice.

We thought this weather event was dramatic, but thanks to the Tongan boys, our car was not damaged.

Walnut-sized hailstones

That day, our hailstones were polite, walnut-sized balls of ice. In comparison, the hail in parts of Sydney resembled white mandarins. Nothing could have prepared Cam and Karly for what they would find waiting for them.

By the time they reached home, much of the ice on the streets had already melted, but piles of white still banked up in shaded areas.

"Looks like it's been bad here," said Cam as they walked up the drive and put the key in the lock.

Their house was large, with big, round skylights letting extra light into every corner of the spacious rooms. The force of the balls of ice had smashed through all the skylights, allowing giant hailstones to pile up on the polished wooden floors, carpets, and furniture. There, the ice sat, melting into puddles of water that soaked into everything. Tables, chairs, sofas, and rugs were drenched. Water had seeped into electrical sockets and lighting fixtures.

Outside was no better. The chicken house roof had been bombed. The chickens were unscathed but must have been terrified throughout the onslaught, judging by the dropped feathers. The little thatched Bali hut with the wooden seating was ruined, and the children's outdoor toys, like the sand-table, were broken heaps of plastic, as though a monstrous hammer had attacked them.

Australia is accustomed to wild weather, and

hailstorms frequently occur. For that reason, hail damage is almost always covered by house and car insurance, so the next step was to contact their insurance company.

Weeks later, the valuers arrived with clipboards and calculators in hand. I was there, and the house was particularly chaotic at the time. Little Winter was crawling at a terrific speed and needed watching every second. Indy, now four years old, had friends round to play. She was Barbie-crazy and every Barbie doll, Barbie accessory, Barbie outfit, car, pony and boyfriend littered the floor.

"I can't find Barbie's other sneaker," Indy announced above the general noise.

It was a full-time job extracting tiny plastic stiletto shoes, or handbags, or other Barbie items from Winter's mouth. LJ, the family dog, had decided that our dog, Lola, was a really annoying little sister, and he was intent on putting her in her place. In the background, the TV played *Frozen*, but nobody was watching.

"I'm sorry about the mess," said Karly.

"That's okay," said the valuers as they took photos of the broken skylights, carefully avoiding trampling the world of Barbie, small children and dogs under their feet.

Indy watched intently, her Barbie temporarily forgotten.

"What's that?" she asked, pointing at something in one of the valuer's hands.

"This?"

Indy's blonde curls nodded.

"That's my measuring tape. We need to know how big this coffee table is."

"Oh," said Indy, underwhelmed. She turned back to her Barbie. "My daddy's got one of those. But my daddy's measurer is *much* bigger than yours."

The valuers didn't take offence and finished their tour of the hail damage. They submitted their report. The result was brand new skylights, new carpets, furniture, outdoor toys for the kids, the Bali hut fixed and a posh new chicken house.

The hailstorm quickly became a distant memory. I hadn't lived in Australia long enough to appreciate the extent of extreme natural events that can occur in this vast continent. I didn't know it then, but the warning signs were already in place.

Drier than normal conditions persisted from the beginning of 2017. We were not aware that Australia was already in the grip of a deadly drought that would produce catastrophic consequences in the future.

RHONDA'S CHOCOLATE WEET-BIX SLICE

Well, this is something I didn't know! The breakfast cereal, Weetabix, is the British version of the original Australian Weet-Bix. Both Weet-Bix and Weetabix were invented by Bennison Osborne, an Australian.

Thanks for this recipe, Rhonda!

Ingredients (serves 4)

1 cup of Weet-Bix

1 cup self-raising flour

1 cup of coconut

1 tablespoon cocoa

6 oz (170g) butter

½ cup sugar

Method

Crush Weet-Bix.

Mix dry ingredients together, then add melted butter.

Place in a greased slice/brownie pan and flatten.

Cook in a moderate oven for 30 mins.

Leave to cool and top with chocolate icing while still warm.

Rhonda says, "I use basic icing made with icing sugar, cocoa, and hot water, and I usually double the mixture which fits nicely in a brownie pan."

2

ALIENS AND A CONTORTIONIST

It was March 2017, and the doctors had pronounced Joe strong enough for the journey back to the UK. The day came for him to leave. The shuttle bus driver who collected Joe to take him to Sydney airport wore a bright Hawaiian shirt. He grabbed Joe's suitcase and heaved it into the bus.

"All aboard," he said and climbed back into the cab.

"Don't worry, I'll be back in no time," said Joe, hugging me. "You know I need to see my specialists, get things sorted out."

"I know. Give my love to the family."

"Lollipop, look after your mistress while I'm away."

Lola's tail became a blur.

The bus swallowed Joe and drove away, up the street and around the corner. Out of sight. I turned back to the house, determined to keep myself busy, not allowing myself to slip into a black hole of depression.

There was still so much to do, and tidying the garden was high on my list. Autumn was coming and most of the neighbouring trees were happily dumping their leaves in our pool. And there was a peculiar growth inside one of our plants that I wanted to investigate.

When I lived in England, I loved gardening. I had my own greenhouse and pottered in it for hours. I planted seedlings, propagated and planned future beds of perennials. I pored over seed catalogues and dreamed of white gardens, and planned raised vegetable beds.

However, when we moved to Spain, everything changed. In our mountain village, the soil baked granite-hard in the summer and froze granite-hard in the winter. Plants in pots soon gave up and died. Only our beloved grapevine, a few very hardy shrubs and some tough Mediterranean geraniums survived. Olive trees and orange orchards thrived, but my garden plants? Not so much.

When we made the decision to move to

Australia, I looked forward to taking up gardening once again. Maybe I'd even have a greenhouse?

That dream didn't pan out as I expected either. Imagine realising that everything you had ever learnt about gardening no longer applies. Imagine gathering up all that knowledge acquired over decades, screwing it up and tossing it into a bin. Useless. Not only is the wildlife endearingly crazy in Australia, but the plants are equally so.

In England, I knew quite a bit about grafting and propagation, for instance. But here in Australia, different rules apply. One can hack off a bit of an old tree trunk, shove it in a random part of the garden and walk away. Or poke a dead stick left lying around into soil. No extra water required, or dusting with rooting hormones, or special attention of any kind. Come back in a few weeks and the stick, or trunk, will still be standing proud and probably already sporting some fresh, new leaves. Miraculous. Fair dinkum.

Before I continue, perhaps I should clear up the 'fair dinkum' question. What does it mean? Hmm. I think it's used to emphasise that something is fair, good, true or genuine. For instance, 'The meal was expensive but fair dinkum considering how rare those mushrooms are. It's a fair dinkum Polish restaurant.'

The origin of the phrase is in dispute. British Melvyn Bragg insists that it originated in the Midlands and referred to a fair day's work. Thus, it means fair play.

"Not so," argues an Australian expert. "Fair dinkum was a response of the early Chinese gold miners to the question: Are you finding a fair amount of gold? They'd answer: Yes, fair dinkum, because *din-kum* means good gold."

It gradually became adopted as a positive response and I've heard it used often. Indeed, our builder, Fred, had a Jack Russell named Fair Dinkum, or Dinks for short.

A while ago, Fred had made me a strong, wooden plant trough. My aim was to plant some bamboos that would grow tall and act as a screen between our neighbours and us. The trough was excellent, and the bamboos thrived. Unfortunately, Fred hadn't realised how strong bamboo roots are, and they quickly pushed out the bottom of the trough. He rebuilt it for me and I applied myself to replanting the bamboos.

It wasn't easy. The bags of soil were heavy and the plants unwieldy. Lola's paws turned black as she helped by digging at the rootballs. Digging is a spoodle trait, I'm told, and I believe it. Soil flew into the air.

"Lola, just stop that!" I said, and groaned at the mess.

Lola's digging had revealed some rather unpleasant tenants. Indignant fat, white grubs squirmed, unearthed by Lola's eager scrabbling.[1]

A slight movement caught my eye. A kookaburra sat on the fence regarding us closely, his head on one side. I'm not sure why, but birds and animals in Australia seem so much tamer than European creatures.

"Are these what you're waiting for, Kookie?" I asked. I had gardening gloves on and a fat grub writhed in my palm.

The kookaburra stretched tall then leaned forward. Before I knew it, he spread his wings and swooped the short distance between us. With the greatest of delicacy, the grub was snatched up and the kookaburra settled back on the fence. Lola noticed nothing.

"Well, Kookie," I said. *Bon appétit.* You've got the job."

We all worked hard that day. Lola stayed in charge of soil displacement while the kookaburra took on pest disposal duties and I carried out the bamboo relocation.

---

[1]. Youtube link to the grubs I dug up and fed to the kookaburra https://youtu.be/XQVbggSI7XQ

"What a team," I said in my best Schwarzenegger voice as I tidied up after the job was complete. It was true: my two companions had made a dull project a delight. And I hadn't had time to miss Joe.

A great, green canoe-shaped leaf fell to the ground, making me jump. It was about the same length as my leg, tough as leather and heavy. I recognised it at once. It wasn't a leaf at all, although it had plummeted from one of our palm trees. It was a protective pod, or casing, for the palm tree's flowers.

And what strange flowers they were! Perfectly folded within the casing like a newborn about to emerge, the flowers developed and swelled. Then, when the pod could contain them no more, it split, allowing the contents to burst out. The empty casing dropped to the ground.

ALIENS AND A CONTORTIONIST

The casing with flowers about to burst out

Within 24 hours, the flowers shook themselves free and hung high above our heads. I call them 'flowers' because I don't have sufficient botanical knowledge to apply the correct name, but the whole set-up is fascinating. Freed from the pod, a spooky white branch stretched out. I imagined that was how a corpse's arm might look. Numerous, long fingers dangled loosely, swaying in the wind. The branch is not wood, nor anything I have ever seen in the plant world. It looks and feels like waxy, white silicon. Clustered all over the silicon fingers cling countless tiny pink balls.

The first time we found a giant pod on the ground and looked up to see the gleaming white arm dangling its pink bobbles high above us, we gaped. It was so spectacularly peculiar that Joe and I named it an 'alien'.

"I've never seen anything like it," declared Joe.

"Nor me. Let's watch and see what it grows into."

The tiny pink balls grew fast until they were the size of peas, then marbles. They flushed to a deep red, packed tight, competing for space on the white fingers.

"Have you seen the alien lately?" I had asked Joe.

"No, why?"

"Look at those balls! They are huge! They look like giant cherries and I can see they've already started dropping."

Lola and I went out to look, and sure enough, they were dropping off in their hundreds. I picked one up, expecting it to be soft, like a cherry. It wasn't; it was as hard as wood and bounced on the dry ground when dropped. Lola tasted one and quickly spat it out.

The wind plucked the red balls from the white arm, tossed them into the pool, and littered the pool area with them. Because of their sheer number, they were a nightmare to clear up. The ones that I missed split open, and happy little palm tree seedlings sprouted everywhere.

I vowed never to let it happen again, as I had no plan to live in a dense rainforest. Learning from that first experience, we sawed off the white arm as soon as it had flung off its protective pod.

The problem was that we had numerous palm trees, although only a few gave birth to these aliens. The ones that did were the tallest and the aliens were well beyond our reach, even with a stepladder. So we bought a saw on the end of a telescopic pole. Even that wasn't long enough, and we had to extend the pole by taping it to our long swimming pool brush.

That did the trick, but it was still a tricky job.

In the summer and autumn, we were on constant alien alert. Whoever pulled up the blinds first in the morning stared through the window, checking for the telltale pods lying on the ground.

"Alien!" Joe would shout and my heart sank.

We had to act fast. If we sawed it down straight away while it was still compact, before it spread its fingers, it would be much easier than when it was a huge flailing structure dropping on us from above. We had 24 hours.

"You get the steps, the tape and twine. I'll get the poles," I said. There was no time to lose.

We worked quickly, joining the poles together and manoeuvring the wheelbarrow into position, trying to judge where the pod would fall.

"Left a bit."

"No, don't put it there; it'll miss it completely."

"Listen to me, left a bit and back a foot or so."

It was hard to guess exactly where the alien would drop, and we always bickered about the barrow's position.

Next came the sawing. Squinting against the bright sky, we placed the saw blade against the gleaming white arm and took it in turns to rasp away, resting frequently.

"It's breaking away! Look out!"

High above us, the arm jerked and plummeted. It seldom fell where we predicted, but we cheered on the rare occasion it landed straight in the barrow.

"Woo-hoo!"

"Yay! Direct hit!"

"Bullseye!"

Each palm tree produced four aliens a year, and we had multiple palm trees.

Every year, the palm trees grew taller, and the aliens sprouted higher. Every year, they were harder to reach. And every year, I was secretly sorry because the waxy, white arms and fingers with their rosy clusters were quite beautiful. And we were killing the tree's babies.

"I'm so sorry, tree," I whispered.

"What did you say?" asked Joe.

"Nothing."

"Silly old fool," he said.

I checked that other plant with the peculiar growth. Surely it had grown several inches since I last looked?

This plant was a big variegated something-or-other, maybe a type of agave, and the growth was like a giant asparagus tip thrusting skywards. It was now waist-high. I vowed to keep an eye on it.

Like a giant asparagus

Not only was the plant growing almost before my eyes, but so were my granddaughters. Winter would celebrate her first birthday in April. How could time fly past so quickly?

Winter had taken her first steps but still crawled most of the time. She was super-fast and slippery as a buttered dolphin, as they say in a well-known Australian TV advert.

"Winter, where are you?"

Watching her was a full-time occupation.

"She's gone again. Joe, did you see where Winter went?"

"Nope."

We usually found her behind furniture or curtains doing something she shouldn't. Everything small enough to fit in her mouth needed to be tasted. Stones from the garden, beetles, earthworms. And bigger things needed to be tasted, too. I still have a video of Winter tasting Lola.[2]

My phone beeped, and I briefly wondered how we ever managed without mobile phones years ago.

My first mobile phone was a Christmas present in the 1980s and it was almost the size and weight of a brick. I was the first one in my circle of

---

2. Winter tasting Lola https://youtu.be/R1XTeqTCmCA

friends to have one, and we all jumped when it rang, which wasn't often. In those days, a mobile phone was just that, except it was too big and heavy to be very mobile. It didn't take pictures, calculate sums, send messages, or play music. It didn't show you maps, or recipes or translate foreign languages. Remember those days?

I recall an occasion when we were having a family barbecue in the garden with friends. Food was plain in those days and barbecues often relied on sausages and burgers, although we tried to be more inventive with our side dishes. I remember we had just discovered sweet potatoes.

The kids at the party were all about the same age, with my son, Shealan, probably being one of the oldest at about ten or eleven years of age.

"Mum, can we go to the shop?" he asked.

"I don't see why not," I said. "Just make sure all you kids stick together."

The shop was on the edge of the estate we lived on, not far away and with no busy roads to cross.

"Mum, can I take your phone?" he asked hopefully. In those days, possession of a mobile phone was an instant boost to one's street cred, especially if you were only ten years old.

I hesitated but decided it was quite a good

idea; he could always ring home if anything went wrong.

"Okay, but tie it to your belt loop so that you don't lose it or drop it."

Shealan did so and swaggered away with the phone sticking out of his pocket. The gang of kids swung down the path. Shealan held his head high, enjoying his status, aware of the envy emanating from his friends. He was cool, the only kid with a mobile phone.

"You should call him," somebody suggested after ten minutes or so.

"Good idea! He'd love that!" I said. "He'll feel really important."

I popped inside and dialled the mobile phone from our landline, smiling as I thought how much he would impress his friends by answering the call. I didn't realise that I was actually destroying any street cred he may have built up.

The mobile phone rang for quite a long time before he answered it and his voice sounded kind of strangled. I could hear hysterical laughter in the background.

"What's the matter?" I asked. "You sound a bit strange."

"How could you make me tie the phone to my belt loop?" he hissed. "I couldn't reach my ear. I had to fold myself in half to answer it!"

ALIENS AND A CONTORTIONIST

Oh dear. That explained the background laughter.

But that was 25 years or so ago; Shealan was approaching his forties now.

The phone in my hand beeped again and a text message flashed up.

> Shealan: Hi Mum, we're all booked and coming over for Easter. We'll be there in time for Winter's birthday! x

> Me: Awesome!!!! Can't wait to see you!

> Shealan: Daria's really excited.

> Me: Me too. I can't wait to meet her!

My son was flying over from the UK with his girlfriend, Daria. I hadn't seen him for ages and I'd never met Daria. I was beyond excited. But before they set foot in Australia and before Winter even reached her first birthday, my youngest granddaughter was the cause of much concern.

BARBECUED SWEET POTATOES

Serve these glistening sweet potato wedges as a side dish at a barbecue. From www.bbcgoodfood.com/recipes/barbecue-sesame-sweet-potatoes

Ingredients

6 sweet potatoes, washed and cut into wedges, about finger length

3 tbsp of your favourite vegetable oil

1 tbsp chopped ginger

1 chopped garlic clove

3 tbsp soy sauce

Juice of 1 lime

1 tbsp sesame seeds, black, white or mixed

50g (1.5oz) unsalted crushed peanuts

1 sliced green chilli

A few spring onions, chopped finely

Method

Lay the wedges of sweet potato on a large metal tray.

Drizzle with the oil, and season. Shake the tray to ensure the wedges are coated.

Cook on the barbecue (or in the oven) until they begin to soften and are a little charred, usually about 25 mins.

Place the lime juice, leftover oil, soy sauce, ginger and garlic into a bowl.

Whisk until thoroughly mixed.

Baste the sweet potatoes using some of your sauce.

Barbecue the wedges for a further 30-40 minutes, basting at intervals.

When the wedges are glazed, they will be sticky. This is the perfect time to remove from the heat and sprinkle with the crushed peanuts and sesame seeds.

Add a sprinkle of chopped chilli and spring onions, then serve.

Create a summer salad by tossing through handfuls of baby spinach leaves, curly kale, rocket or watercress.

3

VERY FRIENDLY

"Don't panic, just thought I'd let you know. We're at the hospital with Winter."

"Oh no! What's the matter with her?"

"Well," said Karly, and I could hear the concern in her voice. "You know how she puts everything in her mouth? We had one of those little round magnets stuck on the fridge and it's disappeared. We've searched for it everywhere and we can't find it."

"You think she's swallowed it?"

"Yup, very likely. You know what she's like."

I sighed. "But it's nine o'clock at night!"

"I know, I'd only just noticed it was missing this evening. Cam was out playing an ice hockey match, so I phoned the hospital for advice. They said swallowing a watch battery is the most dangerous thing, and that swallowing magnets is the second most dangerous thing. I couldn't risk it so I had to wake them both up and bring them in. We're in the waiting room, the girls are in their pyjamas and we're just waiting to get her X-rayed. Indy's falling asleep, but Winter is in holiday mode, having a lovely time. Here's the nurse now, speak to you later."

"Good luck, keep me posted…" But the phone was already dead.

No magnet showed up on the X-ray and the doctor pronounced Winter to be a magnet-free zone.

The offending magnet was never found and the incident was simply added to the ever-growing list of Winter's accident and emergency hospital visits.

"You should have just passed her over some paper-clips first," texted Winter's unsympathetic uncle Shealan. "That would have saved you a trip to the hospital."

By April, the single giant 'asparagus' in our garden had grown taller than me and was still growing. It grew so thick that the fingers of one hand could no longer encircle it. Lumps erupted at intervals on the green, woody trunk.

Easter and the plane carrying my son and his girlfriend, Daria, from London to Sydney arrived at about the same time. What a treat it was to welcome them to Australia, even if it was just for a holiday. So much to show them, so much to see and do! They were based in Sydney, staying with Karly and Cam, but I couldn't wait to have them stay with me and show them our part of the world, too.

The first time I met Daria, she and Indy were wearing matching pink Easter bunny ears and I knew she would fit perfectly into the family. Indy and Winter adored her, and Daria and Karly immediately became close friends.

"Let's all go to the Walkabout Park and spend the day there," suggested Karly, always the organiser. "Indy will love it and Shealan and Daria can go home with you, Mum."

It was a good plan because the Walkabout Park is roughly halfway between Sydney and the Central Coast, where I live. An easy drive. I didn't know it then, but this park was to play a part in my life for years to come.

The Walkabout Wildlife Sanctuary is one of my favourite places.

Ever.

Eighty acres of natural Australian bush with enclosures that visitors can enter and see the animals in their natural environments.[1] Many of the free-ranging rescue animals have grown accustomed to visitors and close encounters are guaranteed.

This beautiful, caring sanctuary was started unintentionally by South African-born Tassin Barnard and her husband, Gerald. Tassin told me that she turned her back on a corporate career in finance and bought the isolated property at Calga "because we didn't want any neighbours." Neither she nor Gerald had any animal background. Starting an animal sanctuary was the last thing on their minds, but that is what their home became.

Tassin's sister, Sally Jane Smith, (author of the Unpacking for Greece travel series) told me about it.

"Honestly," she said, "when I go to my sister's

---

1. Australia Walkabout Wildlife Park has recently changed its name to Walkabout Wildlife Sanctuary to properly reflect their work. Walkabout is the only wildlife sanctuary in New South Wales with both free-roaming Australian animals and heritage-listed aboriginal rock art sites. They do amazing work with endangered animals and it's a fabulous day out. https://walkaboutpark.com.au

house, I never know what to expect. I went to the bathroom once, and there was a tree in there."

"A tree in the bathroom?"

"Yes! Well, not the whole tree, but full-size branches all set up like one. And when I looked closer, I saw a koala sitting there."

"Oh, I remember, that was a very sick koala," said Tassin sadly.

"And right now, they are looking after a blind baby wombat in the house."

"Really?"

"Yes, poor little thing," said Tassin. "He was in his mum's pouch when she was hit by a car. He has two detached retinae, maybe from the impact, or perhaps it's a congenital problem. We don't know."

But this was my first visit to the Walkabout Park, and I didn't know much about the sanctuary then.

I remember the day clearly. We met emus face to beak, and huge red kangaroos that allowed us to pat them. The males really are red, but the females are a beautiful blue-grey. Farmers call them 'blue flyers' because of their speed and ability to leap over tall fences.

We saw wallaroos, wallabies, pademelons (another type of wallaby), wombats, and shy echidnas. Indy, dressed in a pink tutu with matching bunny ears, her chosen outfit for the day, loved it all. And so did I.

Indy patting a kangaroo

I was fascinated by the emus. At more than 1.5 metres [5 feet] tall and weighing in at 45kg [100 pounds] they are quite scary up close, even the friendly ones at Walkabout. The sleepy kangaroos and Waffles the (not so) miniature pig were much more approachable.

"Shame Cam isn't here," said Karly, admiring Waffles. "He's still talking about getting a pig."

"Remember that pig and the emus at that place in Queensland years ago?" I asked Shealan.

"Yes! How can I forget?"

Decades ago, when Shealan and Karly were maybe fourteen and twelve years old, we visited

Australia for the first time and visited a small animal park in Queensland. It was a family holiday and this was our first visit to Australia. We happened to drive by the park in our motorhome and stopped on impulse when we saw the sign. We were the only visitors and the burly Aussie owner and his pet pig, Wilbur, welcomed us personally.

"G'day," said the jovial owner. "Where are you guys from?"

"England," we answered.

The man grinned under his battered, broad-brimmed hat. I noticed he had a big, shiny brooch attached to the front of his dirty, open-necked shirt. It was a hot day and we all wore shorts and open shoes.

"Ah, England!" said the owner. "Heh, heh, heh, you won't have many emus running around there, will you?"

"No," we replied, shaking our heads.

"Right, follow me. I'll introduce you to Edgar and Edith, heh, heh. Kids, wanna feed some emus?"

"Yes, please," said Shealan.

"Eek!" squeaked Karly, jumping as Wilbur applied his wet, suction-pad nose to her bare ankle.

VERY FRIENDLY

"Don't you mind old Wilbur, heh, heh, heh!" said the man. "He's very friendly."

We walked down the dry track until we reached an empty paddock. The man pulled out a bag of sliced bread from a cavernous pocket and handed it to the kids.

"There you go, share that between you. Edgar and Edith will love it. Bring back the bag, emus are greedy buggers and they'll eat anything."

Shealan dipped his hand into the bag and grabbed a big handful of bread for his sister to hold. Wilbur's round, wet nose made contact with my ankle, and it was my turn to jump.

"I can't see any emus," said Shealan as we all shaded our eyes and scanned the paddock for the giant birds.

"Oh, they're probably lying down in the shade," said our new friend, grinning and pointing into the distance. "In you go, kids. You'll soon see them, heh, heh!"

He opened the gate and allowed them through. I sensed both kids were a little reluctant, but they started to head across the field, side by side, bread in hand. At first, nothing happened except their figures shrank smaller and smaller.

"Call me Gav," said the man, making conversation but watching the field intently.

"Gav, are you sure there are emus in this field?" I asked.

"Oh yes! Keep watching. And don't worry, the emus won't hurt them. They're very friendly."

That's a strange thing to say, I thought, but was distracted by the next event.

In the far distance, something in the dappled shade moved. Two small heads on long necks reared out of the grass and swivelled like submarine periscopes.

"There they are, heh, heh!" roared our host, slapping his thigh. "Now watch this!"

The kids hesitated before continuing forward more slowly than before. Two unmistakable emu shapes rose from the long grass. Edgar and Edith. Simultaneously, the giant birds shook themselves. I was shocked to see just how tall they were.

The kids froze.

Gav cupped his hands and took a deep breath. "Show them the bread!" he bellowed across the field. His shoulders began to shake with mirth and I felt distinctly uneasy.

Neither Shealan nor Karly moved.

But the emus did.

They began to trot eagerly towards their young visitors. I'm absolutely sure that it must have been a terrifying sight to see those enormous birds bearing down on them, so I didn't blame our kids one tiny bit when they turned and ran for their lives.

With horror, Edgar and Edith saw their tasty snack beginning to retreat and weren't going to allow that to happen. Heads lowered, necks stretched out, they increased their speed, their long, skinny legs eating up the short distance between them and our kids. Clouds of dust rose into the air. The kids pelted towards us.

Neither of our children had ever particularly excelled at sports at school but I believe they would have won medals that day.

"Run!" shouted our host before dissolving into wheezy bouts of mirth and needing to grab the gatepost to support himself. Then he gathered himself up. "Drop the bread!" he roared.

Suddenly, it was all over. The kids dropped the bread as though it was red-hot and the emus skidded to a halt. Instantly they transformed from nightmarish monsters with madness in their eyes into over-sized domestic fowl pecking the ground.

The dust settled.

We opened the gate and let the kids through, closing it firmly behind them.

"You two okay?" asked their father.

"Yup," they panted, laughing with relief. "That was scary!"

I gaped at Gav. I was quite sure that this

wasn't the first time he had set up this tableau for his own amusement. I had been genuinely concerned for our kids. What if they'd tripped and been trampled by the two rampant, stampeding emus? That would hit the British news headlines, I imagine.

But the kids were unscathed and not particularly traumatised. Shealan gave the loathsome man his bag back and now both kids were hopping about from one foot to the next trying to escape Wilbur's slimy snout on their bare legs.

We were near the entrance and I was ready to leave but Ghastly Gav had another trick up his sleeve. Well, on his shirt.

"Hey, kids," he said. "Wanna see my brooch?"

His fat, dirty fingers closed around the brooch on his shirtfront, and he plucked it off. The brooch reacted in a most un-broochlike way: it let off an extremely loud hiss.

Ghastly Gav waved it under our noses and we all jumped back, alarmed.

"Don't worry," guffawed our host, "he's very friendly, heh, heh, heh!" Tears of mirth left tracks down his dusty cheeks.

The 'brooch' was not enjoying itself any more than we were. It waved its impressive horns, flailed its six legs and hissed louder than ever.

"What is it?" we asked.

"A rhinoceros beetle, heh, heh! He won't hurt you. Anybody want to hold him?"

"No, thank you."

"No, thank you."

"Um, not for me."

"Why is it making that noise?"

"That's his defence. He hisses when he feels threatened. Don't worry, you're not in any danger, unless you're another male rhino beetle, heh, heh, heh!" He roared with laughter at his own joke.

Gav placed the beetle back on his shirt where it stopped complaining and hung on. Now we could look at it more closely. At seven centimetres long, [nearly three inches] it was the biggest beetle I had ever seen, apart from a male elephant beetle in South Africa. I admired its shiny shell, its fierce-looking horns and tight-gripping claws.

"Those claws are designed to hang onto leaves and bark," explained our host. "Sometimes they are hard to get off your clothes and won't let go. If that happens, pat the beetle gently on the back and it will just walk off."

"I'll remember that useful snippet," said my husband drily.

I began to warm to Gav a little. He knew his beetle facts even if he did have a strange sense of humour.

Gav tapped the beetle's back with a fat finger, and sure enough, it began walking up his shirt.

"Hold up, young fella, heh, heh," he said, plucking it off his shirt again. "Hey, kids, did you know that rhino beetles are said to be the strongest creatures on the planet? They can lift up to 850 times their own body weight."

"Wow!"

"That's like your dad lifting up four double-decker buses filled with passengers."

"Wow!"

The beetle, tired of being held aloft as an exhibit, began his hissing protest again. A car drew up, excited children's faces pressing on the windows.

"We must go. Thanks for the guided tour, Gav."

Gav grinned, removed his hat and made a mock bow. Then he popped his beetle onto the centre of his pale forehead where it clung, now silent. Wilbur removed his suction-pad snout from our feet and trotted after his master, happy to help welcome the new visitors.

The new visitors passed us as we exited the park. Three children bounced along, eager to see the animals.

"Don't let your kids feed the emus," I muttered, but the new family didn't hear me.

VERY FRIENDLY

"Well, Mum," said Shealan as we leaned on the railings watching a wombat snoring in his den.

Instantly I left the mid 1990s and was catapulted back to the present, 2017. My grown son stood by my side.

"Yes?"

"I've come to a bit of a decision," he said.

He was watching me closely, and I knew it was important.

Indy and Daria at the Walkabout Park

EASTER BUNNY TAILS

These cute little Easter Bunny tails are made from just three ingredients - marshmallows, chocolate and coconut. They are a fun Easter activity for the kids and a lovely gift idea for friends and family. From kidspot.com.au/kitchen/recipes/easter-bunny-tails/frzyku5w

Ingredients

- 1 cup (190g) white chocolate melts
- 2 cups (170g) shredded coconut
- 2 large packs of marshmallows

Method

Place white chocolate in a heatproof bowl.

Place coconut in a separate bowl.

Microwave chocolate on HIGH (100%) for 1-2 minutes, stirring every 30 seconds, until melted and smooth.

Working with one marshmallow at a time, dip the top of the marshmallow into the melted chocolate and tap off any excess chocolate.

Roll the marshmallow in the coconut to coat.

Place on a plate and refrigerate for 10 minutes or until set.

4

MEXICAN BROTHERS AND A HOLIDAY

I looked at my son curiously.

"You've come to a decision? What kind of a decision?" I asked.

Shealan didn't hesitate. "I want to move to Australia permanently."

I swung round to look him straight in the face.

"Are you joking?"

"No."

"How can you do that? I mean how is that possible?" I knew how hard it was to migrate to Australia.

"I'll start job-hunting. I'll try to find a company in Sydney that needs my skills and perhaps they'll sponsor me to come over."

To be honest, it sounded a bit vague. My heart raced, but I felt it was a rather optimistic plan.

"Aren't you pleased?" he asked when I didn't answer.

I realised I was gaping at him. I hadn't expected that announcement at all. I knew how he enjoyed his London life.

"Of course I am, I'm delighted! But it's not going to be easy, is it? And what about Daria?"

"She'll come too, of course. If I get an employer-sponsored visa, she'll be able to come as my partner."

"I thought you loved London? You won't miss it?"

"Nope, I don't think so. Sydney doesn't have the history but it's a really progressive, exciting city."

I couldn't argue with that. I'm not a city-lover at all and would be unhappy living in one, but I could see the attraction of Sydney and always enjoyed my visits.

"And then there's the weather, of course."

We both laughed. I remembered England's grey skies and grey sea, comparing them with Australia's blue skies and turquoise ocean. No contest. Would we have laughed so carelessly if we'd known what weather extremes were in store for Australia?

I had plenty to tell Joe when we Facetimed next. I told him all about Daria, the day at the Walkabout park, and Shealan's announcement.

"So do you think he'll actually get a job offer?" asked Joe.

"I don't know. I've never really understood what he does exactly, have you? I guess if whatever he does is in demand in Sydney, then it's possible. It's great having him here, though, and great to finally meet and get to know Daria. She's amazing, she's even finished off painting the front door for me."

"That's kind of her!"

"Yes, I'm taking them round to see all the local sights and beaches. We're going to watch the pelican feeding tomorrow. That's always fun."

"Any other plans?"

"Yes! We've booked an Airbnb for all of us at Port Stephens for a long weekend."

"Sounds nice. Will Lola come too?"

"No, dogs aren't allowed, but it's okay, Jasmine will have her."

And then I told him about Jasmine, our new dog minder.

The thought of leaving Lola in kennels didn't appeal to me at all because she's a Velcro dog. She loves everybody but suffers from terrible separation anxiety when left alone. As long as she has human company, she's fine. Kennels were out of the question, and it seemed a little pointless finding a house-minder to stay with her when I'd only be away for a weekend.

What I needed was somebody who would welcome Lola into their own home. I phoned a local pet-minding company and struck lucky. They had a dog-minder called Jasmine who didn't live far from me.

"You'll like Jasmine," they said. "She's training to be a nurse and she's at home with her little one at the moment. She doesn't have a dog herself yet, that's why she's looking after other people's until she can have her own."

I was given her home number, and I called. We arranged a time for Lola and me to go to her house for a meet-and-greet.

"If you'd like to pop round at two o'clock," Jasmine said, "we'll see how it goes. Bring Lola's vaccination papers. If you can leave her for a couple of hours, I'll be able to tell you how she settles and whether it's going to work or not. I should mention, I have a toddler. Is that going to be a problem?"

"Not at all! Lola loves kids and is very used to them. I have two granddaughters, one who is only a year old. Lola is super-gentle with both. Even when Winter grabs her eyebrows and yanks them."

We drove to Jasmine's home and I admit to being a little nervous. Lola had never been interviewed before.

I liked Jasmine immediately and Lola agreed. She liked Jasmine's pats, Jasmine's grassy backyard and particularly liked the tennis ball that Jasmine produced and threw for her.

"Slip out now while I keep her busy," said Jasmine.

It felt like leaving a child at school for the first time. I used the time to do some shopping but I kept glancing at my watch and the minutes ticked slowly.

At last it was time to return and find out whether Lola had passed the test or not. Lola was pleased to see me, but she was clearly already very relaxed with Jasmine and her little boy.

"I can't see any problem at all," said Jasmine. "Marcus loves her and she's been perfect. Is there anything special I should be aware of?"

I thought hard. "Um, she barks at cats. She rolls in mud. Oh, and she digs in her water bowl, I don't know why."

"Well, that's easy," said Jasmine. "There are no cats around here. And it hasn't rained for months

MEXICAN BROTHERS AND A HOLIDAY

so there's no mud. And I'll put her water bowl on a stool so she doesn't dig in it."

Now, why hadn't I thought of that?

She reached for her diary and flicked some pages. "Now, which weekend were you looking at?"

I told her the dates and she examined her diary, her brow furrowing. "Oh," she said, "I already have two dogs booked in. How is Lola with other dogs?"

"She's fine. She likes other dogs but she's nervous of big ones."

"They're two elderly chihuahua brothers."

"Oh, that should be okay," I said, relieved they weren't a big bully breed. "Have you looked after them before?"

"Yes, we've had them a couple of times. Their names are Pancho and Carlos. Actually," she confided, "they are quite, um, bossy. They're okay with other dogs as long as they are the boss. And they're good with adults and children, but…"

She broke off and was trying not to laugh. I waited.

"Unfortunately, they've taken a dislike to my husband. It makes life a bit difficult sometimes. We've got them for a week this time, their owners are getting married in Bali. I haven't told my husband yet."

I smiled. Lola is always the submissive one and has perfect manners with more dominant dogs, so I wasn't worried.

I packed a little overnight bag for Lola. I bagged up her meals. I packed her fluffy platypus with the eggs in its pouch that she loved to work out using her nose. Her favourite blankie. A supply of tennis balls.

When the weekend arrived, we drove again to Jasmine's house. Jasmine opened the side gate and Lola greeted her enthusiastically.

"Hi Lola!" said Jasmine, "I'm pleased to see you, too!"

She let us into the backyard where a grey dog snoozed on a big cushion in the sun.

"Meet Pancho and Carlos," she said. "Let Lola off the lead and let's see what they think of each other."

Lola had already seen the sleeping dog and was keen to say a happy hello. She bounded up to the cushion with an excited *wuff*. The dog on the cushion sprang up and split into two, much to Lola's and my surprise.

Side by side, the two identical chihuahuas yapped in unison, telling Lola exactly what they thought of her. Both grey, except for one black ear, they were like mirror images.

"Yap, yap, how dare you wake us up, you hairy

MEXICAN BROTHERS AND A HOLIDAY

young whippersnapper. We're Mexican, and we don't put up with any nonsense here, yap, yap. And this cushion is out of bounds to you."

Lola understood perfectly. Thank goodness, she has always grasped the strict rules of Dog Etiquette. She knew her place and has never challenged another dog. Wagging her tail frantically to show she was a friendly type, she backed away and began sniffing around the garden. The Mexican brothers relaxed on the cushion again, satisfied they had made their point clear. Twin raspy snores told me they'd resumed their nap.

"I think they'll be fine," said Jasmine, and I agreed.

It was time to hand over Lola's overnight bag and slip away before she noticed I'd gone.

Port Stephens is situated a little north of Newcastle, and is a tourist mecca. This is hardly surprising when you see what the area has to offer. It has beautiful beaches, stunning sand dunes, national parks, pristine waters, and a carefree laid-back atmosphere that invites you to shrug off any cares and woes you may have.

The Airbnb house in Salt Ash was fine, and the main bedroom was big enough for both girls to sleep in the same room with their parents. More importantly, the backyard had a barbecue, so we stocked up on provisions, nibbles and drinks. We were set and ready to enjoy the weekend.

My son-in-law, Cam, has a passion for dirt bikes and he'd brought his along.

"Where are you going to ride it?" I asked.

"Ah, you've never been to Anna Bay, have you?"

"No. Is the beach wide enough to ride on the sand?"

Cam laughed. "Wait and see," he said.

When I saw the dunes of Anna Bay, I immediately understood. I've never seen so much white sand since visiting the deserts of the Middle East. It's not just a beach; it's a monumental, shifting sandscape.

Called the Stockton Bight Sand Dunes, they are the largest moving coastal dunes in the southern hemisphere. They are forever changing, shaped by the wind and weather.

I researched those dunes later and discovered they are made up of three layers, or waves. The current layer is around three thousand years old, but the first wave goes back a staggering 2.5 million years to the Pleistocene period.

MEXICAN BROTHERS AND A HOLIDAY

I mentioned that to Joe later.

"The plasticine period? I don't think plasticine was invented 2.5 million years ago."

"Don't be ridiculous."

The dunes are situated in the Worimi Conservation Lands which the traditional Worimi people still occupy as the custodians. It remains a significant aboriginal site which the Worimi patrol and protect.

It's little wonder that this spectacular area has become a desert playground. Some dunes reach heights of forty metres [130 feet], and steep slopes make ideal launch pads for sandboarding, 4WD tours, quad bike hire, and horse riding.

But before we could head into the dunes, we needed to buy a license from the nearest petrol station, or servo, as Aussies call them. That was easy enough.

Then I followed Cam's ute. (Short for utility vehicle. In the UK and, I believe, in the US, these are called pickup trucks.) Soon, we swung off the main road towards the ocean. Already the tarmac under our wheels was becoming covered with sand, and the further we drove, the deeper the sand became. Then came a signpost warning vehicles not to proceed unless they had four-wheel drive. I parked and Shealan, Daria and I got out. Cam, in his ute, paused.

"Want a lift to the beach?" he called back.

"No, we're fine, thanks! We'll walk."

Off he sailed with the rest of the family inside and the dirt bike behind silhouetted against the blue sky. They soon disappeared, swallowed up by sand. We began our trek to the beach.

Sand dunes rose either side of us, undulating, silent, endless. The sand beneath our feet was deep and powder-dry; no rain had fallen for months. A breeze blew away our footprints as fast as we made them. Sand stretched before us, dunes towered in every direction. We trudged forward through the monotonous, beautiful landscape without speaking.

Such a vast expanse of one colour is almost mesmerising. No vehicles. No other people. No trees, no plants, no structures, no corners, no movement except for sand sliding in silent sheets down the steeper slopes that caught the breeze.

The relentless Australian sun beat down.

MEXICAN STREET CORN

Fire up the barbecue and throw on some beautiful fresh summer corn on the cob.

Ingredients

5 whole corn cobs, with husks and silks removed

2 tablespoons mayonnaise

a good pinch of cayenne pepper or chilli powder

¼ teaspoon smoked paprika

¼ cup parmesan cheese finely grated

2 limes cut into wedges, to serve

Method

Preheat BBQ or a grill pan on a medium to high heat.

Cut corn cobs in half, brush with oil and season with salt.

Grill corn on the BBQ or grill pan until slightly charred all over and the kernels are bright yellow (about 8 minutes).

Transfer to a serving plate and, while the corn is still hot, brush generously with mayonnaise, sprinkle with cayenne pepper or chilli, and parmesan.

Serve with lime wedges to squeeze over just before eating.

5

BIKES

How did the aboriginals, the first inhabitants of this land, the Worimi people, thrive in such harsh conditions? I discovered they were excellent fishermen and shellfish foragers, and naturally, they knew which insects and vegetation were edible. Apparently, the remains of Worimi rockfish ovens, burial sites and ceremonial grounds still exist.

We trudged on. I allowed myself to imagine we were alone, lost in the Sahara desert. It wasn't difficult. I squeezed my eyes closed for as long as I dared to immerse myself in the moment, feeling the heat of the sun on my back.

When I cracked my eyelids open, a movement

caught my attention. Far, far away in the distance, moving in a slow line amongst the dunes, I saw…

No! It couldn't be!

My son's voice broke into my thoughts.

"Hey!" he exclaimed. "Look over there!"

"Camels!" said Daria.

I was relieved. It wasn't a mirage, and I wasn't hallucinating. It really was a caravan of camels with tourists on their backs. Slowly, silently, they plodded along, nose to tail, perfectly at home in this vast sand desert.

Camels at Anna Bay

Gradually, the sounds of the sea grew closer. I could hear waves and the clamour of seabirds. We crested the last dune and there it was, laid out before us. Anna Bay.

Australian beaches always make me catch my breath. Endless variations of white sand, turquoise sparkling water and frothy waves running up the beach. But Anna Bay is special. The beach, stretching away for 32 kilometres almost to Newcastle, bordered by vast swathes of sand dunes, makes one gasp.

If you want a promenade to walk along, ice cream stalls and gift shops, this is *not* the place to come. It's a beach. Very few people, lots of sand, lots of sea and lots of sky. That's it. And I love it.

Cam had already untied his dirt bike and lifted it off the ute. Now he was pulling on his helmet and preparing to ride up the beach.

The tide was perhaps at its lowest point and as we walked towards Karly and the girls, I felt as though I was walking on a mirror. One would need to walk a very long way into the ocean for the water to reach one's ankles. It was the strangest sensation, like walking on glass. The wet sand, interrupted only by the odd seashell or smooth, water-washed pebble, reflected the sky and sucked at my bare feet.

Indy and Winter were having a wonderful time. Indy gathered seashells and excavated holes that immediately flooded with water. Winter crawled, splashed and ate sand when we weren't looking. Shealan and Daria strolled together, deep in conversation, no doubt discussing their exciting future. Far in the distance, a tiny figure zoomed away on his motorbike.

Gradually, the tide crept in and the illusion of walking on glass disappeared. We stayed until the sun sank to the horizon, painting the ocean fifty shades of tangerine.

It was a perfect day.

Returning home after the trip, I couldn't wait to collect Lola from her minder. I knocked on Jasmine's door. She opened it and I was treated to one of Lola's most enthusiastic welcomes. When she'd finished hurling herself at me she trotted back inside, quite at home.

"Come in," said Jasmine and stood aside.

It was then that I heard it: the unmistakable sound of snarling. Neither Jasmine nor Lola seemed concerned, which was odd. The sound seemed to be coming from the kitchen.

"What's that noise?" I asked.

"Oh, give it a rest, you two," said a weary male voice from within. "What have I ever done to you to deserve this?"

Then I understood and Jasmine confirmed it.

"Pancho and Carlos have cornered my husband again," she sighed, but her eyes were dancing with amusement. "They can't stand the sight of him, we have no idea why."

"Jas? Are you there? Call them off, will you?"

"Excuse me, I'd better sort this out," apologised Jasmine.

Off she went and I heard her scolding the tiny twin terrorists.

"Right, you two," she said in a mock-cross voice. "That's quite enough!" The snarling paused. "I'm putting you both outside until you learn some manners."

I heard the back door open, then close again.

A small, bespectacled young man appeared from the kitchen. I couldn't imagine why the chihuahuas felt threatened by him.

"This is my husband, Simon," said Jasmine, joining us.

"Hi," I said. "I hope Lola behaved herself. I'm sorry the brothers are giving you such a hard time."

"Oh, Lola's been great, no problem," they said in unison.

I was pleased to hear that.

"Here's her bag, her toys and stuff," said Jasmine, patting the pile on the table. "She settled really quickly and she stayed well out of Carlos and Pancho's way."

"We'd take her again anytime," said Simon. "Not like those two little Mexican villains outside who …"

He never finished his sentence because two

identical doggy faces suddenly rushed at the sliding glass door, yapping their heads off. They never looked at me, nor Jasmine, or Lola. Their venom was solely directed at poor Simon. I was glad there was a barrier of glass between the predators and their prey.

That evening, Joe and I caught up on the phone. He told me about the medical tests he was waiting for, and the fact that there was no chance of him receiving a lung transplant. Disappointing, but not surprising. I told him all about Anna Bay and the dunes, and Lola's first stay with Jasmine and Simon.

"How's the garden?"

"Oh, it's a bit unruly, I'll spend some more time out there next week. Get it tidied up for the winter. The bamboos are doing fine since I transplanted them."

"How's the 'asparagus' plant?"

"Oh boy, you should see it! It's way taller than me, I'd have to stand on a stepladder to touch the tip. And you know those knobs it grew? Each one of those has grown a thick green stem. And on the end of each of them is a cluster of strange flowers."

"Really? Is it beautiful?"

"No! Not at all. The flowers are very odd, and green. I'll take a photo of it to show you."

"When are Shealan and Daria going back to England?"

"They've still got a couple of weeks left. They'll be here for Winter's birthday. Oh, she's taken her first steps, by the way. Do you think they are serious about coming to live in Australia?"

"Well, remember when Karly announced she was planning to live in Australia all those years ago?"

I laughed. It was a bit of a family joke. When Karly finished university, she spent a gap year in Australia and fell in love with both the country and an Aussie lad. She visited us in Spain and announced that somehow, she was going to go back to Australia. Knowing that young people change their minds frequently, and that getting permanent residency in Australia is not at all easy, we were sceptical.

"It won't ever happen," Joe had said. He was to eat his words.

Karly made it happen. She did return to Australia, and she jumped through all the hoops to become an Australian citizen. And then she married Cam. When the grandchildren started arriving, it was time for Joe and I to also consider leaving our beloved home in Spain and move to the other side of the world. It took two years, a mountain of paperwork and a lot of money to make that happen.

"Well, if Shealan and Daria are serious, it'll take them years before they come over," said Joe, and I agreed.

"Yup, finding a job, and all that paperwork and the visas."

"Yes, it's a nice idea, but it'll probably never happen."

"Have you had any rain?" Joe asked, changing the subject.

"Not a drop. Can't remember when it last rained, months and months ago. It hasn't rained since you left. And it's still really hot even though it'll officially be winter in a couple of weeks."

Lola and I kept ourselves very busy. It was hard waiting for Joe to return, but I knew it would have been even harder for him. He needed to attend his various medical appointments and wait for the results. At least we could Facetime each other, and usually did so every evening.

I could tell him about the celebration of Winter's first birthday and the family visit on

Mother's Day, which falls in May in Australia, not March like the UK.

I'd ordered a garden shed which had arrived some weeks ago. It was still in all of its packaging and I didn't have the courage to open it and try to assemble it by myself. It was just too big, and there were too many pieces. One glance at the instructions scared me rigid.

On Mother's Day, I was given the perfect gift. Not flowers. Not chocolate. Not even wine. For the second time in my life, I was given tokens. Special, unique tokens. Eight of the little beauties.

Each one started the same:

> GIFT CERTIFICATE
> *Happy Mothers' Day*
> *To: Mum/Nanny/Mother-in-law*
> *From: Your favourite daughter, favourite son-in-law*
> *and favourite grandchildren*

But the value was different on each token. They ranged from One Painting Project, to One Lawn Mow, One Carpentry Project, One Tim-Tam Cheesecake and even An Evening of Multiple Glasses of Wine.

Wonderful!

"Would you like to redeem one today?" asked Cam.

Would I!

"Yes! Wow! This one, please! One Flat Pack Assembly."

"The shed?"

"Yes, please!"

And so Cam, in his usual cheerful, capable way, constructed the garden shed as though it was Lego.

Other nice things happened, too, like the RSPCA's (Royal Society of Prevention of Cruelty to Animals) annual Million Paws Walk fundraiser. Starting points are designated on a Sunday in May in different towns all over Australia. It costs a small amount to participate, and many walkers also gather sponsors.

The walk is usually roughly two kilometres, about a mile, and is heaps of fun. I have never, ever, *ever* seen so many dogs in one place. Every colour, every type of coat. Every size from tiny dogs one could carry in one's pocket, to dogs one could almost put a saddle on and ride.

As we waited to begin, we milled around, admiring each other's dogs. Similar breeds gravitated towards each other and compared notes. Lola made a hundred new friends.

I found myself standing next to a lady with a

friendly white dog who she told me was named Patch.

Then, off we went in a glorious, great, long, doggy crocodile. Cars stopped and passers-by gaped. And at exactly the same time, all over Australia, other RSPCA doggy crocodiles set off, too. No wonder it's called the Million Paws Walk, and no wonder it's the RSPCA's biggest fundraiser, year after year.

By the end of the walk, Lola and Patch were best friends, and Jacky and I had exchanged telephone numbers.

"If you're free at all, we could meet for walks and coffee," suggested my new friend.

"I'd love that," I replied.

From that day, the four of us met regularly,

sometimes by the lake, and often on the beach. Jacky and I nattered while Patch and Lola chased each other across the sand and into the waves.[1]

The weather grew cooler. The giant 'asparagus' in our garden passed its Best Before date, turned yellowish-brown and keeled over. I sawed it into foot-long pieces and disposed of them in the green council bin.

Winter now toddled with confidence and Indy was learning to ride her bike without stabilisers.

"Daddy, you won't let go, will you?"

"Of course not, I've got you," said Cam, running behind. "I won't let go. Go on, pedal hard!"

Indy pedalled, and the bike sailed along the path, leaving Cam behind. Indy's head was down, and her eyes narrowed in concentration.

"Yay! You're doing it!" yelled Cam, and we spectators clapped and cheered.

Indy suddenly realised her daddy wasn't holding the bike at all. She promptly wobbled and fell off. But it was a breakthrough. Before long, she

---

1. Lola and Patch at the lake https://www.youtube.com/watch?v=gdvouFZZ9m4

was back in the saddle, and soon riding the bike became second nature.[2]

August brought Indy's fifth birthday. She had heaps of exciting gifts to unwrap, but her main present surprised nobody except the birthday girl herself. Indy unveiled a beautiful, child-sized motorbike, complete with a pink helmet and protective leathers. Cam would have a companion on future rides at Anna Bay.

But August brought another, even bigger surprise to our family.

---

2. Indy learns to ride her bike: https://youtube.com/shorts/LFiGKOsheMU

PAN-FRIED ASPARAGUS

Pan-fried asparagus is yummy and particularly good with salmon or steak.

Ingredients

¼ cup butter

2 tablespoons olive oil

1 teaspoon coarse salt

¼ teaspoon ground black pepper

3 cloves garlic, minced

1 pound fresh asparagus spears, trimmed

Method

Gather all ingredients.

Melt butter in a skillet over medium-high heat. Add

olive oil, salt, pepper and cook and stir until garlic is fragrant, about 30 seconds.

Add asparagus and cook until fork-tender, turning asparagus often to ensure even cooking, about 10 minutes.

6

HOUNDINI

Joe's medical tests dragged on and on. He couldn't return to Australia until they were all complete, but that didn't stop him from applying for his visa in readiness.

"I might as well fill out all the forms now," he said. "It might save time. You know how long visas always take."

I agreed with him.

The next evening when he phoned, I had some astonishing news for him.

"You'll never guess what!" I said.

"No, I very much doubt I will," he replied drily. "But let me try. We've won the lottery?"

"Huh, no."

"Thea has given up baking cakes?"

No cake from our German neighbour and her little bilingual Jack Russell who often popped in with slices of deliciousness? Unthinkable.

"Nope. Thank goodness."

"Okay, I give up."

I was nearly bursting with the news. "Shealan has been offered a job with a company based in Sydney, and they are going to sponsor him!"

"Wow! He's found a job already? That's great news! What about Daria?"

"As his partner, she can come too!"

"Can she work?"

"Yes. Shealan will be on three months probation with his new Australian employer before it's all finalised, but Daria can apply for any job she wants."

"So when are they coming over?"

"Shealan is coming next month! September!"

"Well, that was quick. Where is he going to live?"

"He'll stay with Karly and Cam and the kids until he's finished his probationary period. Then when Daria joins him, they'll find a place together."

"That's really good news." A pause, then, "Has it rained yet?" he asked, as he always did.

"Nope, and it's already getting warm, and it's still winter."

"Any other news?"

"Not really. Except Karly says LJ keeps getting anxious and escaping."

To look at LJ, nobody would think he was a nervous dog. Karly and Cam adopted him from the pound as a puppy when Indy was a toddler. He had very big paws, so they knew he would be a big boy. He turned out to be a handful as a puppy but was extremely gentle with Indy and adored being with the family. He settled down and became the perfect family dog, except he also developed the skills to become a cunning escape artist.

If the family was at home, it was no problem. But if they went out for too long, LJ would escape and search for them. Often, they couldn't even figure out how he got out, but as soon as Cam blocked his latest escape hole, he found another.

Shealan arrived from the UK. The kids were delighted, calling him Fun-cle Shea-Shea.

Before he started work at his new job, he came to stay with me for a while. He caught the train in Sydney and enjoyed the picturesque journey over the Hawkesbury river and all the watery inlets as the train snaked its way north to the Central Coast.

I met him at the station and we hugged. It felt brilliant to have my son in Australia and know that he was actually going to stay and begin a new life here.

As we strolled towards Bruce, parked in the station car park, I handed him the car keys.

"Why are you giving me these?"

"Because you are going to drive."

"What? Mum, I haven't driven a car for about twenty years!"

It was true. He lived and worked in London. There is no need to own a car or drive in London. Most people rely on public transport or taxis.

"You are going to buy a car, aren't you? You might even buy a Jeep, that's always been your dream, hasn't it?"

"Yes, but …"

"You used to be a really good driver and you used to love driving!"

"No, I don't think I'm ready to …"

"As soon as you get going, it'll all come back to you. Bruce is automatic and dead easy to drive. The trip to my house is really straightforward and the roads aren't busy at all. It's the perfect opportunity to get you back into driving."

Shealan gave me a long, hard stare and took a deep breath. Then he climbed into the driver's side. He put the key in the ignition then spent a couple of minutes fiddling with the indicators and familiarising himself with everything. He set off.

I don't think he had even driven a mile before I sensed all his self-confidence return. As I suspected, his driving skills and knowledge flooded back and he was as good a driver as he had been twenty years ago. That weekend, he drove us everywhere.

Back in Sydney, he began work with his new company. It wasn't worth buying a car yet, because he had to make sure that he passed his three-month probation. But he loved the work and made friends with his colleagues easily.

He soon got to grips with Sydney's public transport system and caught the bus to work every morning. All went well until he came home one day, outraged. I may have omitted some colourful language in the following story.

"You'll never guess what happened to me today! I was at the bus stop, minding my own business, and I got dive-bombed by a great big bird! It attacked me!"

"Oh, mate! Was it a black and white one?" asked Cam, trying not to look amused.

"Yes!"

"Ah," said Karly. "I guess nobody warned you about Australian magpies?"

"No!"

"Well, that's what magpie fathers do for about

six weeks this time of year. They attack anybody who comes too close to their nest."

"I was innocently waiting for a bus!"

"Oh dear. The nest must be close to the bus stop."

"What did you say? Six weeks? They attack for six weeks?"

"Um, yes. It's the males who have anger issues. They particularly don't like dogs, or children, or cyclists."

"But I'm not a dog, or a child, or a cyclist."

"You've got a bald head. Perhaps they think you're wearing a helmet?"

"Oh, you are kidding! I have to prepare to be attacked by some demented giant black and white bird for the next six weeks?"

"Yup. Welcome to Australia."

Meanwhile, LJ's frequent escapes were still a problem. Cam left the house early each morning. Shealan headed for the bus stop and his black-and-white nemesis. Karly was the last to leave with the children, and LJ was left to his own devices. It was then that he started to search for new ways to escape.

He squeezed through gaps in the fence panels, which one would have thought impossible for a dog of his size. As fast as Cam found and blocked his exit point, LJ found another.

And where did he go? A phone call provided the answer.

"Hello?"

"Oh hi, do you own a dog called LJ?"

"Yes! Have you seen him?"

"Oh yes. He walked into the house and he's here now, lying on the rug with our dog, Roxy."

"Oh my goodness! I'm so sorry! He keeps getting out and we don't know how he does it. What's your address? I'll come and get him right now."

"That's okay, no rush. He's made himself very comfortable."

Karly dashed round and collected him, full of apologies, but it wouldn't be the last time LJ escaped and went roaming.

Just out of interest, Karly decided to get LJ's DNA checked out. The test would be able to trace their four-legged friend's ancestry back to his great-grandparents. It would be an interesting experiment that might give them a better understanding of LJ's behaviour and characteristics.

The test came back, and the results were interesting. LJ was declared to be part husky, part malamute, part Staffordshire terrier with just a touch of Boston terrier. Fascinating news but probably not terribly helpful.

Whether it was Roxy's charms or the welcome he was given, LJ still carried on escaping and usually ended up visiting Roxy and her owners.

Karly and Cam were mortified. Karly left wine and chocolates on their doorstep with a card apologising for LJ's house calls. Cam checked the fence inch by inch, determined to block any possible escape.

But it didn't stop LJ, otherwise known as Houndini. Nothing stopped him from roaming.

Another time, he got out and visited a different neighbour.

"Hello, I think I may have your dog," said an unfamiliar voice when Karly answered her phone. "I've just rung the phone number on his collar."

"Oh no! I'm so sorry. He got out again, and we don't know how! Did you find him on the street?"

"No, he just walked into our living room when we were watching a movie. We gave him some leftover steak we had. He seemed to enjoy that."

"Perhaps we should get him a friend?" Karly suggested when we were discussing the problem. "Perhaps he wouldn't try to escape if he had company at home."

"No, that's a terrible idea," I said. "You could end up with two dogs roaming the streets together instead of one. LJ could show his friend how to get out."

It all came to a head a couple of weeks before Christmas. One evening, when the family was late getting home, LJ escaped again.

Cam and Karly's house was built on a fairly steep hill. Their next-door neighbours' house was a lot lower than theirs. Their neighbours had two small children, and this particular evening, they'd just been bathed and put to bed. To their parents' astonishment, they suddenly heard both children shrieking with excitement.

"Mummy! Daddy!"

"Quick, Mummy! Daddy!"

The parents rushed to their children's bedsides, surprised to find them in such a fever of excitement.

"What's the matter?"
"It's Santa!"
"Santa's here!"
"He's come early!"
"He's bringing our presents!"
"WHATEVER are you talki…"

Simultaneously, both parents stopped abruptly and looked up at the ceiling. They had heard something, too. The children were on their beds, jumping up and down, whooping, all thought of sleep forgotten.

"We told you!"
"We TOLD you! Santa's reindeer are on the roof!"
"Santa's here!"

The parents looked at each other, eyes wide, completely baffled.

"I'll go and check," said the father at last. He went outside, and, being midsummer, there was enough light to see what was clattering around on their roof.

It was LJ Houndini, of course.

How did he do it? Well, it was easy to work out. He'd used Indy's trampoline as a springboard and leapt over the fence onto the neighbours' roof. Smart dog.

Then another neighbour volunteered some more information.

"I was upstairs once, and happened to look out of the window that overlooks part of your garden. I couldn't believe my eyes. I saw LJ take a running jump up to the fence, scrabble up it, then walk along it like a cat. He should be in a circus!"

Karly and Cam were horrified.

"That's it," said Cam. "I'm going to take a week off work and completely replace the entire fence with a six-foot high one."

And that is precisely what he did. As well as moving the trampoline so that it was nowhere near the boundary. The new fence finally did the trick, and LJ was successfully contained. No more visits to his girlfriend, Roxy, or random neighbours.

Before I set off to join the family for Christmas in Sydney, I was given an unexpected gift.

My phone rang one evening and I saw on the screen it was Joe, making his usual daily call. But this time I didn't even have time to say, "Hello."

"I've got it!" he crowed, before even greeting me.

"Got what?"

"The visa! The visa came through. They've

accepted the letter from the doctor saying I am fit to fly."

"That's brilliant news!"

"I think all my medical stuff is up to date now, so there's no reason for me not to pack up and find a flight. I should arrive soon after Christmas."

Amazing news. When we finished chatting, I put the phone down and took a deep breath.

"He's coming home!" I shouted to nobody.

Lola caught my excitement and began barking as we danced around the room together.

But another family drama was about to take place in the run-up to Christmas that year and it all began with the Christmas tree.

GERMAN BUTTERKUCHEN

Every time I taste this delicious cake with its sugary cinnamon topping, I think of our lovely German neighbour, Thea, and her bilingual Jack Russell. Excellent cake with a cup of coffee.

Ingredients

2 x 7g (0.25 oz) packs dry yeast

½ cup water

¾ cup milk

1½ cup white sugar

1 teaspoon salt

1 cup butter

4 cups plain (all-purpose) flour

3 eggs

½ teaspoon ground cinnamon

Method

Butter a 23cm (9-inch) pan and set aside. In a small mixing bowl, dissolve yeast in warm water. Let stand until creamy, about 10 minutes.

Place milk, ½ cup sugar, salt and ½ cup butter in a saucepan. Heat until sugar dissolves and butter melts. Cool to lukewarm. Add dissolved yeast and set aside.

In a large bowl, combine flour, eggs and yeast mixture. Stir until smooth and blended. Pour into the buttered 23cm (9-inch) pan, spreading dough evenly. Let rise in a warm place for 45 minutes. Meanwhile, preheat oven to 190°C (375°F)

In a small bowl, combine ½ cup butter, 1 cup sugar and ½ teaspoon cinnamon. Mix together and sprinkle over the dough. Bake in preheated oven for 30 minutes, or until the top is golden and syrupy.

7

PAINFUL ARMS AND LEGS

Cam and Karly always buy a real tree to decorate at Christmas time and this year they'd chosen an absolute beauty. It was very tall because their rooms had high ceilings and could accommodate that, but it needed two people to carry it into the house from the ute.

"Okay, kids," said Karly, herding her two daughters into the playroom. "You two stay in here and play nicely while we bring in the tree. Then you can help decorate it."

She joined Cam outside, and together, they unstrapped the tree and manhandled it into the house. The steps up to the house were steep and the tree was heavy and cumbersome.

PAINFUL ARMS AND LEGS

Just as they were trying to get the tree, and themselves, through the front door, they heard it.

A shrill scream of pain from a small child, followed by howls.

Winter.

Dropping the tree and tripping over it in their haste to extricate themselves from its spiky embrace, they raced to the playroom and flung open the door.

The scene that met their eyes seemed totally normal, except that Winter was screaming.

Karly scooped her up but neither she nor Cam could work out what was wrong with her. They examined her closely. Indy watched, wide-eyed and frightened.

"She's not using her arm," said Karly. "Indy, what happened?"

"Nothing! I was just helping her get up onto the sofa. Then she just screamed!"

"Come on," said Cam, "we're going to the hospital. She may have a broken arm."

They fought their way past the abandoned Christmas tree to the car and sped the well-worn route to the Accident and Emergency Department of the hospital.

Because the patient was so young and noisy, and in obvious pain, Winter was seen quickly by the doctor.

"What happened?" he asked, gently feeling her arm and shoulder.

"Indy, tell the doctor what happened."

"I was just helping my little sister get up onto the sofa," she explained. "And then she screamed, really-really-really loud."

"Thank you," said the doctor. He looked from Karly to Cam and stroked Winter's tear-stained cheek. "I'm happy to say that Winter's arm isn't broken," he said, "but, unfortunately, she has a dislocated shoulder."

"Oh no," breathed Karly, white-faced, taking in the information.

Cam waited. He is particularly accident-prone himself. As a regular ice hockey player who frequently witnessed and sustained dozens of injuries over the years, he knew what was coming next.

"You have a choice," said the doctor. "We can admit her, sedate her, then X-ray her and decide what to do."

He paused and took a breath.

"Or?" asked Karly.

"Or I can just pop it back right now. It's very straightforward. It will hurt, but it'll all be over in a second."

Karly and Cam looked at each other.

"Do it now," they said in unison.

Without further ado, the doctor gripped Winter's shoulder and popped it back into place. Winter squeaked, and it was all over.

All was well again.

The family went home to finish putting up and decorating their Christmas tree, and piling the many gifts beneath its branches.

Christmas in Sydney was always wonderful,

and 2017 was no exception. I loved our Spanish Christmases, but nothing beats celebrating the festive season in the bosom of one's own family, particularly when there are children.

We were all up before six o'clock in the morning because Santa had filled the stockings hanging from the fireplace. Out came the little crib that always appears on Christmas Day since I was a child myself. It is a music box, and plays Silent Night. Family rules dictate that nobody is allowed to unwrap any gifts from under the tree until the music slows and finally comes to a jerking, maddening halt. The wait is always excruciating. Indy nearly exploded.

Winter was still too young to appreciate her gifts, but she was very happy to eat the paper and play with the boxes. I clearly remember Indy opening a mountain of gifts, but when asked which were her favourites, there was no hesitation.

She adored the cheerful little plastic toilet, complete with lid, small enough to sit on your hand. The aim was to invite an 'unsuspecting' family member to lift the lid and look inside. As they raised the lid, a little squirt of water hit them squarely in the eye.

Equally tasteful and much-adored was her

new reindeer. Pump its tail and a jellybean poop dropped out.

Both treasures never ceased to amuse Indy, and peals of laughter rang through the house all day.

Karly had catered for an army, and indeed, our party was large. The table looked fabulous, set outside in the shade. The Christmas food was, as usual, partly traditional English with roast turkey and all the trimmings, and partly Australian with oysters, seafood and pavlova. The meal was merry, laughter-filled and loud, the noise competing with the cicadas that hummed in the background.

Cam's parents had brought the daughter of a friend with them, and I was fascinated to find out that Ava was a zookeeper at Sydney's Taronga Zoo.

Of course, I had a million questions.

"What do you do? Are you based in one section or do you move around?"

"I work with the penguins, they are my speciality," she answered, smiling.

I should have guessed because I'd just watched all the children open penguin-themed gifts from Ava.

"Ohhh, I love penguins," Indy squealed. "They are so cute!"

"Me too," I agreed.

Ava's eyebrows twitched. "Everyone thinks that," she remarked. "I love penguins, of course. They fascinate me, and I study them closely. They are definitely my favourite animal which is why I choose to work with them. But cute? Hmm…"

"What do you mean? Why aren't they cute?" I asked, surprised.

Ava shrugged. "Actually, they're extremely cantankerous. Not friendly, homely birds as most people think. I always wear gum boots when I go into their enclosure because, believe me, those beaks slice through skin. Their pointy beaks are tough, designed to grab fish, and human legs are so much softer. Look…"

She lifted the hem of her long skirt. Perfect skin from ankle upwards, until just below the knee.

"Wow! They look like battle wounds!"

A mass of scars crisscrossed her skin. Some were old, healed, pink lines, others more recent angry slashes.

If she'd said she worked with big cats, or Tasmanian devils, I wouldn't have been surprised. But penguins?

"Penguins did that?"

"Yes, you can see where my boots end, can't

you? And what's more, penguins may not have teeth, but they have spikes on their tongues."

"No way! Seriously? Spikes on their tongues?"

"Yes, they use them to grip the fish."

"I had no idea penguins were so dangerous!" I said.

And that wasn't all I learnt about penguins that day. I didn't know that a bunch of penguins on land is called a waddle, or huddle, and if they are in the water, they are called a raft.

And penguins can drink seawater. Who knew? And the oldest penguin fossil ever found was 62 million years old.

Neither did I know that penguins poop every twenty minutes, which is why the penguin keepers are kept busy cleaning up. And that Taronga Zoo (if I remember the number correctly) produces five tonnes of fake snow every day for their feisty exhibits.

Christmas Day and Boxing Day passed in a haze of heat, hilarity, fun, food, family, and penguins. The time came for Lola and me to return home. Our house felt quiet after the days spent with the family, but we settled in quickly and enjoyed each other's company. The days were hot, and I opened all the doors. With the flyscreens in place, I hoped that a summer breeze might waft through the house and cool us.

And then it started. A whirring, grating sound that grew louder and louder.

It was coming from outside, so I stepped outside to find out what on earth it was. Was our air conditioner box outside playing up?

No, it wasn't the air conditioner, but it was definitely coming from that side of the house and was increasing in volume. It wasn't caused by anything on our property, so it must emanate from my next-door neighbour.

I couldn't see over the fence, but I could guess the cause. My neighbours had a covered deck with a table and chairs that ran along that side of their house, and I thought I remembered they had an outside ceiling fan above the table. I was willing to bet that the fan had rusted and developed a fault, which was causing that ghastly, grating, whirring sound.

But why did they not do something about it? Hour by hour, the noise grew worse—deafening—and my neighbours did nothing about it. Perhaps they had gone away?

"You'll have to go next door and complain about it," said Joe from the other side of the planet when he heard my rant.

I knew he was right. I'd taken the iPad outside when we'd been Facetiming, and even he could hear it. How could our neighbours allow that frightful mechanical buzzing to continue? If that broken fan was driving *me* crazy, surely it was even worse for them?

Mercifully, the awful noise stopped when night fell and I hoped I'd never hear it again. With luck, my neighbours had switched their fan off, or had the wretched machine repaired. I'm not the kind of person who complains very much and I really didn't want to march next door and make a fuss.

But morning brought it back again. At first quite softly, then louder and louder until I found I was walking around with my hands clapped over my ears in an attempt to block out the horrendous sound. It was driving me insane.

"It's no good," I said to Lola. "I've got to do something about it. I'm going next door to complain."

CHRISTMAS TREE WAFFLES

Christmas is always a rush, so you can always decide to cheat and use readymade waffle mix. Ssssshh!

www.thebestideasforkids.com/christmas-breakfast-ideas-kids-christmas-tree-waffles/

Ingredients

2 cups plain (all-purpose) flour

¼ cup sugar

3.5 tsp baking powder

2 large eggs – separate yolks & whites

1½ cups milk

1 cup butter, melted

1 tsp vanilla extract

green food colouring

your choice of edible sprinkles

Method

In a mixing bowl, mix the flour, sugar and baking powder.

Separate the egg yolks from the egg whites.

In a separate bowl, lightly beat the egg yolks.

Add the milk, butter and vanilla to the egg yolks.

Add the wet mixture to the dry ingredients.

Now beat the egg whites until stiff peaks form (you can do this manually or with an electric hand mixer).

Add the egg whites to the batter mix and stir to combine.

Add in the green food colouring. Mix until you get the desired green colour. You may need to add a lot depending on the strength of your food colouring.

You can now add your mixture into the waffle maker.

When baking in the waffle maker, make sure to set the waffle maker on the lowest setting possible and monitor the waffles. If overcooked, the waffles will turn brown, so start off really low and keep checking the colouring.

Break the waffle into thirds to form the Christmas tree.

Cut a star out of gold glitter paper and tape to a toothpick to put on top of the tree.

Serve with sprinkles and maple syrup.

8

COMING HOME

I headed for the front door with a purposeful stride, but I never reached it. My phone rang and the screen told me it was Karly ringing from Sydney.

"Hi, Karly, how are you?"

"Hi Mum, just thought I'd catch up while I'm walking LJ. I can hardly hear you, can you speak up?"

"Why, what's the matter? Something wrong with the phone?"

"Nope, it's the cicadas. I'm walking in the woods and I think it's because it's been so hot and they are everywhere. I can't *believe* how loud they are this year! Can you hear them on the phone? Have you got them where you are, too?"

I gasped. "Um…"

"Honestly, they are like a million rusty motors whirring away," said Karly. "You'll have to speak up or I won't hear you."

"Thank you. You have just saved me from making a complete and utter fool of myself."

"Pardon?"

I explained about the broken outdoor ceiling fan next door that was making my life a misery, and the fact that I'd just girded my loins to go and complain.

"It's not a broken fan, is it?" I said in a small voice. "It's a cicada."

"That's hilarious!"

Clearly, this Pommy had a lot to learn. We don't have cicadas in Britain, and the ones we had in Spain were smaller and much more polite than these Aussie whoppers. I made it my business to find out more about these strange creatures.

I guess it came as no surprise to find out that Australian cicadas are the loudest insects in the world, some reaching 120 decibels which is painful to the human ear. I'd discovered that for myself.

In Australia, the nymphs live underground for six to seven years—no kidding, years. Actually, some species spend seventeen years underground. They feed on roots, and grow and shed their skins at intervals. Then, they dig their way to the surface, climb up a tree trunk, wall, or post, and shed their skin for the last time.

That December, when I walked with Lola along the lake under the trees, brittle, empty cicada skins crunched underfoot. Tree trunks were plastered with cicadas, either live ones crawling out of their skins, or empty cases. The heat and drought were the perfect conditions for a bumper cicada year.

Once the cicadas have shrugged off their final skin, the cicada party begins. The males begin to sing, hoping to attract a wife. The louder the song, the more the girls like it. And the boys can keep this up for days and days, particularly through the heat of the day.

Sadly, after the female has laid her eggs on a tree, she will die. The male, having mated, has fulfilled his lifecycle, and he will also die. More cicada corpses join the ones already littering the ground. The eggs hatch in the trees and the nymphs fall to the ground. Many are eaten by birds and insects, but the survivors burrow and grow and the cycle begins again.

But there is another, lesser known fact about cicadas that I didn't grasp until years later.

Cicadas pee.

Profusely.

COMING HOME

Actually, it's not pee, it's ejected tree sap that has passed through the cicada, which I think is just as bad. And they do it all day long. Walking under the trees, one can feel squirts drop from the branches above. Some call it 'summer rain' or 'honeydew', but that doesn't make it any nicer. It's tasteless, odourless and washes off easily, but it's not a good idea to linger, or park your car under trees in summer.

I urge you to check out the photo album that accompanies this book.[1] Shealan took a great close-up photo of a red-eyed cicada and managed to video[2] cicadas squirting. You have been warned.

Australian summers are hot, but it was an exceptionally hot summer that year. In fact, weather experts declared December 2017 to be the end of one of the hottest, driest years on record in the state of New South Wales, leaving fire authorities pinning their hopes on rain before heatwaves could build up any more.

In the year when a huge Arctic chill embraced most of the eastern side of North America, we were officially in the grip of a deadly drought.

---

1. Check out the photos and videos on the Free Stuff page on my website. https://bit.ly/Free--Stuff
2. Cicadas squirting https://youtu.be/JvnH4fLzlZk

TWO OLD FOOLS FAIR DINKUM

Just after Christmas, the familiar airport shuttle bus headed towards our home. Lola and I were glued to the window, watching for it. Finally, it turned the corner and came to a halt outside our house. Of course, I didn't hear the conversation going on inside the bus, but Joe told me.

"Is this your place, mate?" called the driver over his shoulder, slowing down.

"Thank you, yes," said Joe, no doubt scratching himself irritably. "I just hope my wife keeps our dog in. If she doesn't, I'll bet the bloomin' dog will greet me before the wife does."

"He's here!" I said, and threw open the front door.

An orange furry torpedo shot out and flew up the drive to the bus before hurling itself at Joe, who was trying to alight. The driver in his bright Hawaiian shirt guffawed and gales of laughter from all the passengers accompanied Joe's descent.

"Get down, Lola, stop it! Now just behave!"

And then it was my turn. We hugged while Lola danced around us and the driver extricated the luggage. Joe thanked him and said his goodbyes. Then the three of us turned our backs on it, and headed back to the house.

Joe was home.

January stayed hot and marked the beginning of the academic year in Australia. Indy began school. It melted our hearts to see the little girl swamped in her crisp new school uniform. I gazed at the photo. Indy's blonde hair was braided, exactly the same way I used to braid her mother's hair for school, so many decades ago.

"How did Indy's first day go?" I asked Karly that evening.

"She absolutely loved it! Loves her teacher and has two best friends already."

No surprise there, then.

Indy was at that age where she soaked up everything like a sponge. Her teacher said she chattered too much, but Indy's mother had been exactly the same.

"Your daughter is doing really well, she's very bright," Karly's teacher told me, thirty years ago. "And she'd probably do even better if she stopped chatting…"

I guess history repeats itself.

After a few weeks, Indy had settled in beautifully. She had a natural presence and was the kind of magnetic child who was always surrounded by friends. I occasionally went with Karly to collect her from school and was amused to see other children nudging their parents and exclaiming, "Look, Mum, there's Indy from Kindy!" as though she were a tiny celebrity.

I was also delighted to see the sulphur-crested cockatoos interact with the children in the schoolyard.

And Indy had already picked up many things in school. Like teacher-speak, for example.

"Nanny, do you think it'll rain this afternoon?" she asked me once.

I paused, looked at the sky, and considered my answer.

"It's okay, Nanny," she said seriously, her eyes wide and caring. "Don't worry, there's no right or wrong answer."

"Sometimes I feel that time is slipping through our fingers," I said to Joe. "Look at Indy. Already at school. And I really feel we should think about getting out and seeing as much of this beautiful country as possible. Perhaps we could get a little motorhome or caravan?"

"Hold on! I've only just arrived back in Australia. Give me time to catch my breath!"

So I didn't mention it again for a long time, but I couldn't help looking online, and my eye was often caught by For Sale signs in windows of caravans parked by the side of the road.

It was around that time when the word Bitcoin began to pop up frequently on the news. I still don't quite understand how a virtual currency can be 'mined' or have any worth, for that matter. But Shealan not only understood it, he had dabbled in it since its infancy. Suddenly the value of this funny money began to rise and everybody was talking about the Bitcoin bubble.

"Thanks to my Bitcoin investment, I'm going to buy the car of my dreams," he announced.

What would it be? A Porsche? A red Ferrari? Or a Jaguar? We knew better.

"I've bought a secondhand Jeep."

"Really? What colour."

"Um, it's orange and black."

"When do you get it?"

"I have to wait for it to be transported here."

"Why? Where is it? Is it being shipped from abroad?"

"No, it's in Australia. Um, it's coming from Perth."

I don't think I grasped just how enormous Australia is before I moved there. Maybe Shealan hadn't either. The flight from Sydney to Perth is over five hours long, and the journey by road is 2,444 miles or 3,933 kilometres. That's about the same distance as England to Israel, or to Chad in Africa.

Nevertheless, the Jeep finally arrived, and he was delighted with it. Sadly, he didn't research Australian road signs nearly as diligently as secondhand Jeeps and soon acquired three parking tickets. He didn't know it was an offence to park one's car facing oncoming traffic.

And he may have been clever with virtual money, but he wasn't so good at dog-minding, either. One day, when Karly and Cam were out, he left the front door open when he went to empty the rubbish into the dustbin. As usual, LJ took the opportunity to escape and track down his missing family.

Shealan called and searched. No LJ. Cam and Karly returned and went out looking, calling his name. No LJ. Night dropped. Karly phoned all the numbers where LJ had visited before. He hadn't gone to Roxy's house, nor to the family that fed him leftover steak. All the local vets were closed, but she left messages in case he was handed in.

Now it was too late and dark to search any more. LJ had been missing for three-and-a-half hours. Karly, Cam and Shealan were devastated.

Was LJ lost and roaming unfamiliar territory? Had he been hit by a car?

It was time to go to bed and Karly opened the front door one last time.

LJ walked in.

Where had he been for three-and-a-half hours? We'll never know, but he was unhurt. And he was home.

LJ was a very smart dog. For instance, he knew that the chickens were family and not to be disturbed. He also knew that bush turkeys (also known as brush turkeys or scrub turkeys) were *not* welcome in the garden and needed chasing out.

Bush turkeys are very big birds, black and glossy, apart from the crazy-red featherless head and neck, and the bright yellow wattle. This wattle inflates at mating time, and becomes even brighter in colour. Like domestic turkeys, the bush turkey sports a prominent, fan-like tail flattened sideways, making it a flamboyant sight.

So why are bush turkeys so unpopular? The problem lies with the bush turkey's nest. The male works tirelessly to build a great mound of soil and leaf litter, sometimes the size of a family car. If the female approves, she'll lay her eggs in the mound and covers them up. Then she loses interest and wanders off, having nothing more to do with her husband or her incubating chicks.

The mound is tended by the male, but he doesn't sit on the eggs. Instead, he tends the mound, which works like a compost heap. The centre is naturally warm. Amazingly, the male can read the temperature by sticking his beak into the mound and will adjust the heat by adding or removing more leaf matter.

Other females saunter past, and if they like the look of the mound and its guardian, they too may lay their eggs in the same mound. There may be twenty eggs, or up to fifty if enough females approve of the real estate. Curiously, the eggs are positioned standing up, always with the large end facing up.

Eventually, if the eggs haven't been plundered by raiding goannas, snakes or dingoes, they hatch.

And where are the parents?

Gone.

Both have lost interest, leaving their defenceless chicks to fight their way out of the giant compost heap all by themselves. This can take two days, and once they have come up for air they have to learn to forage. They are fully fledged and can fly as soon as their feathers dry.

What remarkable birds! I've always had a really soft spot for them ever since Joe and I were exploring Queensland in a motorhome back in 2008.

I remember we stayed in a delightful campsite for several days. It was full of beautiful Aussie birds of all sizes. Bush turkeys ignored the tourists and scratched in the soil.

Another attraction was the splash of brilliant colour and noise provided by the little rainbow lorikeets that shared the park with us. They were so fearless that we could feast our eyes on their beautiful colours really close up.

Flocks of ducks grazed around the vans and tents. Not your ordinary ducks, oh no. These ducks didn't quack. They whistled to each other. Did you know there was such a thing as a whistling duck? We didn't. The plumed whistling duck is an elegant, long-necked duck, with very prominent long, cream plumes edged in black that flick up in the air. These delightful ducks, and there were hundreds of them, visited the caravan park to graze around the vans every evening as the sun went down. [3]

---

3. Whistling ducks in Queensland https://www.youtube.com/watch?v=DnzfkTQWK68

But the rainbow lorikeets stole the show.

I know that feeding birds with bread or other manmade scraps is not a good idea. Bread swells in their stomachs and can kill little birds. But I yearned to give them something that they liked and would be safe for them so that we could enjoy their company.

"Let's find out what attracts them next time we go to the shops," I suggested.

"Honey water," said a voice. "They love that."

I swung around. Our neighbour in the caravan parked beside us had heard my comment. We'd talked with him before, and he was a fount of wisdom. A well-travelled Aussie, Ollie told us how he had sold his house when his wife passed away and had taken to the road with his dog, Skip.

"I've been travelling for fifteen years," he said, "and I've only seen a fraction of this beautiful country."

I could believe that easily. Australia is an unbelievably vast continent with every climate, from snowy mountains to tropical rainforests.

"Skip and I have lots more to explore, don't we?" he said, gently stroking the greying muzzle of his ancient companion. Skip's tail waved. "She's great company, always has been. Loves people, not so great with other dogs, though."

"Fancy a beer?" said Joe. "The sun's just going down."

"Thanks, mate," said Ollie, "I'll get a chair and join you."

QUEENSLAND VINTAGE UPSIDE-DOWN CAKE

If you've read *Dear Fran, Love Dulcie*[1], you'll understand when I say I'm sure Dulcie would have baked these upside-down cakes. As a pineapple farmer's wife, she must have known dozens of ways to use those delicious Queensland pineapples.

---

1. Title: *Dear Fran, Love Dulcie: Life and Death in the Hills and Hollows of Bygone Australia*

Imagine a true story that unfolds in the harshness of Australia's outback, beginning in 1957 and spanning decades. Imagine Dulcie's battle to keep her family and animals alive in spite of bushfires, floods, cyclones, droughts, dingo attacks and terrible accidents.

The story of Dulcie, a simple Queensland pineapple farmer's wife, has so many twists and turns that it will leave you gasping.

Amazon Link: https://bit.ly/Love--Dulcie

Ingredients

½ teaspoon vanilla

1 cup flour

1 cup sugar

¼ teaspoon salt

3 eggs

½ teaspoon lemon extract

1½ teaspoons baking powder

4 tablespoons cold water

Topping Ingredients overleaf

3 tablespoons butter

1 cup brown sugar

pineapple rings

Method

Beat egg yolks with sugar, add water, lemon and vanilla extract.

Sift dry ingredients and add to mixture.

Beat well for 5 minutes.

Fold in well-beaten whites of eggs.

Preparation of the pan for baking:

In an iron skillet, melt three tablespoons of butter and add one cup of brown sugar. Do not heat.

In this, arrange slices of pineapple until the bottom of the skillet is well covered.

Pour the cake batter on top and bake in a moderate oven for about 45 minutes. When removed from the oven, invert on a platter.

Note: The trick is to have a well-greased cake pan. After removing the cake from the oven, slide a knife or spatula to loosen the cake around the pan. Put a serving plate on top of the cake pan and flip the cake upside down to show off the yummy caramelised pineapple.

Serve with whipped cream.

THIS RECIPE COMES FROM THE STATE LIBRARY OF QUEENSLAND

9

SKIP

Ollie soon returned with a six-pack, a chair, and an old rug for Skip to lie on.

We spent a very pleasant evening swapping stories and watching the night close in. The rainbow lorikeets swooped away to their nighttime roosts, arguing and shrieking. The last whistling duck departed into the gloom. Countless fruit bat silhouettes appeared against the coral sky, and a couple of bush turkeys flapped up into the branches of a nearby tree.

"I didn't know they could fly so well," I remarked, sipping my wine.

"Oh yes, they don't fly much, but they will if threatened, or going to roost," said Ollie, patting Skip's grey head.

"Do people eat bush turkeys?" Joe asked.

"Oh yes, there's a traditional recipe for cooking bush turkey the Aussie way."

Always interested in recipes, I listened carefully.

"It's a very simple, outdoor recipe," Ollie began. "What you do is build a good, hot fire, and half-fill a cauldron with water. Put a couple of stones in the water and wait until the water is boiling nicely."

"Stones? What size stones?"

"Ordinary rocks will do, about the size of your fist. Washed first, of course."

We nodded. Ollie cracked open another tinny.

"You'll have prepared your turkey before that, naturally. When the water is boiling vigorously, it's time to put your turkey in the pot. You can add salt, pepper, spices, whatever you fancy, really. Let it boil for half an hour or so, then your dinner is ready."

"That's it?"

"Yep, that's it. Dinner's ready."

"Really?"

"Yep." Long pause. "So you take out the turkey and throw it away and eat the rocks because they are going to taste a whole lot better than that turkey will. And they're not so tough."

Our laughter woke Skip from her slumbers.

The next day, we checked out the pet shop and bought some special powder made specifically for little birds that feed on nectar. The directions on the back of the sachet advised us to mix it up with water. We bought a couple of rectangular aluminium foil dishes, the type you use to roast stuff in the oven.

I couldn't wait to see what the rainbow lorikeets thought of our purchase. I shook the powder into a glass jug, added water and stirred the mixture briskly.

"Right, lorikeets," I said, "let's see if you like this."

I poured the honey water into the two foil containers and set them out on the grass, then retreated into the shade by the motorhome to sit and wait.

"How long are we going to wait here?" asked Joe after precisely one minute.

"Have patience! They'll be here. Now shhh! I can see something rustling in that bush."

"Lorikeets don't rustle, they screech."

"Of course it's not lorikeets, don't be ridiculous!" I hissed. "Perhaps it's a wombat or something. Shhh, you'll frighten it away."

We didn't have to wait much longer. A muddy nose poked out from the foliage. Joe and I shot glances at each other.

"Wombat?" I mouthed.

Joe shrugged his shoulders and shook his head. We didn't know much about Australian wildlife then, or we would have known it wouldn't be a wombat. Wombats are nocturnal, live in forested or heathland areas and are unlikely to pop out of bushes in broad daylight.

Also a wombat's nose looks nothing like the nose we were watching.

Very slowly, a face appeared, but we still couldn't identify it. Perhaps it might have been easier if it hadn't been caked in mud. We waited.

The creature crept forward, leaving the sanctuary of the bushes, its eyes fixed on the bowl filled with honey water. It hadn't seen us in the shadows.

"It's a puppy!" I whispered, and Joe nodded.

Yes, it was a puppy, but not a cute, fat, roly-poly, happy, healthy puppy. This puppy was dirty and emaciated, its backbone and ribs clearly visible. It was shivering although the day was warm. Clearly thirsty, it lapped the honey water.

"Oh, poor thing!" I whispered. "It must be a stray. It looks starving, I'm going to see if I can catch it."

The puppy was lapping with such gusto, it didn't sense me creeping up behind it. I lunged but it was too quick. I grabbed thin air and the puppy darted back into the bushes.

"Quick, help me find it," I said to Joe. "It can't have gone far."

We peered into the bushes and pulled branches aside, but there was no sign of the pup.

"What are you going to do with it if we do find it? We're on holiday in a motorhome, don't forget."

"I don't know, let's talk about that if we find it."

"What are you looking for?" asked a voice behind us.

I looked up to see our neighbour, Ollie.

"Hi Ollie, we're looking for a stray puppy. It came out of these bushes and when I tried to catch it, it vanished back in here somewhere."

"Ah, was it in a bad way?"

"It didn't look injured, but it was painfully thin, and very nervous."

"Put out some fresh water and a bit of food for it," Ollie suggested. "It'll come back, you mark my words."

"Vicky, can I remind you that we are on holiday? We can't drive around picking up dozens of stray cats and dogs as we go along."

"Not dozens, just one."

"Oh, good grief!" Joe exclaimed as a thought struck him. "You'll be tempting it out with one of those prime beef burgers you bought for my dinner, I'll bet."

Great idea! I thought and quickly changed the subject.

"Where's Skip?" I asked Ollie.

Ollie's eyes saddened. "I've left her snoozing in the sun by the van. Poor old girl. She's not getting any younger and she has bad arthritis in her back legs. I'll leave her be. She'd frighten the pup away anyway, she's not keen on the young 'uns."

That evening, Joe and I talked in hushed tones as we sat outside the motorhome watching the sun go down.

"I can't believe you stole one of my beef burgers to use as bait for some rabid, flea-bitten passing hound," he said for the hundredth time.

I wasn't fooled, he'd hardly put up a fight at all, and he was the one who filled the bowl with water.

"It was only a half. I don't want to make the puppy sick with too much rich meat. I'll give it the other half tomorrow."

"You what? Are you…"

"Sssh!"

I stared at the bushes. Had I seen those leaves, tinted gold by the dying rays of the sun, trembling? Was our little visitor returning?

Yes! Joe's Wagu beef burger was a great success. Lured by the smell of meat, the grimy pup made another appearance. I was a lot younger in those days, so I tensed my muscles and prepared to execute an athletic lunge. One deep breath, and I dived…

Unfortunately, my attempted rugby tackle resulted in grass-stained knees but no catch. The pup seized the beef burger and vanished into the twilight shadows before I had even got back on my feet.

"Well, that did a lot of good, didn't it?" crowed Joe, displaying a woeful lack of empathy. "It clearly doesn't want to be caught, does it? I suggest we pack up and move on to a new caravan park tomorrow."

"We are not moving on until we catch that puppy and sort it out," I said between clenched teeth and threw him one of my Looks. "Tomorrow is another day."

Joe scratched himself irritably but wisely said no more.

Over the next couple of days, the puppy grew braver, but I never managed to catch it. It devoured the food we left out for it and I felt that it was already looking a little healthier and stronger.

"We need to catch it and get it checked over by a vet," I said to Joe. "Then we can hand it over to a local rescue centre, or something. Hey, I bet Ollie knows if there's a pound, or rescue place nearby."

"We mustn't bother him," said Joe. "I saw him this morning and he's going through a really hard time. He told me he thinks he's losing Skip. She's not eating and doesn't want to get up."

"Oh no!"

"She's a very old dog, you know."

"I know. Have they been to the vet?"

"Yes. He said that she isn't in any pain, thank goodness. He told Ollie to spoil her, give her whatever she wants, and keep her comfortable."

"That's so sad."

"I know."

The puppy didn't appear at all that evening and I was worried. The shredded chicken I left out remained untouched until I saw a magpie gobbling it up the next morning.

"It's probably a good sign," Joe said hopefully. "Perhaps somebody else managed to catch it."

"What if it got hit by a car? Or attacked by a fox or something?"

"I'm sure it's fine."

I truly hoped so, but I couldn't get the puppy

out of my mind. The puppy never appeared and I began to search for it. I walked around the caravan park to no avail. The day wore on and I worried, imagining all sorts of horrible scenarios.

"What if an eagle snatched it up? We've seen heaps of huge eagles around here."

"There's no point worrying," said Joe. "I'm sure it's fine."

But I saw his eyes searching the bushes. I fretted until the sun began to drop in the sky. Then a soft call broke into my thoughts.

"Vicky? Joe? Are you there? Come and see this, but come quietly, no sudden movements."

It was Ollie's voice. Joe and I exchanged glances, wide-eyed.

We crept around our neighbour's caravan, towards the voice. Ollie had his back to us but he sensed us behind him. He held up his hand, signalling us to be still. We froze.

"Is it Skip?" I whispered, unable to see Ollie's expression or where he was looking.

"Yes," he said softly. "And a bit of a surprise. Look, they've been like that for the best part of an hour."

He stood aside and we gasped. Skip was curled almost into a circle on an old blanket. She lifted her head at the sound of her beloved master's voice.

And then we saw it. Secure and sleepy in the old dog's embrace, was the little stray. Skip licked the puppy's head and the pup sighed in contentment. We gaped, scarcely believing our eyes.

"What?"

"How?"

Ollie beckoned us away so that we could talk without disturbing the pair. We backed away.

"Don't ask me!" he said shaking his head in disbelief. "All I know is that I put out food for Skip, but she wouldn't touch it, as usual. I always keep an eye on it because the magpies or kookaburras steal it if they can. Then up comes that little urchin." Ollie's hand rubbed his beard as he relived the scene.

Joe and I waited.

"Then, blow me down, but the pup just helps himself to Skip's food, with Skip watching. Did I tell you she's not good with other dogs?"

We both nodded.

"Well, the pup finishes the food, has a good drink of water, and my Skip is watching all the time. And you know what? Her tail is wagging!" He inhaled and blinked with moist eyes. "You know what? That's the first time I've seen her tail wag in a week."

"And the pup didn't run away?"

"Nope, it just trots over ever so slowly, and now both the pup's tail and my Skip's tail are going like the clappers. And the pup just kinda creeps in close and snuggles down. And the old girl is washing its head like it's her long-lost child. If I hadn't seen it with me own eyes, I wouldn't have believed it."

"That's extraordinary!"

"Yup, and she's never had her own litter of pups so I don't know how she knows what to do. But the pair of them are as happy as I'd be if I won the lotto."

"You don't mind? What are you going to do with the pup?"

"I'm not sure, I think I'll let my Skip decide. If she wants to adopt the little tyke, then I'll let her. Looks like she'll make a great foster mum. And the vet did say I should spoil her, give her whatever she wanted. She's been the best dog a man could ask for, so it's the least I can do for her. And she'll teach the little pest some manners, no doubt."

Joe and I returned to our van, our faces wreathed in smiles.

"So," said Joe, "can we pack up and move on now?"

"Yes! But let's stay just one day more. I want to know the end of the story."

HOMEMADE PARROT TREATS

These seed balls are just for occasional treats (once or twice a week) and are not suitable for everyday feeds. Oh, and budgies are (tiny) parrots, too!

Recipe from allpetseducationandtraining.com.au/homemade-bird-treats.html

Ingredients

½ cup quality birdseed

½ cup oats

Plain (all-purpose) flour

¼ cup of honey

1 tablespoon of water

Dried fruit chopped finely (optional)

Method

Preheat oven to 180°C (350°F).

Put the dry ingredients, (birdseed, oats, flour) into a mixing bowl, along with the finely chopped dried fruit.

Mix well.

Add the water and mix well. The mixture will seem dry.

Add the honey and mix well until it becomes a dough.

If the mixture is too sticky, add some more flour and seed, a tiny bit at a time.

Roll into small balls. You may need to wash your hands frequently as they become too sticky.

Line a baking tray with foil and place the balls, not allowing them to touch each other.

Use a skewer or chopstick to push a hole through each ball if you are planning to hang them.

Bake for 20-30 minutes and remove when slightly browned.

Store when cool in an airtight container.

10

DOGS, BIG AND SMALL

Joe nodded. The campsite was in a lovely area near the beach, and there were plenty of places still to explore.

"Another day here won't hurt," he agreed.

Ollie took the mucky pup to the vet the next day, and old Skip came, too. We saw them return and I couldn't wait to hear how they got on. Ollie was carrying the pup and Skip was sticking tight to Ollie's side, glancing up constantly at the pup in his arms, but there was a spring in her step.

"That doesn't look like the same puppy!" I exclaimed looking at the black furry bundle.

"He's had a bath. Turns out he's quite a handsome little fellow under all that muck. The vet gave me this blue collar for him. Suits him, doesn't it?"

"It certainly does."

"Seems he's pretty healthy, too. The vet gave him a good checking over and all the puppy vaccinations. Didn't charge me a cent."

"That was kind of him!"

"It sure was. He said seeing old Skip looking so much better was payment enough."

"Have you decided?" I wondered. "Are you tempted to keep him?"

Ollie looked down at old Skip. Her eyes were bright and had lost their flatness. Her tail waved.

"You know what?" he said, "I think Skip has decided for the both of us. Yep, Lucky stays."

"Well, he was a mucky pup, and now he's a lucky pup. Great name!"

Skip's tail thrashed as though she had understood everything we'd said. There was no doubt about it, that puppy had given the old dog a new lease of life. We finished packing up and left the next day, having watched Skip and her little charge devouring a hearty breakfast together.

And what about the lorikeets, you may ask. Did they come and drink the honey water? Well, yes, they did. But things didn't turn out quite as we planned.

When the puppy appeared, the lorikeets flew away in disgust but soon returned when the coast was clear. Chattering and bickering in a dazzle of colour, they landed on the edge of the metal container, their tiny claws gripping. Tilting forward, they stopped arguing just long enough to dip their orange beaks into the sweet water before tipping their exquisite heads back to allow the delicious liquid to run down their throats.

But not for long. Something else emerged from the bushes and marched with determination towards the colourful, noisy party. The lorikeets chattered louder but showed no fear even though the huge, black newcomer towered over the little parrots.

It was a big, male bush turkey. His feathers gleamed blue-black in the sunshine, and his yellow, pendulous wattle swung as he advanced. The little lorikeets tipped and sipped daintily, but the bush turkey threw his head back, then leaned forward and hammered his beak into the dish.

Within moments, the lorikeets flew away, cursing and screeching insults over their shoulders at the gatecrasher. The bush turkey also lost interest and wandered away.

"I wonder why they stopped feeding so quickly," said Joe, approaching the dish and peering down at it.

"No idea!"

Puzzled, he lifted the disposable aluminium roasting dish I'd used.

"Would you believe it, it's empty! Aha, and I can see why."

He held the dish up against the bright sky and solved the mystery. Dots of white light shone through. The bush turkey had peppered the base with holes from his drumming beak. Every drop of the sweet nectar had drained away and seeped into the grass.

But now it was 2018, and twenty years had passed since we met Ollie, Skip and Lucky the mucky pup. Shealan's three-month probation ended, and his employers were pleased with his work. His partner, Daria, arrived in Australia, having been busy tying up loose ends in England. Karly and Cam took her in, too. Daria had been employed as an au pair many years ago and was brilliant with children. Indy and Winter adored her.

Our family group was growing, and I couldn't have been happier. Joe had settled in well and was following doctors' orders by exercising frequently even though it often became rather a chore.

Happily, Lola appointed herself as his personal trainer and took him for daily walks around the neighbourhood. With her nose to the ground, she led him hither and thither chasing exciting smells. She stopped often to read P-mail on posts and trees which gave him a chance to catch his breath.

All was well until one fateful day when they passed a house they had walked by countless times before. The side gate by the house was high, but something huge was hurling itself against it. Before Joe had a chance to react, the great head of a slobbering dog appeared. After another couple of attempts, the monster was over the fence and charging towards Lola.

Lola screamed as only a frightened dog can, and Joe's grip tightened on her lead.

"Get lost!" he shouted, but the attacking dog paid no heed.

Joe grabbed Lola and snatched her up, but she was a medium-sized dog weighing 12.5 kilos (28lb), and he was frail. Nevertheless, he managed to swing her around out of the brute's snarling reach, which caused it to leap up in an attempt to grab her.

Joe didn't have the strength to fight the dog or protect Lola, so he put her on top of a parked car, out of her attacker's reach.

Neighbours began to appear, having heard the

commotion. One kind, brave lady caught the brute by its collar, and held it back. Another checked on Joe who was collapsing from shock and breathlessness against the car.

"You okay, mate?"

But Joe couldn't answer. It took him a long time to gather enough breath to be able to speak.

"It came from nowhere," he said at last. "Jumped the gate."

The man nodded. "Yep, I just looked. It half-climbed the tree on the other side, and scrabbled up and over the gate. Your dog okay?"

"Yes, she's just frightened."

"I'll take this dog into my house until his owners come home," called the wonderful lady who had caught the escapee. "He's typical of the breed, fine with people but bloody awful with other animals."

"Thank you so much."

When she closed the front door behind her, Joe helped Lola jump down. Lola's legs shook, but she was otherwise unharmed.

"Where do you live, mate?" asked the man. "Can you make it back home okay?"

"I don't think so," admitted Joe, "I'll just phone my wife to come and pick us up."

I was minutes away and came to the rescue immediately, shocked to hear the sorry tale.

"What terrible luck," I said. "You were just walking past. I guess it's the fault of the owners though, not the dog."

"Oh, come on, Vicky! It hardly matters what the owner does. It's all in the breed."

"What do you mean?"

"Genetics! Border collies will always herd, right? Greyhounds sprint if they have something to chase. Poodles are highly-strung and anxious. Labradors are always hungry. Retrievers, um, retrieve…"

"Yes, yes, what's your point?"

"It's in their nature. Some dogs were originally bred for bull-baiting. Stands to reason they regard other animals as prey."

"But we both know they are really loyal to their owners. And great with children. Don't they call them Nanny dogs?"

"Do they? I'll Google it."

When Joe gets his teeth into something, he's like, well, a terrier. He doesn't ever let go, and he was angry.

"There! I knew it!" he said. "It's a complete myth! There is absolutely no fact to back it up, it's just something that lovers of the breeds repeat. And guess what?" He pointed at the screen.

"What?"

"Those dogs are banned in certain countries.

Well done to Germany, Switzerland and the Bermuda Islands. I wish other countries would follow suit."

"Okay, okay. I do understand your point. You and Lola had a horrible scare, but you are both okay now. That's enough now."

Sadly, that incident affected both Joe and Lola. Joe never, ever walked Lola on his own again since that day in 2018. He was too afraid of what could happen and knew he wouldn't be strong enough to fend off an attack on Lola or himself.

And Lola developed a fear of big dogs.

During the summer, that didn't really matter. It was usually too hot to walk or chase a ball anyway. Lola, as Joe's self-appointed personal trainer, was determined that they both kept up a strict exercise regime. As soon as Joe disappeared into the bedroom to change into his swimming trunks, she knew what was about to happen.

Swimming!

Crying with excitement, she stretched herself along the bottom of the bedroom door, body and nose pressed to the gap like a hairy, orange draught excluder, willing him to be quick. Finally, Joe came out and she danced backwards and forwards, urging him to hurry up.

Together, they entered the water. Joe waded in slowly, while Lola threw herself in like a woolly comet. And then the fun began. Races, fetch, or if I was swimming too, piggy-in-the-middle.

Her passion for swimming has never waned and she still delights in throwing herself into water for a swim. Funnily enough, she loves ponds, pools and puddles. But baths? Nope. Not so much.

"Don't tell them that Lollipop usually wins," Joe said when I told him I planned to include a photo of him and Lola racing in the next Old Fools newsletter.

"Of course not," Pinocchio replied.

At the time, Joe was a really good swimmer, but *Lola always won*[1].

We bought ourselves a couple of secondhand bikes that year. The bikes folded up and we could stash them in the boot of the car and drive to one of the many cycle tracks close by.

---

1. Joe and Lola swimming https://youtu.be/spSP5Lh9ljA

Naturally, Lola came too. I bought a gadget called a dog-jogger. It was a rod attached to the bike, with a length of leash at the end that clipped to Lola's harness. This ensured that Lola ran alongside and could not cross in front or get tangled in the wheels in any way.

Lola loved to run, and when she saw us load the bikes into the car, she would bark with excitement.

I was aware that I should never overdo it, and I kept the pace steady. I didn't want to overtire Joe or Lola.

Our favourite ride was the cycle path that hugged the lake. It was flat and easy, and there was always plenty to see. We took picnics and sat and watched the black swans fishing. Herons waded through the water, and fish jumped.

One day, the lakeside path wove us through a little woodland and I caught the sound of cockatoos. I stopped pedalling, looked up and was astonished to see the branches above laden with white cockatoos like exotic Christmas decorations.

"Stop," I called to Joe. "I want to take a photo of them."

Joe obliged and I began to snap photos.

I don't think I'd ever seen so many cockatoos in one group. And they were very vocal. Every tree held dozens of them, and the noise was getting louder.

I switched to taking a video, to catch the sounds, but I didn't know where to point. The air crackled with excitement and the cockatoos shrieked. Clearly, some event was taking place, and I had no idea what the fuss was all about.

Suddenly, they all took to the air, and I realised I wasn't seeing dozens of cockatoos at all, I was seeing at least a hundred. I didn't catch them all, but when Joe shouted, it all made sense.

"Vicky! It's an eagle! It's an eagle!"

You can see the video here[2]. It was a windy day, unfortunately, so there was unwanted noise,

---

2. See the cockatoos chase an eagle on Youtube: https://youtu.be/VAJzALN3QgE

but you'll hear the screech of the cockatoos, you'll hear Joe's shout, and you'll see the focus of the parrots' fury; a huge eagle.

The eagle gave up and flew away, and the cockatoos quietened and dropped back to their perches in the trees.

It wasn't the eagle's lucky day, but it definitely was ours.

I remember that May because we finally did something that we had been promising ourselves to do for ages. We lived just five minutes away from a superb whale-watching lookout called Splinterbone Crag. It's a high cliff, popular with paragliding folk and a perfect vantage point for whale-watchers.

A track from the public road leads through dense bush to Splinterbone Crag, protected national park land. The cliff juts out so there is a view over the ocean on three sides. Look left, and one sees several beaches: some with endless white sand and others crowded with rocks that throw surf up in white fountains. Out to sea, many, many miles away, the distant horizon meets the sky in a long, straight line, only interrupted by silhouettes of container ships heading for Sydney further down the coast.

In the closer waters, small crafts with white sails catch the sea breezes and tiny fishing boats ride the waves. Below us, surfers paddle out, waiting to catch that special roller.

A pair of white sea eagles nest on these cliffs every year and as they wheeled above us, I often thanked that lucky star that brought us to Australia to experience such unspeakably wonderful things.

"Splinterbone Crag? Oh yes, you'll see heaps of whales if you go there," everybody said.

"Really? Which time of day is best?"

"It doesn't matter, they pass all day and night. You can't miss them."

"Hmm, it sounds like Picadilly Circus," Joe remarked, mentioning the place in London where traffic is always heavy. There was doubt in his voice.

Excitedly, I downloaded an app that kept track of local whale sightings. We bought two pairs of good-quality binoculars. We were ready to spot the humpback whales on their annual migration up north to warmer waters to give birth.

Humpback whales have had a rough ride over the years. Sadly, whaling and exporting whale products became Australia's main industry back in the 19th century. Although hunting began in small boats with harpoons, whaling gradually became increasingly sophisticated and, with no control, many species of whale faced extinction by the 20th century.

Thank goodness, the International Whaling Commission banned the slaughter of humpbacks in 1963 but only a pitiful 4% of the humpback population had survived. Illegal hunting continued by whalers from the Soviet Union, who killed more than 48,000 up to 1973.

It was estimated that in 1963, only one hundred individuals remained in Australia's waters. Humpbacks teetered on the edge of extinction.

Thankfully, now living in protected waters, humpback numbers began to slowly rise as the whales began to thrive. By 2006, numbers had risen to approximately 8,000. Each year, numbers increase, and humpbacks are no longer in any immediate danger. They still have to contend with threats such as entanglement in fishing gear, shark nets, or collisions with ships or boat propellors. Pollution and climate change remain a threat. But on the whole, the future is bright, and the wholesale slaughter of humpbacks is shameful history.

"So how many whales are going to be swimming past Splinterbone Crag?" asked Joe.

"Around 30,000," I told him.

"Good grief!"

"Yup! I think we are absolutely guaranteed good sightings."

PAULA'S NONNA'S FRITTATA

Yummy picnic food, or cycling snack. Delicious hot or cold. Thanks, Paula!

Ingredients

8-10 eggs depending on size

1 cup of grated parmesan cheese

½ cup of parsley (chopped)

2 cloves garlic

2 cups of stale breadcrumbs

Salt and pepper to taste

1 cup of milk (measure ½ eggshell for each egg used)

Chopped tomato pieces or cherry tomatoes (optional)

Method

Beat eggs until light and fluffy.

Mix breadcrumbs, cheese, parsley and garlic together. Add mixture to eggs and combine.

Cover base of a heavy frying pan with oil (approx. ½ cup)

Heat on high, then lower the heat.

Fry egg mixture, keeping it moving so that the mixture doesn't stick. After 5 to 15 minutes it will set and come away from the side of the pan.

Remove pan, place a plate over the top, invert and gently slide the frittata back in and cook until the second side is ready.

11

VISITORS FROM OVERSEAS

"Listen to this," I said, reading from my computer screen. "Each January, the humpbacks leave the frigid, food-rich waters of Antarctica and begin the world's longest mammal migration, a 5,000 kilometre, three-month journey to the warm waters of northern Australia where they mate, calve and nurture their newborns."

"What, all of them?"

"Yes, I think so, but apparently, some turn right and swim up the west side of Australia, while the rest mill around Tasmania before swimming up the east coast of Australia."

"Really?"

"Yup."

"Past Splinterbone Crag?"

VISITORS FROM OVERSEAS

"For goodness sake! Yes! Past Splinterbone Crag. Why don't you believe me? Any time from May onwards. They swim all the way up to the barrier reef."

"So we can't miss them?"

"No, there are going to be thousands and *thousands*."

It was May, we had everything prepared, and we couldn't wait to see the migration. We left Lola at home because dogs aren't allowed in Australian national parks.

The first clue was obvious, but we didn't pick it up. We found it easy to park at Splinterbone Crag.

We ignored the fact that there was nobody else there apart from a couple leaning against a tree, so engrossed with each other that a whale could have tapped them on the shoulder with a fin, and they wouldn't have noticed.

We hurried to the railings and looked out over the vast ocean. Left, right, out to sea.

Nothing. No whales, no dolphins. Nothing except some hardy surfers in the waters at the foot of the cliff, and the loved-up couple leaning against the tree.

"Perhaps they are far out to sea," I said, squinting. "We need our binoculars."

So we fiddled with our brand-new binoculars,

attempting to get the settings just right. We swept the area, searching, searching.

Not a sausage.

Not quite true. We spotted two very distant container ships on the horizon, and a tiny fishing boat that rose and fell with the swell.

"Oh yes, 30,000 humpback whales?" Joe scoffed, lowering his binoculars and glowering at me. "So where are they?"

"Well, not 30,000 passing all at once. Not all in one day, that would be ridiculous."

"Listen," argued Joe the mathematician, "the whale season is supposed to last three months, yes? That means ten thousand whales pass each month. That means there are roughly one thousand passing each day."

"Yes, but..." I hated it when Joe argued in figures.

"We've been here nearly half an hour and seen nothing. Apart from that ...um... lively couple behind us."

"Perhaps we are just unlucky today, let's stay a bit longer. You have to admit the view is awesome."

"Hmmph," said Joe, and gave his nethers an irritable scratch.

"Don't do that!"

"What?"

VISITORS FROM OVERSEAS

"Scratch yourself like that."

"Why not? There's nobody else here to see me. Even that copulating couple has gone home now."

"There's a very handsome magpie over there."

Joe swung round just as the magpie flew away.

I gave up and admitted defeat, reminding myself that wildlife doesn't perform to order. And that dedicated naturalists sit in bushes or up trees for hours, days, weeks, or even months, waiting for a creature to appear.

It reminded me of the time we visited South Africa, decades ago. We drove through the Kruger National Park for several days, stopping at rest camps overnight. It was magical. We spotted giraffe, rhino, hippo, elephant, lion and countless other animals, even a leopard.

But one day, we saw *nothing*. All four of us searched the terrain for any movement, but there was no sign of life, all day. Disappointed, we returned to the rest camp that evening, driving slowly in case we caught a glimpse of something.

"Hey, what's that?" exclaimed our friend Barry, who was driving at the time.

He pointed to the road ahead and we all craned forward to see it. It wasn't exactly what we were looking for, but it was a fine sight and we were grateful to spot any native African creature that day.

"What is it?" asked Jacky, Barry's wife, as we drew up closer.

"Our first bit of wildlife today!"

"Stop the car!"

"Wow!" I said, "it's a giant African land snail! I've never seen one of those before."

It was a beauty, easily eight inches long, its shell a grand, conical masterpiece adorned with gleaming ridges and whorls. With its head held high and antennae pointing forward, it was slowly making its way across the road.

The roads in the Kruger National Park were never busy. One could drive for half an hour and not see another car. Even though the snail sighting was hardly as exciting as spotting wild dogs or lions, we were so starved of sightings that we gave it our full attention.

"What a beautiful thing," I said as we all leaned out of the windows to watch the snail labour across the road.

And then a terrible thing happened. A car appeared, heading towards us.

"NO!" we all shouted and waved our arms out of the windows, signalling the driver to stop. But the elderly couple in the oncoming car clearly didn't read our sign language. They sailed past, waving back merrily, probably thinking how friendly we were.

And the snail?

I'm afraid it met its demise. Nothing remained but a wet patch on the road and shattered shell pieces.

I've never forgotten that snail. It was the only African wildlife we saw that day and I'm so sorry it came to a sticky end.

Splinterbone Crag was like a magnet to us, and we visited it nearly every day that May, ever hopeful that we would see humpback whales. We never did see any, but we learned a lot. We learned not to bother going on days when the wind whipped up the waves and made visibility difficult. The same went for grey, cloudy days when the ocean was often cloaked with a silver mist.

And *never* start chatting with fellow whale watchers.

Why? Because conversations always went like this:

> Us: *Seen any whales yet?*
> Them: *No, not now, but a pod of five just rounded the headland an hour ago. Looked like two mothers and some juveniles. The young ones were having a wonderful time, breaching and playing. They stayed around for ages.*

or

Us: *Seen any whales yet?*
Them: *No, not yet. Did you come yesterday?*
Us: *Yes, in the morning, didn't see any.*
Them: *Oh, you should have come in the afternoon. There were loads of them! Some swam in really close. I swear they were putting on a show just for us.*

At this point, I saw Joe beginning to snarl and scratch, and I led him away before he exploded.

"We're doomed not to see any," Joe often said, and I had to agree with him as May drew to a disappointingly whale-less end.

On the first day of June we tried again, and it was like somebody had flicked a switch and opened an invisible gate across the ocean, allowing whales to pass through to swim past our vantage post.

"I think I see one!" I squeaked. "Look straight ahead, where the water changes to a darker blue colour. Wait, there's another swimming behind!"

"I see them!"

I lowered my binoculars to look at him and noted his binoculars were pointing in a different direction. He was watching another pod. The sea was thick with humpback whales.

VISITORS FROM OVERSEAS

Our wide-angle binoculars proved to be worth every penny we spent on them. We could spot that tell-tale spout of water from miles away, then track the whales as they came closer and closer until they passed us.

… So …

… many …

… whales!

Solitary whales, pods of five or more, mothers with juveniles, bachelor boys showing off and leaping out of the water. We saw them all.

Why do humpback whales 'breach' or jump out of the water?

And why do they 'lobtail' or hit the surface of the water with their tails?

Nobody really knows. Some say it's for communication, or to assert dominance. Maybe they do this to warn of danger, or even to remove parasites.

But Joe and I decided that the whales were simply enjoying themselves, leaping and splashing in the vast ocean. Wouldn't you?

During June and July we saw humpbacks every single time we visited Splinterbone Crag, without fail. Mesmerised, we watched until our shadows grew long as the sun sank into the surrounding bush and the sea eagles no longer wheeled overhead.

Now it was our turn to say to other eager sightseers, "Oh, you've just missed them. They were putting on an amazing performance a little while ago."

But we never attempted to whale-watch in May again. We'd learned our lesson. Wait until June and July when the ocean is literally boiling with these giant beauties.

Humpback whale lobtailing

Humpback whales were not the only visitors from overseas around that time. One day, I unrolled the free newspaper, the *Express Advocate*, that had been left in our mailbox and Usain Bolt fell out. It gave me quite a fright to see the fastest man on earth's face on the floor, grinning up at me.

"Joe! You'll never guess what fell out of the freebie newspaper."

"Hmm… A humpback whale?"

"Don't be ridiculous."

"What then?"

"Usain Bolt."

Silence. Then, "Usain Bolt? Now *you* are being ridiculous."

But I'd piqued his interest enough for him to trot over to see what on earth I was talking about.

I picked up Usain's face from the floor, turned it over and examined it. I handed it to Joe, who did the same. Usain's beaming, life-size face was printed on cardboard and appeared to have holes in the pupils of the eyes.

"Is it a mask?"

"Looks like it. But why?"

We found the answer splashed all over the pages of the newspaper, and on the TV News that evening. Apparently, the Olympic champion sprinter and world record holder had set his heart on a sporting career change. He wanted to become a professional footballer and had arrived in Australia to pursue his dream.

Not just Australia, but New South Wales, and *our* local football team, the Central Coast Mariners, was trialling him. The mask was supposed to be an incentive for us to buy tickets for the coming games and wear the mask alongside hundreds of other football supporters, thus forming a sea of Bolt supporters.

The news astonished everybody, and the

excitement was intense on the Central Coast. The newspaper was so excited that it renamed itself the Usain Bolt News. If we didn't receive a mask, we were invited to download one. The superstar, Usain Bolt, was playing football with the Mariners!

Joe watched the Fox News segment with interest.[1]

"I wish him luck," said Joe, who considered himself somewhat of a football expert. "But I can't really see him as a serious player, though. He's the wrong build, really, and just because he's a champion sprinter doesn't mean that he'll make a good footballer."

Sadly, Joe was right. In spite of training with the club for weeks, it seems Bolt's talents didn't transfer seamlessly to the game of football. Marcus Babbel, the Western Sydney Wanderers coach allegedly said, "not in 100 years" would Bolt make it as a pro in the A-Team. Nevertheless, the Central Coast offered him a contract, hopeful that the Jamaican sprinter would attract more fans. But the money they offered was not enough

---

1. News presenters chuckle about the Usain Bolt masks. https://www.dailytelegraph.com.au/newslocal/central-coast/download-your-usain-bolt-mask-here/news-story/2d857a255733a6c060ccf34b292c4488

VISITORS FROM OVERSEAS

to tempt the star. Bolt turned it down and departed with the media circus that had accompanied him from Day One.

That month, hundreds of cardboard Usain Bolt masks were tossed away into bins all over the state. Mike Charlesworth, chairman of the Central Coast Mariners Football Club, summed it up.

"Whilst we understand that Usain will not be part of the club going forward, the Central Coast Mariners wish him all the best in his future endeavours."

"Hear, hear," said Joe.

When we lived in Spain, years before Whatsapp was a thing, picking up the phone and calling Sydney was not only expensive, but difficult because of the crazy time difference. Now we lived just an hour away from the 'kids' and phoning was easy.

"Hi Mum, what's the weather like on the Central Coast?"

"Good, but still no rain. Everything looks so parched. Our grass is all brown, and the sports fields around here look like sandy deserts. How's Sydney?"

"Same."

"Girls okay? Any news?"

"Both girls are fine, thanks, and Cam's busy at work. Um, we didn't plan it, but we've got a new kitten."

"Oh? How did that happen?"

"You know what it's like… She was in the window at the RSPCA shop…"

"And you couldn't resist her."

"Exactly! She's tiny but sooo feisty! She has no problem putting LJ in his place and he's about twenty times bigger than her. If he gets too close, all her fur fluffs up and she hisses and lashes out. Her claws are like needles."

"Poor old LJ. What colour is she?"

"A beautiful tabby like Bandsaw."

"Lovely! What does Bandsaw think of her?"

"Actually, Bandsaw isn't impressed with her at all, we're already wondering whether it was a rash decision."

"I'm sure they'll get used to each other eventually."

"Hope so. Actually, you know I told you that Bandsaw seems to have been putting on a ridiculous amount of weight recently? She's like a barrel on legs, seriously!"

"Yes, have you discovered why? Does she have a medical condition?"

"Nope! She's got two homes! We've discovered that she goes round to our neighbour in the next street, and makes herself at home there. She sleeps on their bed and they feed her. No wonder she's so chunky. She's been doing it even more since the kitten arrived. She may explode soon."

"Have you thought of a name for the kitten yet?"

"Um, we let Winter choose."

"Oh, was that wise? What did she come up with?"

"She's named her Burgers."

"Right."

But of course.

Some readers may remember that Karly and Cam's first cat, Bandsaw, was supposed to be called Banjo, but Indy couldn't say the word. She called her 'Bandsaw' which was quite fitting as her kitten's purr was particularly loud. The name stuck.

Bandsaw grew up with Indy and tolerated being carried endlessly, dressed in dolls' clothes, and pushed in prams. However, she wasn't the first in line when intelligence was handed out. For instance, when Cam replaced the door leading from the kitchen into the garden, she never really coped with the idea.

In her opinion, this new door was not to be trusted. She behaved as though it was protected by an invisible force field and refused to use it. To enter the garden, she would miaow at the front door, go outside and pad all the way around the house to the back garden.

To come back inside, she headed for the open kitchen door, but only up to a certain point. Then her amber eyes widened as she hit the electromagnetic field. Backing away, she changed her course and circled the house back to the front door to wait to be let in. It took months before she passed through the new kitchen doorway.

Meanwhile, Shealan and Daria found a flat in Sydney and moved in. It was amazing to have all my family within visiting distance and, apart from Joe's health causing so much concern, life couldn't have been better.

Joe didn't feel up to visiting, nor socialising much, which I understood. But I was able to see the family often, and join them on trips.

"Mum, are you doing anything next weekend?"

"No, not really, why?"

"Well, we've booked an Airbnb in the Hunter Valley, and there's a spare bedroom. Would you like to come?"

HUMMINGBIRD

Maybe Usain Bolt is familiar with this drink from www.allrecipes.com/recipe/21676/hummingbird/. Apparently, this alcoholic drink is served in Jamaica and contains rum cream liqueur, coffee liqueur, strawberry syrup, banana, and milk. It has a smoothie consistency.

Ingredients

30ml (1 fl oz) rum cream liqueur

30ml (1 fl oz) coffee-flavoured liqueur

30ml (1 fl oz) milk

15ml (½ fl oz) strawberry-flavoured syrup

½ banana

1 cup crushed ice

Method

In a blender, combine rum cream liqueur, coffee liqueur, milk and strawberry syrup.

Add the banana and crushed ice.

Blend until smooth.

Pour into glasses and serve.

12

TERRIBLE NIGHT, PERFECT DAY

We had a plan. On the Friday night, I would babysit Indy and Winter while Shealan, Daria, Karly and Cam went on ahead to settle into the Airbnb they had booked in Polkobin, a picturesque area in the centre of the Lower Hunter Valley wine region. They'd been invited to a friend's party that night.

I would hand the little girls over to Cam's parents the next morning, then drive up and join them in the Hunter Valley.

But everything went wrong that Friday night in the Sydney home. I hadn't been there very long before I heard a loud yowling coming from the guest bedroom. Opening the door, I found

Bandsaw asking to come out. I let her out, my nose twitched and my heart sank.

"Nanny, Bandsaw has done a great big poo in the middle of your bed," said Indy, stating the obvious.

"She certainly has."

"It's so smelly!" Indy rolled her big blue eyes and made a face.

"It certainly is."

Bandsaw had probably been shut in the room for hours, so it wasn't her fault, but I hadn't reckoned on cat poo removal and laundry tasks that evening.

Poor little Winter was recovering from an ear infection and was super-cranky, and didn't want to be put down. I added floor-pacing to my list of duties.

It didn't help that Karly and Cam had just bought a brand-new TV. It was huge, and I had no idea how to control it. A pile of remote controls sat on the coffee table, but I had no idea which controlled what, which were old or new, or whether one needed a combination of two or three. Even six-year-old Indy, who usually solved techie problems easily, gave up trying.

I didn't even want to watch the TV, I was just trying to switch it off, but that TV was having none of it. Every time I left the room, it burst back into life, blaring at full volume. I couldn't work out how to change the channels, so I was stuck with a Punjabi soap opera. I couldn't even turn down the volume. The Off button worked, but the TV jumped back to life almost instantly, and my hope for a TV-free evening was fruitless.

"This time you will stay off," I growled at the TV as I clicked the Off button yet again.

But the TV thought otherwise. While I was checking on Winter in her bedroom, it exploded into life again, and clearly some kind of violent argument was kicking off in the Indian state. I reached the Off button just as knives were being unsheathed while sari-clothed ladies wailed in horror. The screen went black, and blessed silence reigned.

But not for long.

Burgers, the kitten, was also making a nuisance of herself. Hyperactive and fearless, she took a flying leap from the sideboard to land on my back as I passed, needle-sharp claws unsheathed.

I reached around and managed to grab and remove her. Not a painless procedure, and blood was drawn. Mine, not hers. I put her back on the floor but she leapt for my leg, trying to run up my jeans. Wherever I put her, she found me again.

I'd brought my laptop, but I didn't write a

word that night. Burgers wouldn't let me. If she wasn't leaping at me from various pieces of furniture, she was on my keyboard, her paws typing long sentences of gibberish. Even when I tried to make myself a coffee she was on the counter in seconds, threatening to knock over cups and generally tormenting me.

The TV switched itself on every half hour or so and treated me to more colourful snippets of Punjabi life before I reached the Off button yet again.

"That's it," I told LJ who had been no trouble at all. "I've had enough. I'm going to pull out the plug."

Not an easy task because the TV was huge, and the table it stood on was heavy. I heaved it aside and managed to single out the TV cable from the twisted cluster, followed it to the socket and pulled out the plug. Burgers was using my kneeling figure as a springboard to the coffee table and I cursed those claws as they dug into my skin again.

"Shame I can't pull your plug out, too," I told her.

Eventually, I shut both cats out of my bedroom, went to bed and fell asleep quickly. The baby alarm was set up in case Winter awoke, but all was peaceful apart from the call of night birds

TERRIBLE NIGHT, PERFECT DAY

and the cackle of fruit bats feasting on a nearby palm.

At exactly midnight, I sat bolt upright. All noises sound louder at night and this was no exception.

I froze. There was something moving in the house. Something that hummed and clattered. And it was getting closer.

"Hey Siri, turn on the torch," I said quietly, and Siri obliged.

I shone the light around the room. Everything seemed to be in order, if you didn't count the slight, lingering smell of cat poo.

I slipped out of bed and opened the door. The noise was louder now, and it sounded as though it was approaching. Just before it came into sight in the dim glow of the hall light, I suddenly knew what it was.

The robot vacuum cleaner. Obviously set to start cleaning at midnight when everybody was asleep, it had begun its nightly toil.

Relieved, I went back to bed and dreamed of Bollywood dancers, robots and giant kittens with unsheathed knives that never slept.

Next morning, Karly messaged me.

> How was everything last night? Is Winter okay?

> Yes, all good. Winter slept through, didn't wake at all.

> Good, glad you had a nice quiet time. See you later. You'll love it here in the Hunter Valley, it's fabulous. xx

> OK. Setting off soon. See you in a couple of hours. xx

Nowadays, the Hunter Valley is one of Australia's main wine regions, home to acre upon acre of vineyards and wineries. However, in the late 18th century, it was an established penal colony belonging to the British Empire. Running along this massive, fertile valley is the Hunter River which meets the sea at Newcastle.

The Hunter River, although well known to the aboriginals who had populated the area for at least 30,000 years, was discovered by accident in 1797 by British Lieutenant John Shortland as he searched for escaped convicts.

How one can stumble upon a watercourse the size of the Hunter River by accident is remarkable, but Australia is like that. It is so vast that there is a surprise past every hill crest, beach or bend in the river.

Polkobin, where our Airbnb was situated, is neither a town nor a village. It's a lush green area abundantly populated with wineries. Some are family-run boutique wineries, others are world-famous brands, and all offer cellar doors.

"Cellar doors? What does that mean?" I asked.

Nobody really knew, except Cam, the only true Australian amongst us. Tall, strong and capable, my son-in-law is affectionately known as Aussie Cam, especially when summoned to remove huntsman spiders, lift something heavy like a case of XXXX (pronounced 4-ex, a popular Aussie beer) or translate Aussie-speak for us.

"Hey, Aussie Cam, do you know?"

"Yeah! A cellar door in Australia is like a tasting room. You sit at a bar, or around a table, and the host will tell you all about their winery, and you get free tastings."

"That sounds good!"

"Yes!" announced Karly, ace organiser. "I happen to have arranged for us to get picked up by a man who owns an e-bike hire company tomorrow. We've got an e-bike each, and we can ride to some wineries and visit some cellar doors. But today, we're going to have a barbecue at home."

Nobody argued with that. The Airbnb had a verandah with seating and a barbecue. It overlooked rolling slopes of endless vineyards stretching away as far as the eye could see. The grapevines looked healthy, probably thanks to the black irrigation tubes that ran along every row, delivering life-saving water to plump the future grapes. The grass wasn't faring so well, suffering from lack of rain.

I was interested to see that at the start of every row of vines, a rosebush bloomed.

"Why is that?" I asked.

"Because if the rose bush doesn't flourish, that's an early indicator of something amiss with the vines," replied Aussie Cam.

He explained that it was traditional to plant white rosebushes. Apparently, roses and grapes share the same soil and sun requirements, but roses are far more fussy. Both are susceptible to aphid attacks and other pests and diseases, but roses show signs first, giving grape growers early warnings of problems to come.

That evening, as the sky streaked orange, and silver rose-tinted puffy clouds hung motionless, we barbecued. We raised a toast to family time and Australia. Then Daria spotted something.

"Can you see something moving between the vines?" she asked, pointing.

We all squinted, then I saw it too. "Yes!"

"Kangaroos!" said Karly. "Shall we see if we can get any closer?"

"Oh, I'd love some close-up photos!"

So Karly, Daria and I walked along the lines of vines towards the group, or mob, to use the correct term. The kangaroos grazed, pulling at the parched grass, but soon noticed us closing in on them. At first, they just froze, staring at us over their shoulders, and then three or four of them bounced nervously away over the hillock.

Two of them stood their ground and watched us. I don't think I'd ever realised just how big kangaroos can be, and my steps slowed. One roo bounced away, but the biggest one didn't move. Now he was only a few yards away.

"He's huge!" I said quietly. "He's taller than any of us."

Indeed, the roo regarding us with expressionless eyes was a magnificent specimen. He towered over us, and I couldn't help but notice his powerful back legs, which I knew he could use to disembowel us if he felt like it. He towered above the vines, his head and shoulders silhouetted against the darkening sky. A breeze fanned his fur, but he remained statue-still, unblinking.

I sensed I wasn't alone in my fears because Karly and Daria's steps had also slowed to a stop.

None of us really wanted to get any closer and risk the wrath of that roo. Without a word, we quietly backed away. The kangaroo had won the staring match and we retreated. The hillock was his again.

"Did anyone get any photos?"

We all shook our heads. None of us had taken a single shot. It didn't really matter, because kangaroos came close to where we sat outside, anyway. They arrived silently, stared at us, then hopped away.

It was a wonderful experience to get so close to wild kangaroos, but that was quite close enough for me.

The other thing that sticks in my mind about that weekend is also related to size. Not only were the kangaroos enormous, but so were the lemons —gargantuan fruit that I could hardly hold in one hand.

TERRIBLE NIGHT, PERFECT DAY

The next day, as promised, we were collected by the e-bike man, who told us his name was Glenn. I was squashed in the back seat of his ute with Karly and Daria.

"I was just thinking," mused Karly. "Do kangaroos have territories? And do they have burrows or something?"

We all shouted with laughter, but in the rearview mirror, I saw Glenn roll his eyes, although the crinkles showed he was grinning. I didn't blame him for his reaction. Karly is one of the brightest people I know, but she knows nothing about kangaroos. Of course, we teased her mercilessly about her ridiculous remark for the rest of the day.

Glenn took us to his depot where he chose e-bikes for us individually and kitted us out with helmets. He showed us the controls, and features, and we all had a practice ride. The e-bikes were surprisingly powerful. One flick of the lever and the e-bike surged forward. I tried it on the gravel drive and sent an arc of small stones into the air as the e-bike leapt forward. It was a new experience for all of us because it was 2018, and e-bikes, now commonplace, were a novelty then.

"Right," said the owner when we all felt comfortable. "The bikes are fully charged. You have four hours to ride wherever you like. There are heaps of wineries to visit, and if you buy any bottles, the wineries will let me know. I'll pick them up for you and have them ready for you to take home when I drop you off."

"Wow, thank you!" we chorused.

"Now remember, if you want to pedal, that's fine; just treat the bike like an ordinary bike. But if you want some assistance up the steeper hills or want to go faster, just use the lever, and the bike will take you effortlessly."

"Sounds wonderful," I said, then turned to Karly, already knowing the answer to my question. "Do you have a plan?"

"Well, funnily enough, I do."

No surprise there, then. Karly spread out the map from a brochure we'd picked up.

"I think we should ride up this road here, pop

into a few cellar doors, stop for lunch here, and come back on this road here via these wineries. Does that seem like a good idea to you, Glenn?"

Glenn nodded, clearly impressed. This tourist knew nothing about kangaroo behaviour, but she could certainly organise.

"Perfect," he said.

And it *was* perfect. Utterly, beautifully perfect. The roads were completely empty as we sailed our carefree, effortless way from winery to winery. A cloudless blue sky stretched overhead and we passed dozens of kangaroos grazing in the fields. The wineries welcomed us and plied us with free tastings at their cellar doors, and we purchased bottles of the wine that we liked.

Lunch was delicious and the e-bikes were such fun to ride. As I got braver, I sped along, smiling at the roos that stopped grazing to watch us pass. I was with my beloved family, in a beautiful country, having the time of my life. All cares were forgotten and my heart swelled with happiness.

"Well, you did have a good time," remarked Glenn later as he loaded the fourth box of clinking bottles into the ute, ready to take us home.

He was right.

The end of the year approached. I wondered what the brand-shiny-new year ahead would bring, unaware that my simple routine dental appointment would result in something almost life-changing.

EASY LEMON SPRITZER

So refreshing on a summer's day! And you can give it an alcoholic kick by replacing half the soda water with sparkling wine.

Ingredients (makes 6 glasses)

1 cup caster sugar

1 cup of boiling water

1 lemon, rind peeled into strips avoiding white pith

1 cup lemon juice from (4 large lemons) chilled

9 cups (approx) chilled soda water (about 2.5 litres or 4.5 pints)

Crushed ice to serve

Mint leaves to serve

Lemon slices to serve

Method

Combine the sugar, boiling water and lemon rind in a large jug. Stir until the sugar dissolves.

Place in the fridge for 4 hours to chill.

Stir the lemon juice into the sugar syrup. Strain into a sealable jar or jug.

Divide the lemon mixture into serving glasses. Top each glass with the chilled soda water. Add ice, mint and lemon slices.

13

A NICE SMILE

"Had any problems with your teeth?" asked my hygienist when I went for my usual check up and teeth-cleaning appointment at the dentist's surgery.

"No, all good, thank you."

My dentist's surgery is modern compared with the dentist's surgery we left behind in Spain. Joss sticks burn on the reception counter and they sell bamboo toothbrushes. Patients type all the necessary forms and details on an iPad and the waiting room is as cool and white as the models' teeth on the posters framed on the walls.

In the consulting room, there is a large TV screen fixed to the ceiling. When I lie back in the reclining chair, I'm handed headphones, and the assistant asks me what I'd like to watch. I always choose *Friends* or David Attenborough. I love it. It takes my mind off what is going on in my mouth, and I can't hear that high-pitched machine that polishes my teeth.

But there is another screen I don't like. It's large, and shows a great blown-up image of the latest X-ray of my teeth.

"Oh my goodness," I said, staring at it in horror. "Is that really my teeth?"

"I know, it's a bit confronting seeing your own teeth in such detail," said the hygienist.

"It's awful, and I swear the gap between my front teeth has grown even bigger."

"Yes, they do tend to drift apart a bit more with age."

"Really? I've always hated the gap between my front teeth."

"Well, if it really bothers you, you know we could fix that, don't you?"

I looked at her in amazement. I've had that huge gap all my life. People told me it was lucky if one could pass a sixpenny coin through the gap. I think one could drive a double-decker bus through my gap, and that didn't make me feel lucky at all.

"I'll tell you what, I'll ask the dentist to pop in

and have a look when I've finished cleaning your teeth," said the hygienist.

My gap fixed? No gap? Nope, I couldn't believe that was even possible. After all, I was in my sixties, and nobody had ever told me before that my gap was fixable. I thought I was doomed to put up with it forever.

But I guess I'd never actually asked.

For once, I couldn't concentrate on David Attenborough's explanation of why sloths only climb down the tree to poop once a week.

The dentist came in and stared at the X-ray on the other screen. Then he peered into my mouth.

"Yes, I can fix that for you," he said. "It could all be done and dusted by Christmas if you want to go ahead."

I gaped at him. It was early December now.

"All fixed by Christmas?" I squeaked.

"I think we'll need to make you six crowns," he explained, pointing at my giant teeth on the monitor, "and we can do it all in one day. In the morning, we'll set up a little mould of your teeth for you. And in the afternoon, you'll come back, and we'll finish the job."

It all sounded so easy.

"By Christmas?" It was hard to believe.

He gave me a price. I blinked rapidly. He

suggested I think it over and contact the receptionist if I wanted to go ahead and book it.

I left the surgery with my head reeling. Questions spun around and around. I was in my sixties, was I being ridiculous to want nice teeth? What would Joe say? What about the price? Was I being terribly vain? What if something went wrong?

It occurred to me on the way home that getting the dental work done would cost the same as getting a carport built on the house, something I had always wanted. How could I justify spending money like that on a nice smile?

I met my friend, Debbie, for coffee.

"Guess what? This morning, my dentist said that he could fix the gaps between my teeth if I wanted, by Christmas."

She didn't look surprised. "With crowns?"

"Yes!"

"Yes, it would be like mine," she said, baring her teeth for me to see. "I had mine done nearly ten years ago."

"Really? I had no idea! I've always admired your teeth, was it expensive?"

"Yes, but worth every penny."

"But we could build a carport with what it would cost."

"A carport doesn't give you a lovely smile.

Well, maybe when it's first built, but you'd soon not even notice it."

I phoned my daughter.

"Karly, you know we were planning to get a carport built?"

"Yes, what about it?"

"Well, I've just been to the dentist. He said that he could fix the gaps between my teeth if I wanted, by Christmas."

"You are kidding! That's awesome! When are you booked in?"

"I'm not booked in yet. I just wanted to think about it first. It would cost about the same as building a carport on the house. What do you think, carport or teeth?"

"Teeth, no contest."

"Really?"

"Really. Absolutely. One hundred per cent."

Gosh. Two down, just one to go… I decided to go straight for the jugular.

"Joe, what would you say if I said I wanted to blow the carport fund and get my teeth fixed instead?"

Joe blinked. "Is there something wrong with your teeth?"

"My gap!"

"I like your gap."

"But I hate it! And it's getting bigger. I'm embarrassed to smile."

"Really? Then you should get it done."

"But what about the carport?"

"The carport can wait. Getting your smile back is much more important."

Wow. I turned away. I had something in my eye.

I phoned the surgery and booked my appointment for the following Tuesday. I couldn't wait! As the days slipped by, I kept looking at myself in the mirror, trying to imagine how I'd look without that gap, then feeling deeply ashamed that I was behaving in such a vain manner.

The bright, young dentist's assistant settled me into the chair and I tried to relax. The TV screen on the ceiling was blank. She handed me the earphones.

"What would we like to watch today?" she asked.

"*Friends*, please."

"Good choice!" She swished her blonde ponytail and fiddled with the TV remote.

"I'm going to give you a series of six injections," said the dentist. "You shouldn't feel any pain at any stage, just vibrations. If you feel any pain, just raise a hand, and we'll stop. I'll just pop this mouth prop into your mouth, and we'll get started."

Mouth prop? I had no idea what that was, but soon found out.

"Here we go," said the cheerful assistant, and suddenly I was wearing a kind of plastic guard that forced my mouth to stay open wide. Not my best look, I imagine.

"Are we comfortable?" she asked. "Mouth props stop our jaws from getting fatigued. We wouldn't want to be closing our mouth in the middle of things, would we?"

We wouldn't.

Nobody likes injections, but it was soon over, and work began in earnest. As I watched Ross trying to interest Rachel in dinosaurs, I felt numerous vibrations, as I had been warned. At first, I guessed he was cleaning the teeth, ready for the mould. However, judging by the smoke, the smell of burning, and the sprays of water and splinters, something much more dramatic was happening. I was grateful for the prattle of the cheery assistant, even though I couldn't hear much of what she said, and the comforting, familiar humour of *Friends*.

For two and a half hours, I lay with my mouth propped open. Ross and Rachel had become an item and then split up. Joey landed the part of neurosurgeon Dr Drake Ramoray in *Days of Our Lives,* and Phoebe wrote and performed Smelly Cat, badly.

I suddenly realised that, apart from *Friends* still running in my earphones, the room had fallen silent. And why had the dentist stopped working? Why wasn't the assistant prattling? Was it all over? Or was something wrong?

The assistant's chatter had dried up, and she suddenly left the room in a flurry. Next, the receptionist swept in, white-faced. Out of my line of vision, I heard a conversation taking place in barely concealed code. It was hard to understand with the earphones on, but I was sure something had happened.

I was right.

"We're really sorry," said the dentist, after the now-silent assistant had removed my earphones. "We've had a computer malfunction. Normally we'd be able to finish the whole job in one day, but that isn't going to be possible this time. I'm going to put in some temporary teeth, then you'll be able to go home. As soon as the computer is up and running again, we'll phone you and get you to come back in."

I wanted to ask how long that might be but the mouth prop prevented speech, and he'd gone back to work in my mouth.

A NICE SMILE

When I finally got home, I was a little shaky after the day's events and my face was still paralysed. The dentist had glued on temporary teeth, as promised, and I couldn't wait to see how they looked. Although temporary, they would be the first glimpse of myself without the hated gap.

"Come on then, show me," said Joe.

I hadn't looked in the mirror yet, but I faced him, drew my lips back and bared my teeth. Joe leaned forward and stared.

"They look exactly the same as they used to," he said at last.

"What?" I flew to the mirror.

Yup. Huge gap between the front teeth. Big gaps between all the others.

I expected to see how my new teeth would look, but the mould was a replica of my old ones. I would need to wait a bit longer.

The receptionist phoned me two days later. She told me that the computer software problem had been solved, and that the job could now be finished.

Thursday came.

"What would we like to watch today?" said the cheery assistant, fanning me with her fake lashes.

I picked David Attenborough this time because I didn't expect to be there very long and wouldn't need to shut out drilling and splintering sounds. I was sure they would just slip the new teeth on and use some kind of super-glue.

Nope. I had six more injections, two halfway through the job, because I felt my feeling coming back. Another two-and-a-half hours in the chair.

This time, the assistant handed me a mirror.

"Would we like to see our new teeth?" she asked, smiling.

We would.

I held the mirror up and gasped.

I sensed both the dentist and his assistant were holding their breath, but they had no need to worry.

The teeth were beautiful and I wore the biggest smile in Australia. It may have taken sixty-three years, but it was worth the wait.

"What do you think?" I asked Joe later.

"You look gorgeous, as always."

We still don't have a carport, but I have a confident smile.

In Sydney, Christmas flew by in a flurry of wrapping paper. Dolls strewed the floor, delicious smells tormented the animals, crammed fridges gradually emptied, older family members disappeared for naps and laughter rang in every room.

The new year arrived. It was exceptionally hot and January brought no relief. Some days, temperatures soared to 45°C [113°F], and even the cicadas sounded weary. Lawns were non-existent, replaced by brown, baked earth, split by jagged cracks as the yellow sun sucked the life out of every growing thing. Rain was a distant memory.

The TV brought us more terrible images of farmers in despair. Of dried-up rivers, scorched, ruined crops. Livestock like walking skeletons. Lush acres transformed into dust plains.

Apart from the soaring price of fresh produce, we were relatively unaffected by the drought, unlike the farmers who were forced to watch their animals and crops die. Such suffering. I wept when I watched the evening news.

We were so lucky. The whole family looked forward to the long weekend we had booked together at Port Stephens. We dreamed of lively sea breezes and cool waves washing over our hot, bare skin.

But before we packed our swimming costumes, hats, and sunscreen, Shealan and Daria issued an invitation.

"Come and see our new apartment," they said.

WHITE CHOCOLATE SNOWFLAKES

Here's a Christmas activity that both adults and children of almost any age will enjoy making and eating.

Ingredients

1 large block of quality white chocolate

Cake decorations of your choice

Method

Search online for a snowflake pattern that you like, repeat it on a blank piece of white paper, then print out.

Melt the white chocolate in the microwave, or a heat-proof bowl over a saucepan of simmering water, stirring until smooth. Transfer to a zip-lock or piping bag.

Lay a sheet of baking paper over your snowflake template.

Carefully snip a tiny corner from your bag of melted chocolate and pipe snowflakes onto the baking paper using the template as a guide.

Don't worry if the first one or two don't work out perfectly. Keep trying, and you'll soon work out how hard to squeeze the bag and how to trace the snowflake pattern. If any go wrong you can eat the mistakes or return them to the bag for another go.

Decorate however you like with edible silver balls or hundreds and thousands.

Leave to set.

14

PRANKS

Shealan and Daria had no problem settling into Australian life. They were both employed and had finally left the temporary shelter of Cam and Karly's home to find one of their own.

"Are you free next weekend? Come and have drinks and nibbles at our new place," they said.

Indy and Winter were having a sleepover at their other grandparents' house so an adult evening was planned. Joe wasn't feeling well and stayed at home.

We arrived and were given the grand tour. Their new apartment was on the ground floor of a large building set on the edge of a national park, yet still convenient for both of them to commute to their jobs. They'd furnished the rooms tastefully and a big outdoor table was set up on the verandah.

"Make yourselves comfortable," said Shealan. "What would you like to drink?"

Daria brought out a cheeseboard and we grazed, sipped and chatted as the sky darkened. Moths danced a fandango around the outside lights and kookaburras out-laughed each other before retiring to their roosts in the dense bush.

"I've got some really hot corn chips, if anybody is brave enough to do a taste test with me," suggested Shealan.

"I'll do it," said Aussie Cam. No surprise there.

"Yup," said Karly, "bring it on."

Lent courage by my third glass of wine, I heard myself saying, "I love spicy food, I'll give it a go."

"Are you sure, Mum?" asked Karly, and she rolled her eyes.

Shealan and Daria smiled.

"Okay, if you're sure, this is what I'm going to do," said Shealan. "I'm going to lay the tortilla chips out in rows, in order of hotness. We'll each try them at the same time. Of course, anybody can back out at any time if you find them too hot."

Red rag to a bull.

Shealan went inside to organise the board,

while Daria splashed iced water into glasses for each of us. Just in case.

Shealan reappeared and put the board down in the centre of the table. We eyed the rows of innocent-looking chips.

"There are five corn chips to try each, each one a bit hotter than the last. These ones in this row here are the mildest. Is everybody ready?"

"Yes," we chorused.

"Okay, let's begin. Altogether, taste!"

Obediently we reached for a corn chip from the first row and popped it into our mouths.

"Easy," said Aussie Cam, crunching.

"Done," said Karly.

"That wasn't too bad," I said, trying not to cough.

"Well done, Mum," said Karly. "Do you want to go on?"

"Of course!"

"Okay, everyone," said Shealan, "grab chip number two. All together now, taste!"

I really didn't want to, but I couldn't let the side down. I put the chip in my mouth. Within seconds, little red flames danced on my tongue.

"Easy," said Aussie Cam.

"Done," said Karly.

I tried to speak but my tongue wouldn't behave. Part of it had gone numb, and my eyes were beginning to sting. I looked longingly at my glass of water.

"Don't drink the water," hissed Karly, "it'll make it feel worse. Do you want to stop?"

My head said YES. My heart said YES. But my pride wouldn't let me tap out. I shook my head. No.

"Chip number three, halfway through the taste test!" crowed Shealan. "Are you ready? Grab your chip, altogether, taste!"

A kookaburra laughed hysterically through the darkness.

I forced myself to receive the third chip in my mouth. Hot flames spread to the inside of both cheeks and my eyes watered. Gasping, I opened my mouth wide and sucked in the night air in the hope that it would cool the furnace that was my mouth.

I looked at the others who were clearly busy fighting their own battles.

"Easy," said Aussie Cam, but for the first time his voice lacked conviction and his cheeks were inflated as he blew out.

"Done," whispered Karly, eyes wide.

I couldn't speak. All I could do was close my eyes and endure the pain, waiting for the burning to subside. I sounded like an old-fashioned steam train as I puffed and blew, attempting to cool my mouth.

And all the time, chip number four was waiting.

"Mum, you don't have to have any more," said Shealan.

"I'll try just one more," I rasped. My iced water sparkled alluringly. "I won't try number five, but I'll give number four a go."

The kookaburra cackled and swooped away on silent wings. I saw him silhouetted for a brief moment against the silver moon before being swallowed by the black Australian bush.

The night was silent. The easy chatter had died away and nothing stirred in the bush. The only movement came from the ice cubes shifting in the water jug and moths whirling their endless dance around the lights.

"Right, chip number four, altogether, taste!"

I ordered my reluctant fingers to pick up the chip and put it in my mouth, aware that my companions were doing the same.

It was done. For a split second, nothing.

Then my mouth exploded. I felt as though I'd taken a bite out of a red-hot meteor. A burning sensation spread across my lips and ignited my tongue. Tears spurted from my eyes and my nose ran. I knew my face was beetroot-red and my body was sweating.

Enough. I grabbed the glass of water and gulped it, I swilled my mouth out and leaned over the verandah wall, evacuating the contents of my mouth.

Slowly, slowly, my mouth cooled. I heard shrieks of laughter and turned to see my family. Cam and Karly were just about getting their breath back from the latest devilish chip, but Shealan and Daria were laughing so hard they could barely stand up.

"How could you do that?" asked Karly, aghast. "That was so mean!"

"Do what?" I asked, confused.

Shealan couldn't speak, so Karly answered for him.

"He's just told us that he switched the fourth and fifth chips."

"You mean…"

"Yes, your beloved son, my brother, has just tricked us into tasting probably the hottest chips ever invented."

I still haven't forgiven him. And I now understand why professional hot sauce tasters use just the tip of a cocktail stick to dip into the sauce and onto the tongue.

Of course, this wasn't the first time my son

had played pranks on me over the years and I should have seen it coming. But sometimes I manage to pay him back...

I played my favourite trick on him when he was about fourteen years old. I promised myself I would confess on his eighteenth birthday. But it was too good, and I didn't want to tell him the truth, so I delayed my confession. He's in his forties now, and although I'm sure he suspects, I have never actually told him the truth. He doesn't read my books, so I can safely explain here.

You see, I told my fourteen-year-old son that his middle name was Doris.

I remember his face turning white with shock and disbelief as he gaped at me.

"You are kidding?"

"Um, no."

"Doris? DORIS? Why would you do that?"

"I'm sorry, we didn't have any choice really. Your grandmother was called Doris and the name has been passed down the family for generations. We didn't know if we'd ever have a daughter so we had to give the name to you."

"I don't believe it."

"I'm sorry."

"How come I never knew before?"

"Well, we guessed you probably wouldn't like it very much, and we'd already chosen Robert as a middle name, so we just tacked it on the end. Nobody needs to know, unless you tell them, of course. Oh, and if you were to join the army, or get married, or need to sign the official secrets act, or something like that. They'd probably need to know then."

Speechless, he stormed off to school. The news clearly preyed on his mind because that evening he broached the subject again.

"Were you serious about my name? You didn't really call me Doris, did you?"

"I'm sorry. We did."

"Can I see my birth certificate?"

"Yes, of course. We only keep the short version at home so it might not be on that, though. It'll definitely be on the long version that's kept at the bank with all the other important papers."

Disgusted, he turned away. As far as I know, he still believes his middle name is Doris. I doubt I'll ever tell him now. He deserves to suffer…

"Won't you come with us?" I asked Joe. "It's only for the weekend, and the change of scenery would do you good. You know how you love Port Stephens."

Joe shook his head. "I don't feel up to it," he said. "I get so breathless, and I don't want to hold you back. I'd rather just stay at home and look after Lola."

"Well, it's a pity. Are you sure?"

"Yes. You go and enjoy yourselves."

"Are you looking forward to our little holiday to Port Stephens?" I asked Indy.

"Yes, yes, yes!" she said, jumping up and down. "We're going to hunt for a pipi!"

"Are we? What is a pipi?"

"Um, I'm not sure, Daddy is going to show us. And if we catch any, we're going to EAT them!"

"Right, okay."

We arrived at our Airbnb and unpacked. Of course Cam had brought his dirtbike again and couldn't wait to ride it along the sand, and the kids and I couldn't wait to hunt a pipi, so we soon set off for the beach.

Anna Bay, with its endless white sand dunes, never disappoints, and it was particularly attractive in the heat of that drought-gripped summer.

When we drove down to the beach, we seemed to have even more baggage than usual to unload. Along with Cam's dirtbike and Indy's little pink dirtbike, the rugs, the buckets and spades, the sunscreen, hats and snacks, were

PRANKS

several large empty eskies, as Aussies call coolboxes.

"These are for the pipis," explained Indy, dragging one across the sand leaving swirly tracks in the virgin sand.

"But what are pipis?" I asked again.

"Um, er, I'm not sure," said Karly, shrugging her shoulders. "Aussie Cam, what are pipis exactly?"

"Pipis are little, edible saltwater clams. Little triangular shells. You find them under the sand at low tide. They taste great and they are easy to catch."

"Do we dig for them?"

"No need! I'll show you how to dance for them."

"Dance?" Indy was instantly interested. Dancing is her middle name.

"Dance?" I echoed, knowing I have two left feet.

"Yup. Dance. Dance the twist."

He showed us how to stand at the water's edge, then twist our bodies from side to side at the waist, digging our heels into the sand.

"When you feel something hard under your foot, that'll be a pipi. Dig it up and throw it in the eskie. Keep the big ones and leave the babies to grow."

So we all stood in a row, three generations, doing the twist and singing loudly as the waves lapped our ankles.

> *"Let's twist again, like we did last summer,*
> *Let's twist again, like we did last yeearrrr…"*

"Got one!"
"Me too!"
"Look at the size of this one!"

We finished up with about a hundred and took them home to cook. But that day was probably my first and last pipi dance.

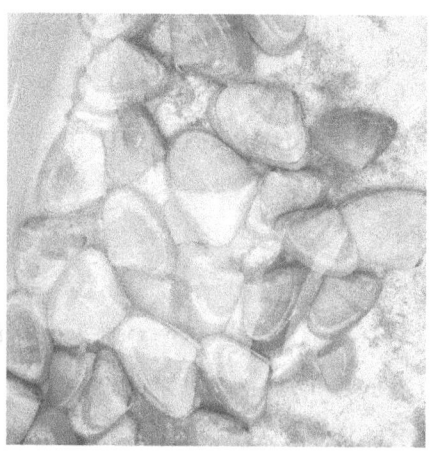

Days later, as I browsed Google to check the

spelling of the word pipi, I found myself on an official New South Wales website.

```
Pipis must not be collected by
any method and for any purpose.
Anyone caught collecting pipis
risks a heavy fine.
```

Oops. Too late. We're sorry, we didn't know.

I'm not sure whether this rule applies to just the state of New South Wales, or the whole of Australia. I also don't know if the law was made to protect the pipis, or the humans who may be consuming contaminated shellfish.

Whatever, the pipis we cooked that evening were very tasty. And I'll always treasure the memory of pipi dancing with my family as the white sea foam washed our toes and the wet sand sucked at the soles of our feet.

"I'm sorry you didn't come with us, you'd have enjoyed it," I said to Joe.

He shrugged. "I think it's all too much effort for me now. I have to work so hard to breathe.

And the thought of staying away from home makes me anxious."

I thought about all the wonderful places we had visited together in the past and felt sad. The house exchanges we had with home-owners from South Carolina and Australia. The river cruise down the Nile, the bus trip across the desert in Egypt, visits to Malta, Spain, France, the Netherlands, and Thailand. Multiple visits to the US, the road trips, the year in Bahrain. So many adventures.

"Well, what about if I had an idea. A way we could explore Australia and you would never even move out of your comfort zone?"

PIPIS IN GINGER AND SWEET CHILLI SAUCE

I discovered that pipis can actually be bought from certain supermarkets and fish markets so there is no need to break the law like we did.

Ingredients

1 tbsp olive oil

2 garlic cloves, finely chopped

3 cm (1 inch) piece ginger, peeled and finely chopped

60 ml (¼ cup) sweet chilli sauce

80 ml (⅓ cup) chicken stock

2 tbsp soy sauce, or to taste

1 kg (2.2lb) pipis, soaked and rinsed

2 spring onions, roughly chopped

1 handful coriander leaves, roughly chopped

Method

1. Heat a heavy-based saucepan over medium heat. Add the oil and cook the garlic and ginger for 1 - 2 minutes or until fragrant. Add the sweet chilli sauce, stock and soy sauce, then simmer until slightly thickened.

2. Add the pipis, stir to coat well, then cover and cook, shaking the pan regularly for 5 - 6 minutes or just until the pipis open. Transfer to a serving dish, scatter with spring onion and coriander and serve on sourdough toast or fluffy rice.

15

SHEILA

As the weeks of 2019 slipped by, Australia dropped deeper into drought. The state of New South Wales had already been declared 100% in drought during August of the year before, and Queensland and other regions soon followed. Reservoirs stood almost empty, farmers despaired as their livestock and crops died, and the famous Murray Darling basin was drying up.

I'm ashamed to admit that I'd never heard of the Murray Darling basin before I moved to Australia and had no idea of its significance. I didn't know it covers over a million square kilometres in south-eastern Australia, an area even larger than the combined size of Germany and France. 77,000 kilometres of rivers run through expansive wetlands, and this rich area is responsible for at least one-third of Australia's food supply.

The basin is home to cotton and rice growers, grain and cereal crops, oranges, apples, cattle, sheep, and pigs, amongst a long list of other foods and human needs.

The Internet tells me that apart from its agricultural importance, it is also home to at least 35 endangered species of birds, 16 endangered species of mammals and 46 known species of native fish.

As the Australian sun continued to scorch the earth, more water was diverted from the Murray Darling basin to supply towns and industry. Of course, the inevitable happened. Rivers ceased to flow, and dried up. Terrible, confronting images of dried river beds where millions of dead fish lay rotting in the heat began to air on our TVs.

In vain, people searched the sky for rain clouds. There was nothing anybody could do except conserve as much water as possible, and wait. We all knew this drought was the worst for 120 years, but we didn't know there was much worse to come.

I diverted myself by dreaming of exploring Australia before Joe's health worsened and we could no longer travel. I was determined to make it happen.

"You'd like to see more of Australia, wouldn't you?"

"Well, yes, of course, but I can't see how. I need my breathing machine at night. And I'm too weak to do much."

He was right, his breathing machine was vital. It was like the common CPAP machine which many people with sleep problems use. But he needed the more powerful BIPAP which would breathe for him as he slept. I'm told the main difference between BIPAP and CPAP machines is that the BIPAP delivers two levels of air pressure, one for inhalation and one for exhalation, while CPAP delivers a continuous, single level of air pressure throughout the breathing cycle.

"I know, but there is a way, and you'd always have your BIPAP."

"Really? How do we do that? How do we explore Australia without leaving home? Watch travel shows?"

"Don't be ridiculous. I've mentioned it before. Why don't we buy ourselves a nice little caravan…"

"A caravan? No. That would be really hard work. You know I can't do much."

"I don't think it would be hard. I'd do it all,

anyway. And you can do the driving. You love driving, don't you?"

"Yes, but…"

"And Lola could come, too."

"Caravanning?"

"Yes, of course. There are loads of caravan and campsites that welcome dogs."

"No, I don't think it's a good idea."

I expected this reaction. The disease had robbed him of his self-confidence.

"Well, there's no rush, is there? We can just have a think about it, and maybe look around to see what's available."

I changed the subject quickly. I had sown my seed and I let it sprout and take root and grow in Joe's mind.

Of course, Joe didn't 'look around to see what's available' at all. Nothing could have been further from his mind.

But I did.

Obsessively.

Did we want a motorhome or a caravan? We loved the motorhome trip that we had taken up the east coast of Australia more than a decade before, but I remember that we found it annoying having to take our whole home everywhere, even for grocery shopping or collecting a takeaway meal. No, it might suit us better to hitch up a caravan.

Just out of interest, I checked out the price of new caravans. Oh dear, way out of our price range. I widened the search and explored local adverts and Gum Tree for used vans. There were plenty to choose from.

There was one in particular that caught my eye, advertised by somebody living a bit further up the coast. I waited until Joe was out of earshot, then rang the number supplied.

"Hi! I'm just enquiring about the caravan you have for sale. Is it still available?"

A male voice with a strong Welsh accent answered.

"Yes, indeed it is."

"Oh good, can you please tell me about it?"

The man told me his name was Evan. He and his wife had recently bought a motorhome, which was why they were selling their caravan. He assured me that although the van was 24 years old, it was all in perfect working order.

"Could we come and take a look?" I asked.

"Of course. We're free this afternoon if you want to drive over," said Evan.

"I'll check with my husband, Joe, and I'll ring you back," I said. "My name's Vicky."

I found Joe outside in the garden.

"Joe, do you fancy going for a drive?"

"Sure. Anywhere in particular?"

"Um, well… I just happened upon an advert for a little caravan and …"

"A caravan? We're not buying a caravan."

"Yes, I know! I just happened to see it, and I gave the number a quick ring. Just out of interest, you know."

"We haven't discussed this at all."

"Oh, I know! Don't panic. I just thought we could go for the drive, just to look, of course. We haven't actually decided to get a caravan yet."

Joe scratched himself irritably but I sensed I was making progress.

"It would do us good to get out of the house for a couple of hours, wouldn't it?" I said. "Are you feeling up to a drive?"

"Yes, but…"

"I'll get the car keys."

Twenty minutes later, we were heading north along the freeway.

"He sounded very nice, very Welsh. His name is Evan," I prattled as we passed brown fields. It was autumn and still warm, but crisp, dry leaves lined the sides of the roads. "He said the caravan is in perfect condition."

"We're not buying a caravan today."

"No, no, of course we're not!"

We found the address easily and shook Evan's hand.

"Nice to meet you, Don," said Evan, "and you, Becky. Did you have any trouble finding us?"

"It's Joe and Vicky," corrected Joe, smiling. "No, no trouble at all. And this must be the caravan?"

To be perfectly honest, the caravan was no beauty. Maybe 25 years ago, when it had been manufactured, it might have been impressive. However, over the years, its white finish had dulled to a curdled, sour-milk cream. Over-enthusiastic previous owners had stuck stickers all over it. There were badges, kangaroos, go-faster stripes and all kinds of unrecognisable shapes. Bleached by the sun, they had faded, flaked and half-peeled off.

Joe and I exchanged glances. *Not in a million years.*

"Vanessa, come and look inside," invited our host. "I think you'll be surprised."

I didn't bother to mention that he'd got my name wrong again and followed him obediently.

"George, come and see," said Evan, holding the door open for both of us.

I could just about stand up, but Joe couldn't straighten up; he had to bow his head.

"Allow me," said Evan, and reached above my

head. He pushed on a lever and the ceiling raised up. "Excuse me, Jeff," he said and pushed the other lever above Joe's head. "That's the pop-top up! I'll let you take a look round."

He left us in peace, and something strange happened. With the pop-top roof raised, the inside of the caravan felt spacious and light. Sunlight streamed in through the windows. At one end was a sink, hob, and oven, with a tidy little fridge and clean countertop. Neat rows of cabinets ran all around the walls. There was even a full-height wardrobe with a mirror and plenty of hanging space.

Twin beds were separated by a decent dining table, and I guessed rightly that there was even more storage space under each mattress.

I realised I'd been holding my breath. Oh, the possibilities! I could actually picture Joe, me and Lola exploring Australia in this caravan. I could almost see the red earth tracks we would drive down, the beaches we would visit, the bushland and waterfalls we would see. What adventures we could have! And this elderly but charming caravan felt both homely and inviting.

SHEILA

Bruce and Sheila

"What are you thinking?" asked Joe, studying me carefully.

I'm not great at hiding my feelings and I imagine my hands clasped in rapture under my chin and my faraway expression as I planned our future had already given the game away.

"I love it!" I whispered.

Okay, I didn't love the shag-pile carpet on the floor, or the lacy net curtains, but they could easily be changed, couldn't they?

"How are you doing?" asked Evan, popping his head in. "When you've finished, Gary, I'll show you how the awning works." His face vanished again, reminding me of Lewis Carroll's Cheshire cat.

"Joe, not Gary," muttered Joe, but his heart wasn't in it.

"What do *you* think?" I asked Joe. "Do you like it?"

"Well, I'm pleasantly surprised…"

"Shall we make an offer?"

"But we're not ready to buy a caravan, are we? We just came to look!"

"I know! But Sheila's perfect!"

"Sheila?" Joe's eyes were wide. "Sheila?"

"Yes," I hissed. "Sheila. The name suits her perfectly. Just think of the fun we'll have! Think of the places we'll see, all in the comfort of our own little home on wheels. We have to work quickly, make an offer before anybody else grabs her!"

Joe's mouth had dropped open. He shook his head and rolled his eyes before backing out of the caravan to discuss awnings with Evan. I happily opened some more cabinets, admired the dinky little cutlery drawer and switched some lights on and off.

"It's perfect!" I whispered to myself and joined the men outside.

"Oh, there you are, Verity," said Evan. "James and I have just been putting up the awning. You can see it's very roomy."

"I love it!" I said and caught sight of Joe shaking his head in defeat.

"Ah, there's Bronwen, my wife," said Evan, introducing us. "*Cariad*, meet Vera and Jim. I think they may be interested in our caravan."

To cut an inevitable story short, we made an offer, which was accepted. All four of us shook hands and I couldn't wait to take Sheila home.

Unfortunately, we had overlooked the fact that our car didn't have a tow hitch, so we had to leave her behind and arrange for one to be fitted.

"That's just the most perfect caravan for us," I crowed as we headed home.

Joe nodded. "I think it'll suit us just fine. But you know you'll have to do most of the fetching and carrying."

"Yes, I know."

"And the heavy stuff, like lifting gas bottles."

"That's okay, I don't mind."

We fell into silence, each lost in our thoughts. I was dreaming about the bedding we'd need, and the camping crockery, pots and pans. I couldn't wait to fit Sheila out and embark on our first adventure.

"Evan really struggled with our names, didn't he?" observed Joe.

"Yes, he did. Nice man, though. I liked him."

"He couldn't even get his wife's name right. One minute he was introducing her as Bronwen, then he was calling her *Cariad*."

"I think that's Welsh for 'darling'."

"Oh. I bet her real name is Belinda or something."

"Probably."

I didn't really care what Evan's wife's name was. I was dreaming of introducing (caravan) Sheila to her husband, (car) Bruce. What an exciting partnership that would be! I imagined hitching them together for the first time and heading north to explore Australia.

"We could travel around the whole of Australia if we wanted," I said.

"We could."

"We could even go across the Nullabor. Imagine! Days of travelling across the desert from one side of Australia to the other."

"I'd love that. Do you know why it's called that?"

"Yes, it means 'no trees'."

"I knew that."

"So many places to explore! Places that are just names to us. Like Dubbo or Broken Hill. We could go panning for gold in Queensland, or explore the wilds of the Northern Territory!"

"Yes, that's true," said Joe drily. "But let's concentrate on getting a tow hitch fitted first."

"Okay."

SHEILA

"Then you can plan a nice, gentle, local maiden voyage."

I was so excited I couldn't sleep that night.

WELSH RAREBIT

Welsh rarebit is a dish of hot cheese sauce, often including ale, mustard, or Worcestershire sauce, served on toasted bread.

But beware! Wikipedia states that Welsh rarebit supposedly causes vivid dreams. The 1902 book Welsh Rarebit Tales is a collection of short horror stories supposedly from members of a writing club who ate a dinner which included a large portion of rarebit immediately before sleeping in order to give themselves inspiring dreams.

Ingredients (serves 3)

¼ cup butter

¼ cup all-purpose flour

½ teaspoon salt

¼ teaspoon pepper

¼ teaspoon mustard powder

¼ teaspoon Worcestershire sauce, or more to taste

2 drops Tabasco, or more to taste

1 cup whole milk

½ cup beer

225g (½lb) sharp Cheddar cheese, shredded

6 slices bread

Method

Melt butter in a saucepan over low heat. Stir in flour, salt, pepper, mustard, Worcestershire sauce, and Tabasco. Cook and stir until smooth and bubbly, about 5 minutes.

Remove the saucepan from the heat.

Gradually stir in milk, then return to heat and stir continuously until mixture comes to the boil.

Slowly pour in beer; cook and stir for 1 minute.

Melt Cheddar cheese into mixture in small portions until completely incorporated.

Under a grill, toast bread slices on 1 side. Arrange on a baking sheet with the untoasted side facing up.

Spoon cheese sauce over untoasted side.

Cook under the grill until cheese sauce is bubbling and golden, 2 to 3 minutes.

Serve hot.

16

MAIDEN VOYAGE

A nice young man came out and fitted our tow hitch. He did a great job and showed us how we would connect it to Sheila so that her indicators and brake lights flashed when required.

Off we went back to Evan and Bronwen's house to pay the balance for Sheila and bring her home.

"Good morning, Jonas, good morning, Vi. Lovely day!"

I nearly said, *We've come to introduce Sheila to Bruce*, but stopped myself just in time. If Evan had trouble remembering our names, expecting him to absorb our car and caravan's names was probably a bridge too far.

With papers signed and exchanged and a

lesson from Evan on how to connect Sheila to Bruce, we set off. We'd tested the brake lights and indicators, and everything worked perfectly. Evan and Bronwen (or was she Belinda, or *Cariad*?) waved us goodbye.

"How does it feel, pulling Sheila?" I asked Joe. "Is it harder to drive?"

"No problem at all. It all feels fine."

The sun beat down from a flawlessly clear sky, and the world was our oyster. With Sheila, we could go anywhere, do anything. The excitement of future possibilities made me shiver.

Joe had some experience pulling a caravan decades ago, back in the UK, and was full of confidence.

"There's nothing to it," he said. "Just remember to take sharp corners wider than you might normally. And reversing is a piece of cake. Left hand down if you want to go right, and vice versa."

All went well until we reached home. Lola saw Sheila pull up and went frantic. We couldn't hear her through the window glass but we saw her barking furiously at the white monster that was attempting to reverse up our drive.

"Are you sure you can remember how to reverse?" I asked Joe after his fifth failed attempt. "I'm worried you may hit next door's tree."

Next door's tree was large, and both a blessing and a curse. Its branches were strong and thick, and the foliage was dense. Children from the neighbourhood were drawn to this tree like a magnet and it was common to see bikes thrown on the grass, shoes discarded and bare feet dangling from the branches above.

Sometimes children fell out. Howls ensued and parents raced to scoop up their youngsters, the relief that their child was only bruised turning their concern to anger.

"I *told* you not to climb that tree! You're lucky you didn't break an arm or leg. Don't you *ever* let me catch you climbing it again."

But of course the children always came back. The tree was irresistible. I was often tempted to climb it myself.

When the children were at school, the wildlife took over. The tree bore swathes of white berries every year that dozens of sulphur-crested cockatoos feasted on. Screeching to each other, they snipped off bunches with their secateur-like beaks. Then, standing on one foot, they would hold the bunch up with the other claw, examine it, select the juiciest berry and drop the remaining clusters to the ground. Because the branches of the tree spread over our driveway, the twigs and berries landed where our car drove out, to be crushed by the tyres. Sweeping the drive was a daily chore for me in season.

Autumn was no better. When the tree lost its leaves, the wind gathered them in swirls and dumped them in our swimming pool. Another chore for me.

But I enjoyed watching the cockatoos argue and feed, and the children climb. At dusk, the kookaburras were the last to leave the tree's embrace, and with a final raucous laugh, they allowed the tree to transform into a possums' playground.

With the big tree standing to attention on one side of the driveway, and our mailbox on the other, one might be forgiven for thinking it would be easy to gently reverse Sheila between such markers.

"You'll have to get out and direct me," Joe snapped. "I can't see where I'm going."

I jumped out and began waving, pointing, and trying to help.

"What are you saying?" shouted Joe. "What does that frantic waving mean?"

"It means you're getting close to the tree!"

"Oh, for goodness' sake, how was I supposed to know that?"

He pulled forward and tried again. It took a

long time, but eventually, Sheila was parked (almost) straight in our driveway.

"You'll have to unhitch her," said Joe. "I'm too breathless."

I did so, trying to remember the steps that Evan had taught us.

"We need practice," I said when we'd settled down. "I need to make lists. I'll write a step-by-step idiot list for hitching and unhitching. I'll get it laminated. And I think you should teach me how to reverse her, too. You never know when I might need to do that myself. It can't be that difficult."

Joe snorted and scratched himself.

I made a hitching/unhitching list and used it every time. I now knew what a jockey wheel was, coupling pins, chocks, D-shackles and 7-pin connections. I was proud of my new skills and vocabulary.

However, my first reversing lesson didn't go so smoothly.

We drove to our local oval carpark, a spacious area. Only one other car was parked there, so we had plenty of space.

"Right, get in the driver's seat, and I want you to reverse straight back until you are in line with that tree."

I looked over my shoulder. Just reverse straight back? Easy-peasy!

But it wasn't.

Every time I inched back, Sheila would begin to veer left. Or right. She never went straight.

"Never mind, drive forward. Let's start again. Right, start reversing… Left hand down, no! Left hand, not so fast. Good, swing right. Not that much! Slow down, try again. No, stop! You're heading for that parked car again!"

It was a nightmare. Why was it so hard?

I'd like to say I finally mastered it, but I never did. I never managed to reverse Sheila successfully, ever. But I did become much more sympathetic towards Joe's efforts, which, although often haphazard, were infinitely better than mine.

I had already bought a beautiful book which showed all the campsites in Australia. It had maps and suggestions, and every site was star-rated with a full description of facilities and prices. That book was my caravanning bible and I loved it.

I set to work kitting Sheila out with everything we would need for our trips. I bought pots, pans, plates, pillows and pantry items. I bought bedding, blankets, a bed for Lola and balls. I washed the curtains and found cushions. It felt like setting up a little house in miniature, and I really enjoyed myself.

"So when are we going on our maiden voyage?" asked Joe, having watched me trot backwards and forwards with armfuls of stuff umpty-nine times. "You're making me dizzy."

"I've decided we'll be ready next week. We're going to Jimmy's Beach."

"Who is Jimmy?"

"I have no idea. That's what it's called. Jimmy's Beach."

"Where is it?"

"In the Port Stephens region."

"Oh."

"Near Hawks Nest. Not far from Tea Gardens."

"Are you making these names up?"

"No! Of course not. Do you want to see the map?"

"No, I'll leave it to you. What's it like?"

"Well, it sounds perfect, but we'll just have to wait and see."

Our first adventure! Apart from a niggling worry that we would have to reverse into a space at the caravan site under the scrutiny of experienced caravaners, I couldn't wait to hit the road.

The drive to Jimmy's Beach was pleasant and

uneventful. We were lucky that the plot we were allocated was drive-through, therefore no tricky reversing was required. We parked Sheila on a nice flat spot under the shade of a tree. Using a very long leash, we tethered Lola so that she could explore without getting lost while we sorted ourselves out.

"I can hear the sea," I said. "I can't wait to look!"

But two surprising things happened in quick succession which delayed our exploration of the path that led into the bush in the direction of the beach.

Lola alerted us to the first surprise. She suddenly began to bark frantically.

"Whatever is the matter with that dog?" said Joe. "Stop her barking or we'll get thrown off the site before we've even unpacked."

"Lola, stop that," I said, trying to work out what she was barking at.

And then I saw it.

"Joe, look!"

I pointed at a four-legged animal strolling calmly past the parked vans, down the track, heading for the beach. Bold as brass, it ignored us and turned its back on Lola's outraged barking.

Joe verbalised exactly what I was thinking.

"That looks like a dingo!" he said.

Wildlife is my passion and I knew a little about dingoes. Apparently, they arrived in Australia from Asia, maybe 4,000 years ago. It is thought humans brought them, and dingo numbers gradually spread across the continent from that time. It seems that the aboriginal people recognised their usefulness and bred them, and soon dingoes also began to populate off-shore islands. Dingoes have been blamed for the extinction of the Tasmanian tiger, and the Tasmanian devil from mainland Australia.

But was this a dingo? And if so, why was a dingo marching through the campsite?

The answer was in the toilet block. Signs warned visitors not to feed the dingoes that sometimes passed through the camp. Apparently, the dingoes were losing their natural fear of humans and becoming unafraid. It was feared that if hungry, they might become aggressive and attack domestic dogs or humans.[1]

---

1. Picture by News of the Area - Modern Media

Wild dingoes resting in the afternoon sun at Jimmy's beach

Now we had a worrying wild dog situation, but another concern soon replaced it. Although we had hooked up all the electrical connections, nothing seemed to be working. The lights wouldn't turn on, and even the fridge was not functioning. We were in an unfamiliar location at the beginning of the weekend, and we had no idea where to find an electrician. Spending our first night in Sheila was not supposed to be like this.

"I'll see if Reception is still open," I said. "Maybe they can advise us."

It wasn't open.

"Okay, we still have some time before dusk. Let's finish unpacking and make the beds. Do everything we can while we still have light. Then we'll drive out to the nearest shops and buy a couple of big torches. On the way back, we can pick up a take-away. Good idea?"

Joe nodded.

I quickly made the beds and laid out everything we would need later. Then, as twilight deepened the shadows and the trees and vans became silhouettes, we drove out of the campsite in search of shops.

We discovered that there were small shops nearby, and a little further there was a mall with big late-opening supermarkets. We would have reached them sooner but were distracted on the way.

The road we took had dense bushland on either side, with tall gum trees whose branches met and formed a canopy over the road. It was like entering a tunnel, the roof of which was made up of a random latticework of living intertwined branches and twigs. Stark and black against the cinnamon sky, it was a surreal experience.

Joe drove slowly into the tunnel and we became aware of a clamour of cries and squeals. And then we saw them.

"Fruit bats!"

"We're right in the middle of the colony!"

"And they're just waking up!"

Yes, the smell of ammonia was stifling, and the noise of a thousand bats beginning their day was deafening. But what fantastic timing!

Joe crawled along at snail's pace as we stared upward. Black shapes hanging from the branches wriggled and swung. They yawned, scratched and stretched one wing, and then the other. Finally, each bat launched into the orange sky, now silent black shapes, like a vampire movie backdrop.

Impatient motorists honked their horns as we slowly drove through that magical tunnel. They yelled and waved their fists as they overtook us.

But we didn't care. We must have watched scores of bats flap away to begin their journey in search of food that night. The bats, also known as flying foxes, knew which bush fruits would be ready to feast on, but they had no idea how vital their feeding forays were. Without the flying foxes, the forests of Australia would die. Koalas and all the other forest creatures would perish. Fruit bats are the main pollinators of trees and carry out the vital job of forest regeneration.

Flying foxes migrate along the east coast of Australia in large groups, following the fruits in season. Their habits haven't changed in thousands of years, but now they suffer from habitat loss.

Sadly, flying foxes are no match for developers who are fast bulldozing the trees that sustain them.

All too soon, the tunnel opened out and we left the trees behind. High above us, already far, far in the distance, we saw the black specks flying into the night.

I dived into the brightly lit supermarket and found a couple of huge torches, complete with batteries. The shop was not busy and the check-out girl was deep in conversation with a colleague.

While I waited for them to make a decision about which nail polish colour they preferred, I noticed they looked like clones of each other. Both had brassy blonde hair extensions cascading down their backs, both had inch-long sweeping black lashes that caused a draught when they blinked, and both had inflated lips like ducks' beaks that they could hardly close.

Reluctantly, one girl began scanning the barcodes of my purchases, still carrying on her conversation over her shoulder.

"So he said to me, what are you doing tomorrow, babe? Well, I just stared at him!"

"He never!"

"He did!"

"What a cheek! Bet he's a Sagittarius."

I coughed politely, and the girl suddenly remembered me and rang up my purchases.

Having paid for the torches, I climbed back into the car.

"How did you get on?" asked Joe.

"Success! They had two big torches. Let's try them out!"

The torch and batteries were tightly blister-packed and we struggled to get into the packaging. We wrestled, we tore, we bit, but all in vain. We could not break in.

"I'll have to go back in and ask one of the zombies to lend me some scissors," I groaned.

"Zombies?"

"Yes, well, clones. Never mind, I'll explain later."

Back in the shop, nothing had changed, and I was still the only customer. I walked up to the counter and paused. Neither zombie took any notice of me.

"So I said to him, you can take that look off your face."

"You never!"

"I did!"

I coughed. Both girls turned and blinked at me with their black eyelashes.

"Excuse me, but I wondered if you could help me? Do you remember me? I just came in and bought these." I waved the torches in the air.

The zombies silently stared at me, their botox-injected faces unable to create any expression.

"I need some scissors, please," I said.

"Aisle twelve," they chanted in unison.

"No, no," I explained quickly, worried they might lose their concentration if I didn't hurry. "I can't get into the packaging of these torches. Could I borrow a pair of scissors, please?"

They stared at me, wide-eyed, as though I'd asked them to hand over the day's takings, but eventually one opened a drawer and put some scissors on the counter.

That did the trick. A few snips and I was able to extract the torches.

I thanked them, although I doubt they noticed, then headed back to the car, dropping the cardboard and plastic in a bin on the way.

"Success!" I said again.

I spoke too soon because we failed the next task: opening the torches to put in the big square batteries. We pulled, twisted and struggled, but the torches wouldn't give up their secret.

"Well, these torches are absolutely no good to us, are they?" Joe snorted. "If we can't open them, they're pointless. You'll have to take them back."

"But there's nobody in the shop apart from a pair of zombies. And they don't know anything about anything, except star signs and nail polish."

"Pardon?"

"Oh, never mind."

I retraced my steps back to the shop.

Both zombies looked up, faint recognition in their otherwise empty eyes. They looked at the torches as I laid them on the counter.

"I'm so sorry," I said, "but we can't open the torches to put the batteries in."

"Are you bringing them back?" asked one. "Are they faulty?"

"No, we just can't open them."

"We'll need the packaging and the receipt if you want a refund."

"No, I've thrown those away. I don't really want a refund anyway, I just need some help opening the torches."

Despite the botox, I recognised the expression that flicked across both girls' faces. *Poor old dear*, they were thinking. *She can't work out how to put the battery in.*

Each girl stretched out a manicured hand and began to examine, then grapple with the torches. I couldn't help feeling a tad triumphant when they struggled. So it wasn't a senior problem. Good!

But I was worried. There were no other torches

on the shelf, we had no light apart from the torch on our mobile phones, and the night was now inky black. How were we going to cope at the campsite, our first night in Sheila, in pitch darkness?

A ZOMBIE HAND FOR HALLOWEEN

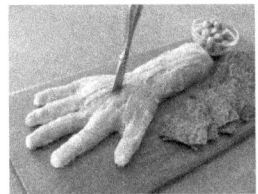

This ghastly hand will definitely be the centre of attention on your cheese board! Recipe from allrecipes.com.

Ingredients (serves 2)

About 10 prosciutto slices, depending on size

700g (1½lbs) cream cheese, softened

⅓ cup finely chopped roasted red pepper

2 tablespoons chopped fresh Italian parsley

½ teaspoon freshly ground black pepper

¼ teaspoon garlic powder

¼ teaspoon salt

1 pinch cayenne pepper

Method

Add cream cheese, red pepper, parsley, black pepper, garlic powder, salt, and cayenne to a bowl and mix thoroughly.

Cover with plastic wrap, and chill until firm, about 30 minutes.

Trace your hand on a piece of parchment. Turn parchment over, and place on a baking sheet.

Use two teaspoons to fill in the hand template with the chilled cheese mixture. Build cheese up and sculpt it to form the 3-dimensional shape of a hand and wrist.

Cover with plastic wrap and freeze until very firm, about 2 hours.

Use a knife to separate fingers from hand and hand from wrist. Wrap each piece with prosciutto, tucking extra meat underneath.

Cover, and place in the freezer for about 1 hour or until ready to complete assembling the hand.

Place the hand section on a serving board first, then attach the fingers and the wrist. Use your own hand as a reference for placing parts of the hand. Use more prosciutto to cover seams, and to add detail and definition.

Refrigerate until ready to serve with crackers.

17

KARMA

Try as we might, we couldn't open the torches to insert the batteries.

Salvation arrived from an unexpected source. A young man dressed in tradie neons plonked a six-pack of beers onto the counter. We all jumped.

"Are you ladies having trouble?" he asked.

The zombies tried to fight the botox and smile. The result was more of a pout than a smile, but their fluttering eyelashes made up for it and I think he recognised that we were all friendly.

"I've just bought these two torches," I explained, "but we can't work out how to open the battery compartments."

He picked one up and examined it closely.

"Ah, you have to unscrew the glass lens, I think," he said at last.

He tried it and that worked. Now I had two working powerful torches. Hooray!

I thanked him and was just leaving when a thought occurred to me.

"You don't happen to know of an electrician, do you?" I asked. "We are at Jimmy's Beach caravan site, and all our electrics have failed."

"Well, funnily enough, I do," he replied and gave me a friend's number retrieved from his phone. "Bono will help you if he can, he's a good sparky."

I couldn't thank him enough, and walked away, leaving him in the zombies' clutches.

"How did it go?" asked Joe.

"Excellent. I have two working torches and a sparky's telephone number."

We stopped to pick up fish and chips, then enjoyed our first night, torchlit, in Sheila.

"Those fish and chips were delicious," I said, as I packed up all the paper.

Joe nodded.

The sky was black and huge, apart from the thousands of bright, white pin-pricks that twinkled above us. The tide must have been high because we could hear the waves crashing up the beach not far away.

KARMA

"You know what," observed Joe, pouring us another glass of red wine each. "Wine tastes the same whether you can see what you're drinking, or not."

He was right.

We phoned Bono the next morning, but he said he couldn't get out to us for a couple of days. We decided that didn't really matter, our torches were sufficient. We would wait. We had plenty to explore. As yet we had heard the ocean and knew it was close, but we hadn't seen it yet. According to the campsite map, we could access the beach directly through the bush.

"Right! Let's investigate," I said, and led the way.

The path that led through the dense bush towards the beach was punctuated by strange peaks of sand with a round hole in the top, like mini volcanos. Judging by the size of the hole in the crater, the inhabitants were worryingly large.

"Ants," I said. "Big ones. Best avoided. Lola, get your nose out of that or you'll get it bitten off."

Lola was thoroughly enjoying herself. So many new scents to check out. Rabbit trails, giant ants, dingo footprints and a host of other exciting sniffs. We crested a sand dune and all three of us stopped.

It's happened many times in my life,

particularly since we moved to Australia. That moment when you reach the top of a hill, or dune, or cliff, and suddenly catch sight of a view so unexpected and magnificent that it makes you gasp.

Five kilometres of gleaming white sand curved in an arc, lapped by gentle waves that frothed and slid back into the sapphire waters. Out to sea, a green island rose from the calm ocean. Sea met sky in a symphony of blues.

There was no other human in sight.

Joe stood by my side, and together we marvelled without saying a word.

Lola paused with us, but not for long. She galloped down the sand dune and onto the beach, picking up speed as she reached firmer sand. Her ears flew out behind her as she ran, ran, ran, each joyous step resulting in perfect prints at the water's edge. We joined her at a more leisurely pace, but our enjoyment matched hers.

"I think we've found paradise," I said as the warm water washed over my bare toes.

KARMA

Lola and me

We didn't mind waiting a couple of days for Bono to fix our electrics. It turned out that our fridge was faulty, resulting in a short circuit, but as soon as we switched the fridge off, our lights, sockets and microwave worked again.

We had plenty to keep us occupied in the area. We discovered that the green, forested island we could see was called Cut Feet Island, but we had no idea why. We watched a pair of cheeky pink and grey galahs nest in a hole in a hollow tree. The dingo returned often. It had much better manners than Lola and ignored her hysterical barks as it passed.

Of course, we had to visit Tea Gardens, too. It proved to be a quaint little town that runs along the bank of the Myall river.

"Why is it called Tea Gardens?" asked Joe.

"I looked that up, and it seems nobody really knows. Some think it's because they tried to grow tea here in 1826. Or it could be because there are heaps of tea trees growing along the banks of the river."

It wasn't the tea trees that charmed me, it was the signage. For instance, the tiny police station sign had a cutout painted pelican perched on it, complete with a pair of handcuffs dangling from its beak.

Spanning the river to the town of Hawks Nest is a road bridge commonly known as the Singing Bridge. It earned this name because its railings act like a wind harp and the bridge sings during strong winds.

A ferry drew up and moored, and a stream of chattering passengers disembarked.

"Oh look," I remarked. "This ferry goes to Nelson Bay several times a day. And it's dog-friendly. Let's do that tomorrow."

We made our way back to the car, only stopping to chat with an elderly couple who wanted to pat Lola. The lady was wearing a headscarf dotted with red and white striped rectangles which I recognised to be the flag of Poland.

"We are havink a dog quite the same as this one at our home in Poland," exclaimed the lady.

Lola enjoyed the pats and wagged her tail furiously.

Another beautiful day dawned, and we drove from our campsite to the Tea Gardens ferry wharf, where passengers were already waiting in line. We joined the queue, which was beginning to board the ferry.

"Ah, you are waitink too?" said a heavily accented voice behind us. I recognised the red and white scarf immediately. It was the Polish couple we had met the day before.

"Hello again," I said.

Lola swished her tail, knowing more pats would come her way.

"You are takink your beautiful dog on the boat? We are takink our dog on a boat in Poland. She was likink it very much," said the lady.

The couple waved cheerily as they entered the lounge room of the ferry, and we found a bench on one of the open decks. As the engines rumbled into life, Lola looked at us anxiously but soon became accustomed to the strange noise. The ferry swung around and moved away from the wharf, churning the river water into an arc of white froth.

Lola, now the salty sea dog, stood on the bench between us, her front paws resting on the handrail. I kept a tight hold on her leash, aware of her passion for water and swimming. Her ears flapped in the breeze, and her nose pointed into the wind absorbing all the exciting, fishy river smells.

Perched on tall poles, pelicans watched us pass, while cormorants dived out of sight only to reappear somewhere completely different.

"Dolphins on the starboard side," announced our captain on the loudspeaker.

"Oh, three of them!" I said, watching them leap out of the water in an elegant synchronised curve. "How lovely!"

"Where?" said Joe.

But it was too late, he missed them.

Nelson Bay is the name of the town, and also the bay. We disembarked just behind the Polish couple.

"Your dog, she likink the boat?" asked the lady, her red and white headscarf stirring in the breeze. "Our dog in Poland she always likink the water and also she is likink the swimmink."

We assured her that Lola had enjoyed herself

and waved the couple another cheery goodbye as we parted ways onshore.

The walk along the harbour was very pleasant. Judging by the many beautiful, expensive-looking craft moored in the marina, Nelson Bay is favoured by millionaires and Joe and I enjoyed ourselves imagining which boat we would buy if we won the lottery.

The water was crystal clear and we were delighted by the variety of fish that darted amongst the seaweed at the little fish feeding station.

"Oh, you are seeink the little fish," exclaimed a familiar voice. The Polish couple had appeared yet again, right beside us. "Our dog in Poland she also is likink fish to eat!"

She nudged her husband and they both laughed as though she had just cracked the funniest joke.

Joe groaned and scratched himself irritably, but they didn't seem to notice.

I smiled and nodded politely and we moved away.

"You are kidding," growled Joe. "Are they following us? We met them yesterday, now wherever we go, they pop up like jack-in-the-boxes. Come on, quick, let's lose them."

I trotted after him as he dived into one of the many seafood cafes that lined the harbour.

Safely tucked away from the pavement, we ordered lunch and gazed at the view. The waitress placed our plates before us and I realised how hungry I was. I picked up my knife and fork.

"Oh, good grief," hissed Joe, and to my astonishment dropped down as though he'd been shot. I gaped down at him on the floor.

"Did you lose som…" I asked, but, to my horror, he grabbed my sleeve and dragged me down with him.

"Duck!"

"What are you doing?"

"It's THEM again."

"Don't be ridiculous!" I whispered. "We can't crouch behind a table in a cafe. What if they see us hiding?"

Lola, sensing Joe's excitement, misread the situation and thought we were playing a lovely game. She barked joyfully, eager to join the fun. Two pairs of sensible open-toed sandals, complete with beige socks had appeared beside us.

"Oh, it *is* you!" said the Polish lady, looking down on us. "I am hearink your dog. She has the *woof* just like my dog in Poland when is makink the bark! I am thinkink it must be my dog!"

Husband and wife laughed merrily together. I

was aware I was gaping up at them and collected myself.

"Um, we were just looking for our, er, keys," I said. "Joe dropped them, didn't you, Joe?"

It was Joe's turn to gape.

"No, no!" squealed the Polish lady. "Look! You are makink a mistake! Here are your keys. They are lyink on the table."

Indeed, she had picked up Joe's car keys from the tabletop. She dangled them from her fingers, rattling them a little in case we didn't believe her.

"Oh, thank goodness," I gushed, straightening up. "Joe, stand up. Panic over."

"Is everything okay?" asked the waitress, probably wondering what on earth was going on.

"This lunch our friends are havink is lookink very good," said the Polish lady, wagging her head. "Please we are orderink that."

Her husband beamed and nodded.

"Shall I bring two chairs so you can all sit together?" asked the waitress.

"Oh, yes!" said the Polish lady, clapping her hands in delight, the Polish flags on her headscarf fluttering in the brisk sea breeze.

"No!" said Joe. "Absolutely not."

"What my husband means is that he'll move the chairs," I said quickly.

Husband and wife beamed, and the waitress

hurried away to prepare their order. Joe sullenly brought two more chairs for our new friends. I looked sadly at our waiting plates of food, already cooling and losing their appeal.

Much later, Joe and I were leaning on the ferry's handrail as Nelson Bay receded, watching the water rush by as we headed back to Tea Gardens.

"How did we get lumbered with them?" asked Joe, scratching himself with annoyance.

"It was your fault! If you hadn't dived under the table, Lola wouldn't have barked."

"No, it was your fault! If you'd reacted quicker when I told you to duck, they wouldn't have seen us."

"Well, never mind. At least they aren't on this ferry. They weren't so bad, really. Actually, I feel a bit better now knowing we could help them a bit. They had their hearts set on buying a ship in a bottle, didn't they? How did you know there was a little shop on the other side of the harbour that specialises in ships in bottles?"

Joe stared intently at a point on the opposite side of the river.

"Joe?"

Silence.

"Joe, you made that up, didn't you? How could you! You gave those poor people fake directions to a non-existent shop to get rid of them, didn't you?"

Joe was saved by the captain's voice booming out, cutting into our conversation.

"Dolphins on the port bow," he announced.

Lola and I rushed over and caught a glimpse of a school of dolphins, their fins cutting through the water. But Joe was too slow.

"Where are they?" he asked.

"Oh, they're out of sight now," I said.

"Dammit, I missed them again!"

"Yes. Serves you right. That's Karma."

So much to see! So much to do!

"What's on the itinerary for today, then?" asked Joe, the next day.

"Well, I fancy an exploratory trip along Mungo Brush road," I said.

"Good. Let's see if we spot any mungos," said Joe.

BEER-BATTERED DEEP FRIED FISH

A gorgeous, classic fried fish recipe.

Ingredients

About 2 litres (or 2 quarts) vegetable oil for frying

8 fillets of cod or similar flaky fish

salt and pepper to taste

1 cup plain (all-purpose) flour

2 tablespoons garlic powder

2 tablespoons paprika

2 teaspoons salt

2 teaspoons ground black pepper

1 egg, beaten

1 can or bottle of beer, or as much as is needed

lemon wedges for serving

Method

Heat oil in a deep fryer to 185°C (365°F).

Rinse cod fillets, pat dry, and season with salt and pepper.

Mix flour, garlic powder, paprika, salt, and pepper in a large bowl; add egg and stir well to combine. Gradually mix in enough beer to make a thin batter.

Dip cod fillets into the batter to coat.

Carefully lower fillets, one at a time, into the hot oil.

Fry several fillets at a time, turning once, until cooked through and golden brown, about 2 minutes per side.

Drain on paper towels. Repeat to cook remaining fillets.

Serve hot with lemon wedges.

18

TRIPS

From Tea Gardens, heading north, we found Mungo Brush road. Barely more than a track, it snaked through the bush and scrub, hugging the curves of the coastline. I don't believe we saw another car.

"Ah, Dark Point," I said as we passed a small signpost.

"What's that?"

"I think it's important aboriginal land. All this area belongs to the Worimi people and they've been using Dark Point and surrounds as a gathering place for over 4000 years."

"Should we take a look?"

"No, but let's stop at one of these lookout places."

"Here we go, Hole in the Wall picnic point. Will that do?"

There were no other cars or people when we parked.

"You go," said Joe. "I'm a bit out of breath. I'll wait here."

Lola and I explored a sandy track and I could smell the sea. I thought I knew what to expect, and I wasn't disappointed. We climbed a dune and the sand, so white it almost burned the eyes, stretched and meandered both left and right for miles. The ocean sparkled in a million shades of blue. In the distance, Broughton Island reared out of the water like a giant, jagged deep green emerald.

"Did you see a wall with a hole in it?" asked Joe when we returned.

"Nope, just a beach."

But it *wasn't* just a beach. That's the thing about Australia. It has thousands of stunning beaches, but each one is unique. I couldn't begin to describe the shades of blue my eyes feasted on, or the blinding white sand, or how the sparkling water danced in the sunshine.

"A nice beach?" asked Joe, and I grieved that his illness robbed him of the energy to share my little adventure.

"Yes, a lovely one. I can see why the Worimi

people have thrown their parties here for 4000 years."

I don't think we saw it, but our road was also echoing the curves of the Myall River to our right, which emptied into a large lake. We rounded a bend and came to an abrupt stop. Cars queued in front of us, and we waited our turn.

"It's the Bombah Vehicular Ferry," I said, reading the sign. "And it's a national park on the other side of the water."

In the back, Lola woke up and sat up straight, aware that we had stopped. The dry, sandy scrub of Mungo Brush road had given way to cool green, leafy shade trees reflected in the lake.

Our ticket cost just $2.50 and we waited in line. There was space for about six cars on the ferry, and we drove on without mishap. It was just a short trip and we were told to stay in the car, but I don't think there was space to open a door anyway, we were so tightly packed. It was more of a raft than a ferry, propelled by chains. Vehicles parked behind us, and we were ready to go.

The car next to us had two elderly ladies in it. I saw them looking into our car and Lola wagged a greeting. Then their window descended and the lady in the passenger seat turned to us, a severe expression on her face.

"We see you have a dog," she said. "Dogs aren't allowed in the national park."

Joe said nothing, leaving me to reply. I leant across him to answer.

"Oh, it's okay, she won't be allowed out of the car at all," I said.

Now it was the driver's turn to add her pennyworth.

"Dogs are not allowed in the park at all. Period. Even if you keep them in the car. If you continue you are risking a hefty fine if a ranger catches you."

I tried to think of a reply but the window had already zoomed up and both women were staring straight ahead, their thin lips pressed together, emanating disapproval.

Joe scratched, rolled his eyes and spoke to me from the corner of his mouth.

"Well, what are we supposed to do? Ask everybody to reverse off the ferry?"

It was too late anyway. The little ferry rumbled and began its short journey across the water.

The trip was spoilt for me as I imagined uniformed rangers marching between the vehicles, checking for smuggled dogs.

"What do we do?"

"Can't you make her lie down?"

"Lie down," I ordered Lola but she looked at me as though I was crazy. Why should she lie down? She'd only just woken up after a nice long sleep and she wanted to see what was going on.

I rustled about in the glove compartment and found a dog treat. It wasn't very big and it may have been in there for years. Age had made it soft and bendy, so I tore the tiniest fragment off it and tossed it on the floor behind.

That did the trick. Lola jumped off the seat, into the foot well, and sniffed the morsel out. I kept repeating the action, whilst furtively scanning the ferry for approaching rangers, praying that I had enough to keep her hidden on the floor until we drove off.

I can't tell you about the Myall River, the waterway or the scenery because I was too busy breaking the law to take note. But eventually, we drove off on the other side undetected. Once there, we drove straight through the national park and out of the other side as fast as possible.

I remember we stopped in a town called Bulahdelah and parked by the wide river to picnic. We didn't know how to pronounce the name of the town, and I'm still not sure.

That maiden voyage with our car, Bruce, and his new partner, Sheila, was a huge success. When we arrived home, we splashed out on a new caravan fridge and I set to work planning more trips.

I don't remember it ever raining when we went off in Sheila to explore pastures new, and that should have been a sign to even us novices. The prolonged drought that had begun two years before in 2017 had ensured that Australia was crisp and dry.

The clock was ticking.

In order to renew Joe's visa, he was required to exit Australia before he could enter again. He had previously flown to New Zealand for the day, which was allowed. However, due to his need to attend appointments with British medical specialists, and get his Bi-Pap serviced, he decided to fly back to Britain for a few weeks.

In hindsight, that decision probably saved his life.

But before his departure date arrived, we wanted to cram in as many trips in Sheila as we could. Cam and Karly also had a caravan so it was ideal to meet somewhere for a family holiday and spend time together.

There were so many places to visit and so much fun to be had. I remember One Mile Beach where the waves roared as we slept. At twilight, rabbits popped out of their burrows and hopped around the tents. Kids to play with, rabbits to chase: Lola was in doggy heaven.

This campsite had many attractions, and one of our favourite was definitely Albert. Next to the reception building was a very large enclosure built around a tree and bushes.

"Mummy, what's in there?" asked Winter, pointing.

"No idea!"

Later, we had more time to explore and check out the enclosure again. We walked around it, peering in.

"Is anybody there?" I asked, searching for a resident.

"Anybody at home?" called Indy.

"Anybody at home?" echoed Winter.

"Hellooo?" said Karly.

"Hello," came the reply from within and we all jumped.

A large sulphur-crested cockatoo stepped out of the foliage and peered at Karly, its head on one side. He ignored the rest of us.

"Hello," he said again.

"Mummy, he likes you!" squeaked Indy. "Talk to him!"

"Hello!" said Karly again.

"Hello, hello," came the squawked reply.

It wasn't a deep, meaningful conversation, but the two were definitely communicating.

After numerous exchanged 'Hellos', we entered the reception building.

"We've just been talking to your cockatoo," Karly gushed, proud that she was the only one of us to get a response from the parrot.

"Oh yes, Albert," said the receptionist. "He's a cantankerous old bastard."

Indy and Winter absorbed this, mouths open, unblinking.

"He only talks when he feels like it, and he prefers people with an English accent."

"Oh!" said Karly, disappointed that she didn't have any special Dr Dolittle powers after all.

As we closed the door behind us, seven-year-old Indy piped up.

"Shall we go and visit the cantankerous old bastard again later?" she asked.

Karly and I looked away, trying desperately hard not to laugh.

Another attraction was the large, square, metal fire pit provided to all guests. Cam gathered extra firewood for ours. Unfortunately, he collected it in the dark, and much of the wood that he piled up was green and sappy and challenging to set alight. Finally, in best Boy Scout style, he managed to set it on fire. Sadly, instead of a healthy, flickering flame, acrid smoke billowed out.

"Hey, mate, would you mind doing something about your fire?" said one camp neighbour.

"Sorry, mate! Will do," said Cam.

But our fire just blew out black smog, making us all cough. Joe retreated behind a distant tree.

Cam did his best, but the fire wouldn't cooperate. Our sausages remained anaemic, only half-cooked, and the smoke was so dense we couldn't get near them.

"Listen, mate," called another camper. "D'you think you could tone your fire down a bit?"

"No worries!" said Aussie Cam cheerfully, ever resourceful.

He grabbed a tow rope from his ute, hitched it to the smoking cast iron fire pit and slowly dragged the whole thing to the edge of the clearing, earning applause and cheers of "Good on yer, mate!" from our fellow campers.

Problem solved.

Meanwhile, Joe was having a little adventure of his own. It was almost dark, and as he sat in his chair behind a tree, escaping the evil smoke of our fire pit, he heard a little scratching sound. Quietly, he turned his head towards the trunk of the tree. Motionless, with its dark, glittery eyes on the same level as Joe's, a possum stared back at him.

Joe and the possum stared at each other for a full minute. Native Australian wildlife is notoriously tame on Australian campsites.

Joe was fascinated by the possum's claws, which were exquisitely designed to grip tree bark. He was also captivated by its soft, silver fur and dark eyes, which allowed the animal to see in the dark. The possum's prehensile tail served as another hand, allowing it to wrap around a branch and support its weight.

"Hello, little guy," he said softly. "We've got one of your cousins at home in our garden. His name is Percy."

But the possum didn't want to hang around and chat. With a twitch of its tail, it scampered up the tree and was swallowed up by the dark, leafy mass.

At last, the fire began to behave. The smoke

died down, we picked up our chairs and relocated to finish cooking and eating our sausages as the ocean roared in the background.

"We have some news," said Karly after the children had been put to bed.

The fire was dying down and the waves crashed behind us.

Joe and I waited.

"We've just put our house on the market," said Cam.

"Really? Why?" I asked, surprised. I thought about their beautiful house, the pool, all the work they had done on it, and the Happy Birthday bird they would be leaving behind.

"Cam's seen a house and fallen in love with it. It's in the same area, but it would give us more space. We'd love more land, a bigger garden for the kids to play in."

"Maybe we could have pigs?" Cam mused, and we all smiled, knowing he had always dreamed of having pigs.

As we sat around the fire we didn't know that in less than a month, all fires of any kind, whether fire pit, barbecue or birthday candle, would be totally banned.

Oblivious to future catastrophic events, Joe and I carried on exploring New South Wales and enjoying nights in Sheila. We found a little place called Boat Harbour. There was not a single boat to be seen, but we watched humpback whales cavorting in the waves as they headed north for warmer seas to spend the winter.

But time was running out. Joe would be heading back to the UK soon. We had time to organise one last jaunt in Sheila before he had to board the plane.

"So, where are we going next?" asked Joe.

"Um, a place called Darawank."

Joe blinked. "Really? Are you sure?"

"Yes. I'm not making it up. Really."

SAUSAGES WITH ONION AND APPLE

Absolutely perfect for campsite cooking or any meal at home. Serve with mashed, fried, boiled or roast potatoes or with bread rolls or hunks of sourdough.

Ingredients

8 sausages

2 tablespoons butter

2 medium onions, halved and sliced

3 large apples - peeled, cored, and cut into thin wedges

2 tablespoons apple cider or red wine vinegar

2 heaped tablespoons brown sugar

salt and pepper to taste

Method

Prepare a barbecue or grill for high heat.

Prick sausages several times with a fork. Place in a large pot, cover with water and simmer for about 7 minutes over medium-high heat, until cooked through. Remove from heat and set aside.

Warm butter in a large skillet over medium heat. Stir in onions and cook until soft and translucent. Stir in apples, vinegar, and brown sugar. Cook, stirring gently, until caramelised for 10 to 15 minutes. Season with salt and pepper.

Meanwhile, place the boiled sausages on the barbecue and brown them.

Serve on a mound of caramelised apples and onions.

19

DRAMAS

Darawank may sound strange to us English speakers, but it actually means 'dark waters' in the local aboriginal language. Drive along the Lakes Way road, blink and you'll miss the little village of Darawank.

Situated where the Wallamba River meets the road, Darawank is about ten kilometres from the popular twin seaside towns of Forster and Tuncurry. Forster and Tuncurry are tourist magnets boasting beautiful beaches, a turquoise ocean and a bustling resort vibe with cafes and restaurants. However, I immediately fell in love with the secluded caravan park cradled within the curves of the river.

The site was perfect. I'd asked for a quiet spot

to park Sheila and we were given a riverside plot under a shady tree with no neighbours and minimal reversing. We arrived late in the afternoon but had time to explore the campsite after setting up our temporary home.

To our delight, the site offered all kinds of treats for dogs, like an off-leash dog play area, Sunday Bark Walks along the river path and an auto dog-wash. There was a cafe and restaurant, and we found information about local beaches, national parks and lookout points. We understood that summer was their busy time, with the river offering fishing, kayaking and all manner of water sports, but we were staying out of season and could enjoy the peace.

Typical for Australia, although it was June and officially winter, it wasn't cold at all.

"Let's pour ourselves a glass of something and watch the sunset," I suggested.

We set up our chairs and prepared ourselves to watch the glorious spectacle unfolding in front of us.

As the winter sun slowly sank, the sky caught fire, turning the river-water deep orange. Ducks hurried along the banks and plopped into the water, intent on getting home before dark. As they paddled past, they created ripples like molten lava. The distant trees became black silhouettes, and the sky darkened until no orange streaks remained. Darkness closed in. The birds fell silent. The show was over.

But not quite. Frogs began to chorus, and, lit by a nearby campsite lamppost, we caught sight of a movement on a branch in the big tree above us.

"I think it's an owl!" whispered Joe.

"Yes, I think there are two of them! Come on, let's see if we can get any closer."

The owls were not in the slightest bit alarmed by the two humans with upturned faces creeping towards them. Huddled together, they gazed down at us with round eyes, as we crept closer.

"I know what they are!" I whispered. "They aren't owls at all, they're tawny frogmouths!"

"Looks like an owl to me."

"And me, but they aren't. They belong to the nightjar family or something, not owls."

Tawny frogmouths are utterly adorable, and their expression is so comical that it's impossible not to smile when you see one.

Actually, it's rare to see just one because they are usually found in pairs and like to cuddle so closely to each other it's hard to see where one frogmouth starts and the other begins.

Tawny frogmouths have definitely earned

their place in my personal Top Twenty list of Australian birds.

Darawank had cast its spell over us and we stayed for five days, much longer than we'd planned. By day we walked Lola along the river path, spotting eagles that hung motionless in the sky before dropping like stones on unsuspecting prey. We became familiar with a family of three, with their white underbellies, black-tipped wings and red backs. We visited beaches and local lookouts and had coffee in quaint cafes.

We didn't have a TV but we had something much better. We watched the fiery sunsets play over the river as darkness dropped, blissfully unaware how orange skies and fire would become part of our future in a few short weeks. But for now, we enjoyed our time together before Joe had to leave.

Time sped on. Joe's appointment with Dr Patterson in the UK approached.

Lola and I bid Joe yet another farewell as our favourite driver from the airport shuttle service drew up outside our house. His bright Hawaiian shirt failed to cheer us as he jumped out to stow Joe's luggage.

"Off to the UK again?" he asked. "Looks like your dog wants to go with you. Has she got a passport?"

But the driver's quips barely raised a smile from us and Lola cried when the bus rounded the corner, out of sight.

"Cheer up," I said, as we walked back up the drive. "He'll be back in no time."

But he wouldn't be.

Years of drought, no moisture in the soil, parched grass and tinder-dry foliage had set the perfect stage for a calamity. That June, bushfires ignited in central Queensland and continued to rage and spread. No rain was forecast and we were informed by the media that the situation could become critical.

"Are you coming down to us this weekend?" asked Karly. "Cam's going to be out back-burning."

"What's back-burning, exactly?" I asked Aussie Cam when I saw him.

Cam had been a volunteer fireman for many

years, working with other volunteer and permanent firemen. They had been kept particularly busy this year. As yet, there were no fires in New South Wales, but the threat was always imminent.

"Actually, what we are doing at the moment is 'prescribed burning', or hazard reduction. It's not the same as back-burning. We're hazard burning, which means we're targeting areas where there's lots of fuel for possible bushfires. Open land, usually, where there's a lot of dead wood or dry leaf litter. If we can reduce this, bushfires have nothing to feed on, no fuel."

"So, what's back-burning?"

"Ah, that's a technique we use actually to suppress or redirect an existing fire. We purposely light a fire close to the edge of an active fire. That way, we may starve it of fuel or try to control which direction it's moving."

Fascinating. And in line with ancient aboriginal traditions.

Although the unfolding Queensland bushfire stories were aired on our TV daily, other crises were affecting our family more. Cam's lovely grandmother, known to us all as Nana, had a silly, but serious accident.

Nana was 88 years of age but active and full of life. She'd bought herself a new bedspread, and as she was making her bed, she stood on a corner trailing on the floor. Then she caught her other foot in it, tripped and fell awkwardly. We've all done the same thing but Nana's bones were brittle and she broke her collarbone.

Nana was rushed to hospital, and the doctor examined her.

"We can operate," he told the family, "but there are risks. In addition to the fact that the patient is 88 years old, there are other factors to consider. The shoulder is dislocated and putting it back may make it shatter even more."

"Just do it," said Nana, and we all held our breaths, waiting to hear the outcome.

I'm delighted to say that the operation was a complete success.

This happened during the school holidays, and Indy had come to stay with me for a few days.

"Do you think it would be a good idea to make Nana a nice Get Well card?" I suggested.

"Yes!"

Indy sat down at the dining room table, thinking hard.

"I'm going to make Nana a present AND a card," she announced at last. "Have you got a box you don't need any more?"

"I expect so, what size? Like a shoe box?"

DRAMAS

"Yes! And I need scissors, glue, paint, lots of cardboard, all that kind of stuff."

I hurried away to gather the items, keen to encourage the young artist as best as I could.

"I'm going to make Nana's bedroom," she said, busily cutting paper.

And so she did. Nana's room in miniature. Complete with wardrobe, bed, chair, window, door, bedside table with a book on it, and mat. She'd even put Nana in the bed, complete with a sad face and unruly woollen hair.

I loved it, and so did Nana when she received it. Apparently, it cheered her up no end, and so did the card Indy made.

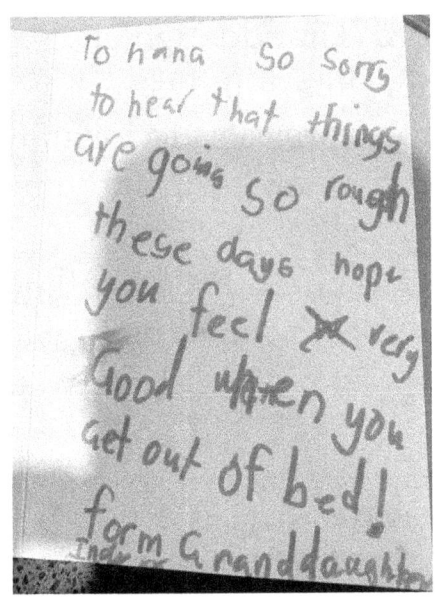

In case you can't read it, it says:

> To nana so sorry
> to hear that things
> are going so rough
> these days hope
> you feel very
> Good when you
> Get out of bed!
> form Granddaughter
> Indy xx

Indy had signed it 'form Indy' and then helpfully added the word 'Granddaughter', I'm guessing in case Nana knew lots of Indys.[1]

The tiny room was so successful that when the next family drama arrived, Indy knew just what to do.

"How will the Tooth Fairies know where to come when my tooth comes out?" wailed Winter.

"They just know," said Indy, the wise big

---

[1]. Indy also sent a Facetime message to Grumps (Joe) in the UK. https://youtube.com/shorts/TeREaC9a_VY or go to the Free Stuff page on my website and browse through the Fair Dinkum photobook.

https://bit.ly/Free--Stuff

sister. "They are probably just waiting for it to fall out. You keep wobbling it and we'll make them a Tooth Fairy Airbnb so they'll have somewhere to stay while they're waiting."

So, in preparation for when Winter's tooth came out, they built a beautiful tooth fairy Airbnb.

Meanwhile, Joe was creating his own drama in the UK.

"How come you didn't answer my phone call yesterday?" I asked. "Are you okay?"

"I'm sorry, I couldn't, I had a bit of a mishap." His voice sounded even gaspier than usual. "I'm actually in hospital."

"What? Why? What happened?"

"All the family was visiting, and we were cooking a big curry. All I did was lean over the frying pan to smell the spices heating up, and suddenly, my heart started pounding, and I couldn't breathe. I dashed outside to get some fresh air, and that's where they found me."

"Oh no!"

"I couldn't get a proper breath. They called an ambulance and the paramedics worked on me until I was breathing properly again. Anyway, they admitted me to hospital with a suspected heart attack."

It was my turn to gasp.

"Don't worry, it wasn't that, it was apparently

a panic attack, but my oxygen level had plummeted."

"Oh, how awful. How are you feeling now?"

"Better, but not quite right yet. They are keeping me in the hospital for tests and further observation for another couple of days. Anyway, enough about me. How are you doing? I hear bushfires are breaking out in Australia."

"Yes, but they're nowhere near us. I think they're all up in Queensland."

"No, other news?"

"Yes, quite a bit, really. Nana is doing really well after her shoulder operation. Oh, Karly and Cam have sold their place. The house they have their eye on is absolutely gorgeous. And Shealan and Daria moved."

"Shealan and Daria left that lovely apartment on the edge of the national park? Why?"

"I think it was too quiet, you know how they love the city vibe. Also, I'm willing to bet that Shealan's constant fear of the huge spiders that kept marching in from the forest was a factor in the decision, too."

"So where are they now?"

"They found a penthouse apartment right in Sydney's city centre, only two streets away from Central Station."

"Wow."

"Yes, great city views, two balconies, they love it. Anyway, they've just had a housewarming party with all their friends. I went down to Sydney to babysit the girls so Cam and Karly could go."

"How was the party? Did they enjoy themselves?"

"Oh yes. It was a Mexican-themed party. It wasn't supposed to be a costume party, Shealan hates dressing up, but Karly and Cam dressed up anyway. Can you guess what they dressed up as?"

"No, I can't. Mexicans in sombreros and ponchos?"

"Nope."

"A pantomime *burro*?"

"Nope. Do you give up?"

"Go on, then."

"A couple of baggies of cocaine."

Joe burst out laughing and I was glad I had cheered him up.

"What about you and Lola? Have you both been okay?"

"Oh yes, we're fine. Nothing to report."

"That's good. I'm going to start looking for a flight home soon. Glad everything is okay. Okay, the nurses are on their rounds, I'd better go. Chat tomorrow."

But I had lied. I did have something to report;

I'd had a domestic drama all of my own. But I didn't admit to it then. I was too ashamed of myself and mortified by my stupidity.

MEXICAN BEEF PIZZA

Who doesn't love pizza? This one has a Mexican theme, but vegetarians can skip the beef.

Ingredients

230g of minced beef (½lb ground beef)

1 medium onion, diced

1 clove garlic, minced

1 tablespoon chilli powder

1 teaspoon ground cumin

½ teaspoon each of paprika, salt, black pepper

1 can refried beans

4 flour tortillas

½ cup salsa

1 cup shredded Cheddar cheese

1 cup shredded Monterey Jack or other semi-hard tasty cheese

2 green onions, chopped

2 tomatoes, diced

¼ cup thinly sliced jalapeño pepper

¼ cup sour cream (optional)

Method

Preheat the oven to 180°C (350°F). Coat 2 pie plates with non-stick cooking spray.

Place the minced beef, onion, and garlic in a skillet over medium heat. Cook until beef is evenly browned and crumbly, 5 to 7 minutes.

Drain and discard the grease. Season beef with chilli powder, cumin, paprika, salt, and pepper.

Lay one tortilla in each pie plate, and cover with a layer of refried beans. Spread ½ of the seasoned minced beef over each one, and then cover with a second tortilla. Bake in the preheated oven until tortillas are crisp, about 10 minutes.

Remove pizzas from the oven and set aside to cool slightly. Then spread ½ of the salsa over each top tortilla.

Cover each pizza with ½ of the Cheddar and Monterey Jack cheeses.

Place ½ of the tomatoes, ½ of the green onions, and ½ of the jalapeño slices onto each one.

Return pizzas to the oven and bake until cheese is melted, about 5 to 10 more minutes.

Let pizzas cool slightly before slicing each one into 4 pieces.

20

MORE DRAMAS

Do you ever drive your car on autopilot? I mean when the route is so familiar that you navigate it without thinking?

I've done that many times and am unable to remember much of the journey I've just completed, even if traffic lights are involved. It often happens when I'm deep in thought about something else. Writing, for instance. Or when something peculiar grabs my attention. While my mind is wrestling with that, my hands and eyes carry on driving as usual. My Auntie Jean used to watch her favourite TV shows, or read a book whilst her hands knitted away, needles clacking. She rarely glanced at the knitting and never made mistakes.

MORE DRAMAS

You may remember the beautiful tree that grew on the strip of grass between the entrances of our driveways, on the boundary between our house and our next-door neighbours. During school holidays, it was the climbing tree for the neighbourhood kids, a seasonal feeding station for sulphur-crested cockatoos, and Percy the possum's playground by night.

One day, as I returned from a shopping trip, something looked all wrong, but it took me some seconds to figure out what it was.

As always, I drove Bruce slightly past our house and stopped, preparing to reverse. Then I turned the wheel and began to reverse into our driveway so that I would face the right way when I drove out again.

But something felt seriously different.

And then it dawned on me. The tree! The climbing tree had gone! I'd only been out an hour or so, and in that time, the tree had been cut down, leaving a big, round, raw-looking orange stump at ground level.

As I gaped at the space where the tree should have stood, I carried on reversing the car as I had done countless times before.

Kerrrunchhhhhh!!

I can hear it now, that sickening sound of metal crunching. But how could I have hit anything? I knew that driveway like the back of my hand and could reverse down it with my eyes closed.

My foot jammed down on the brake, and I forced myself to look in the reversing mirror. A big white shape loomed behind me.

I had forgotten Sheila! I was so shocked by the disappearance of the climbing tree that I'd reversed into our new caravan. The coupling hitch had embedded itself into the back of poor Bruce. Luckily, Sheila was unscathed.

It was an expensive mistake. And it was embarrassing to admit that nobody else was involved in the accident and that I had reversed into my own caravan, in my own driveway.

"I just can't believe I did such a stupid thing," I confessed to Joe on the phone eventually.

"Never mind. At least Bruce is insured. I can't believe they cut the tree down, though."

"Me neither."

Claiming the insurance and booking Bruce into the car hospital was a bit of a palaver, but when he was discharged, he looked brand new.

Meanwhile, as I had told Joe, Karly and Cam's home had sold. They accepted an offer from buyers and were in that difficult, precarious position where they hadn't yet found anywhere they liked. The beautiful house they had set their heart on was snapped up by buyers with much deeper pockets. Sydney properties were flying off the shelves, selling as soon as they hit the market and Cam and Karly lost out on several houses.

But, at last, they heard of a home that hadn't been advertised yet. Both the location and size were perfect, and Karly and Cam crossed their fingers when they went to look at it.

"It hasn't been styled at all yet," the estate agent told them. "The owner hasn't even started to declutter or change anything."

That didn't bother Karly and Cam at all. They didn't need huge vases of flowers and the smell of baking bread and coffee brewing to woo them. They fell in love with the house immediately, warts and all. They made an offer, and it was accepted.

"It's perfect! And it has so much potential," Karly told me excitedly. "Cam can't wait to get his hands on it."

"Does it have a pool?"

"Yes, and a pond, and it has a fabulous view over the valley. We'll be able to see the sun setting over the bush every night. Oh, and it has heaps of garden space for the girls and all the pets. Who knows, we may even get a pig in the future."

I rolled my eyes. Not that again. I wasn't convinced getting pigs was a good idea.

I went to see the house as soon as possible and loved it. Each of the girls now had her own big bedroom with a beautiful shared bathroom, and there was a guest room with another bathroom, a big living area with an open fire, and a huge rumpus room with a bar and pool table. Cam and Karly's spacious bedroom, walk-in wardrobe and ensuite was almost as big as our own home's whole footprint. Big trees stretched to the sky, providing shade.

That evening, we sat on the back deck drinking wine and grazing from a cheeseboard. We watched the bush turkeys flap up into the trees to roost and flocks of rainbow lorikeets and white cockatoos make their noisy way across the valley to bed. The sky turned bright orange, silhouetting the trees.

"You are right," I said, "this house is perfect."

"Just look at the colour of that sky."

We all nodded, yet again blissfully unaware that we would stare at orange skies in horror very soon.

The next day, when I arrived home after my visit, my phone rang.

"Oh good, you're home safely," said Karly.

"Yes, it was an uneventful drive. Everything okay with you?"

"Actually, no. Winter again."

"Oh no, what has she done this time? Another accident? Is she okay?"

"Yep, but feeling very sorry for herself."

"What happened?"

"She stuffed a crayon up her nose."

I rolled my eyes. Typical Winter. There was no doubt she took after her father, Cam, who has had more stitches than the Bayeau tapestry.

"You are kidding."

"Nope."

"A crayon?"

"Yep! A purple one."

"Did you have to take her to the hospital to get it removed?"

"No, but we thought we would have to because she stuck it up there good and firm! We bribed her to keep still by promising her chicken Mcnuggets and Cam managed to get it out with tweezers."

"Oh well. That's good. Let's hope she won't have another accident for a while."

But less than twenty-four hours later, Winter was worrying her parents yet again.

"She's done it again!"

"Who? What?"

"Winter of course."

"Not another crayon up her nose? What colour was it this time?"

"Nope. Not a crayon. This time, she got a paralysis tick."

"You are kidding me. I didn't even know paralysis ticks attacked humans!"

> "Neither did we! Apparently, it's quite unusual. Trust Winter to pick one up!"

Everybody knows that Australia teems with dangerous animals and insects, and these little horrors are some of the nastiest. I was aware of them because they are such a danger to dogs and I always made sure Lola was up to date with her medicines.

According to the Australian Museum, the Australian paralysis tick, *Ixodes holocyclus*, is a common parasite found in Eastern Australia's bushy coastal habitats. It happily infests native mammals, livestock, pets, and occasionally even humans. Although it prefers mammals on its menu, many birds and sometimes reptiles also fall prey to it.

With a flattened, oval-shaped body, these ticks are seed-like in appearance and have six legs during the larval stage, while they have eight legs during the nymph and adult stages, like its arachnid relatives.

Paralysis ticks are the stuff of nightmares, and I can't help but think that they could easily inspire horror film-makers.

To find suitable hosts for their growth and development, ticks wait on leaves or long grass with their legs outstretched, waving slowly until they make contact with a living, juicy passer-by.

SASH (Small Animal Specialist Hospital) website describes what happens next:

> *After attaching, the tick feeds on the host's blood, injecting small amounts of saliva into the dog or cat. The tick's saliva contains a toxin that disrupts the connection between the nerves and the muscles of the body, causing weakness and paralysis. Not only does this affect muscles that help the animal to stand and walk, but it can also affect muscles used for breathing and swallowing, leading to serious and life-threatening conditions.*

A paralysis tick, before and after feeding

Often, pet owners are not even aware that their pet has been bitten until the poor animal begins to stagger and suffer from partial paralysis. Then it's a wild dash to the vet to get treatment before it's too late. Long-haired pets sometimes need to be shaved all over to ensure no more ticks are feasting in their fur, unseen.

Sadly, I have met people who have lost their pets to paralysis ticks. In one tragic case, a beloved elderly chihuahua was found drowned in a swimming pool. Its owner was mystified because the little dog never went near the pool. It wasn't until they found the attached paralysis tick that they understood. The poor little dog must have been bitten, then staggered, half-paralysed, into the pool.

> Where did the tick bite her?

> Just under her eye.

> Poor thing! Hospital?

> Yep, again! The Dr used a freezy thing to kill it then pulled it out with forceps.

> Yuk.

> He put her on antibiotics. So far no ill effects.

> Whew.

September came, not my favourite month. Multiple bills always arrive in September, and I needed to book Bruce in at the garage for his annual service. I had so much to do, books to write, emails to answer, but I had to put the day aside to take the car to the dealership.

The year before, I had taken my laptop, but I hadn't got much work done. The waiting room was too busy, and the laptop kept slipping off my knees. So this time, I decided to use the courtesy bus which shuttled backwards and forwards to the local mall. I could do some shopping until Bruce was ready. Karly had told me all about water-flossers and I thought I might treat myself to one.

Every seat on the little bus was filled as we set off.

"Anybody want to be dropped off at Bunnings?" asked the bus driver, "or are we all bound for the mall?"

I love Bunnings, and there's nothing quite like it in the UK. It's a massive DIY chain, but so much more. I love the charity sausage sizzles that are held near the entrance doors. I love the fact that you can browse up and down the huge aisles and can buy anything from a pot of live pet grass to soothe your dog or cat's upset stomach, to paint, timber, a hook to hang your hat, or a miniature screwdriver.

I also love the fact that they have a cafe, and dogs are welcome in the store. I even own a Bunnings umbrella. Actually, it's the best umbrella I've ever had. Not only does it open with a satisfying click, but it's large and has a special skirt which prevents strong winds from turning it inside-out.

But I didn't need anything from Bunnings that day. However, the man in the seat in front of me raised his hand.

"Me, please," he said.

"Righty-ho," said the driver. "First stop Bunnings."

His wife, sitting next to him, swung around to face him.

"What on earth do you want to go to Bunnings for?" she snapped, loud enough for everybody to hear.

Her husband didn't reply but stared out of the window.

His wife leaned forward and hissed. "I asked you a question. Why do you want to go to Bunnings?"

The man shrugged.

"Well, I'm not going into Bunnings with you, that's for sure. If you want to go to Bunnings, you can go by yourself."

"That's fine," the man replied quietly.

"And don't you go buying something ridiculous that we don't need."

The man's eyebrows twitched but he said nothing.

The woman kept up the attack all the way to Bunnings. I was cringing, and I saw several other passengers roll their eyes and look away, embarrassed.

The bus drew up outside Bunnings, and the man disembarked, politely thanking the driver.

"I'll pick you up at quarter past two," the driver said.

"Do you hear me? Don't you go wasting good money on anything!" called the woman as her husband strode away and entered the store.

Mrs Grouch settled herself in her seat, still huffing, her hands tightly gripping the handles of the bag on her lap. She stared straight ahead.

"Honestly!" she announced to the bus in general, "That man! Nobody has any idea what I have to put up with."

I spent a relaxing few hours in the mall and bought myself a new gadget: a water-flosser. Once, I caught sight of Mrs Grouch in the Dollar

Shop. She was buying a large, pink, plastic flamingo. It was so big that its head peeped out of the plastic shopping bag. I sped past before she saw me.

At two o'clock I climbed back on the waiting bus. Humans are creatures of habit, and I noticed that everybody was sitting in exactly the same seats as they had on the outbound journey. Again, I was sitting behind Mrs Grouch.

I couldn't wait to see what happened when we picked up her husband from Bunnings.

SUNSET COOKIES

These little savoury parmesan cookies need only three ingredients and are great as a homemade nibble with wine. We called them 'sunset' cookies because we enjoyed them with a glass of red as we watched the sun go down.

Ingredients (makes about 36)

1¼ cups plain (all-purpose) flour

½ cup salted butter, softened

1⅔ cups grated parmesan cheese

cracked black pepper (optional)

Method

Mix the flour (and optional cracked black pepper for an extra kick) and butter together.

Add parmesan cheese and work into a solid dough.

Preheat the oven to 175°C (350°F). Line a baking sheet with parchment paper.

Roll out the dough between 2 sheets of parchment paper until it is thin. If you find it too crumbly to work, add a few drops of water.

Use a small cookie cutter to cut rounds.

Place on the prepared baking sheet.

Bake in the preheated oven for 10 to 15 minutes. Transfer to a wire rack and cool before serving.

21

GADGETS

I saw the box before I saw the man. It was huge. The man was sitting on a bench and I could just see the top of his head.

Mrs Grouch gasped in horror.

"I knew it!" she shrilled to her captive audience in the bus, "I just knew it!"

Furiously, she swept her shopping bag aside, preparing space for her husband on the seat beside her. The pink plastic flamingo's head bobbed alarmingly.

Meanwhile, the bus driver had hopped out of the bus.

"I'll give you a hand with that, mate," he said, "I'll put it in the back for you."

"Wait until he gets on this bus," said Mrs

Grouch, staring straight ahead. "I'm going to have words with him!" Her lips pressed together in a thin, bloodless line.

Her husband stepped up into the bus. Nobody looked at him, or his wife, but I think we were all listening.

"Hello, dear," he said mildly. "Did you have a good time? I see you bought a flamingo."

"Never mind the flamingo! What on earth have *you* just bought?"

"Nothing much."

"Don't give me *nothing much!*" the woman exploded. "I'm not blind, I saw the size of that box!" She had turned an interesting shade of greenish-purple, rather like an unripe plum.

The flamingo wisely ducked its head.

"I'll show you when we get off the bus," said the man.

"What is it? How much did you spend? I *knew* I couldn't trust you in Bunnings by yourself. Whatever it is, it'll have to go back. We don't have the money or the space for stuff that you insist on buying when my back's turned."

And so it went on, all the way back to the dealership. Nag, nag, nag. The man never raised his voice but neither did he tell her what he'd bought. I bet the plastic flamingo wished it could go back to the peace and sanctuary of the Dollar Shop.

"You get out first, dear," said the man when the bus parked. "Sort out the paperwork and get the car keys. I'll unload the box and wait for you here, outside."

Without a word, Mrs Grouch stomped off the bus, her expression thunderous.

There was a small silence, and I caught sight of the man smiling to himself.

"Hey, mate," said the bus driver curiously. "Would you mind telling us what you bought in Bunnings? I think we'd all like to know."

We all nodded. He'd asked the question each one of us desperately wanted the answer to. The man was grinning now.

"Nothing," he said. "Absolutely nothing. It's an empty box. I wanted to teach her a lesson."

I hope Mrs Grouch didn't hear our laughter.

Still chuckling, I collected Bruce and drove home to unpack my latest gadget, the water-flosser.

I'm very fond of gadgets. I remember my first microwave, back in the 80s.

"It'll never catch on," said my friends, staring at it doubtfully.

Before that, I was a fan of pressure cookers when they first became popular. Nowadays, I love

GADGETS

my new air fryer with its glass door and three shelves, which easily outclasses my old one with the bucket drawer.

Karly shares my love of gadgets and has introduced me to many of her finds. One of my favourites is definitely House Botty. Karly was so enamoured with her first robot vacuum that she couldn't wait to show me how it worked.

"I just press this button and off he goes," she sang. The robot hummed and began work, neatly avoiding the furniture. "I can go out or do something else, and when I get back, all the vacuuming is done and he's taken himself back to his charging station. All I have to do is empty his stomach and he's ready to go again."

I was impressed. No more boring vacuuming? I secretly wanted one, too, but I would need to think about it. Top-of-the-range robot vacuums weren't cheap, and I had to justify it to myself.

As it happened, I didn't have to wait long. Karly had discovered that a new type of robot vacuum had been invented. One that not only vacuumed the carpets and rugs but also mopped the floor using water and high-frequency sound vibrations. Irresistible.

"I'm going to get one, Mum. You can have my old one if you like."

I welcomed House Botty 1 (HB1) with open

arms and marvelled at the way he busily swept and sucked his way around the house. Mesmerised, I watched him methodically cover every inch of the floor space before finally returning to his dock for a well-deserved rest and recharge.

Lola, on the other hand, was not at all keen on the black, humming, circular intruder. Outraged, she barked at it until it rolled towards her, whereupon she fled and hid behind me.[1]

Lola barking at HB1

Gradually, however, she grew accustomed to his habits and just ignored it.

House Botty 1 was superseded by House Botty 2 who proved to be even more efficient.

"There you go," I often said to him. "We're going out, so make sure the house is clean before we get back."

---

1. Lola challenging House Botty 1. https://youtu.be/Y95oF_sY4wU

GADGETS

HB2 whizzed his way around the house while I was out, vacuuming under beds and furniture before mopping the hard floors.

When I returned, he'd be waiting patiently at his docking station, only a slight film of dust on his white casing showing how hard he'd been working.

I checked his stomach, and as usual, it was crammed full of hair, dust and fluff. Sometimes I was convinced he'd popped next door and vacuumed their place, too. Surely our house couldn't have been that dirty?

Lola gradually accepted that HB2 was here to stay. Sometimes she picked up a toy and placed it carefully on him, hoping he might want to play a game of Fetch with her. Then, as he hummed around the house with the toy on his back, she followed him, just in case he wanted to take a little break from cleaning and felt like throwing it for her to retrieve. Eventually, when HB2 showed no signs of any interest in a game of Fetch, she collected her toy and retreated sadly to her bed.

Our next robot was Pool Botty, the pool-cleaning marvel that chugged over every inch of the bottom of the pool, and climbed nimbly up the perpendicular walls sucking up leaves, berries, mud and algae. Compared with the awful creepy-crawly pool vacuum with its thick tubes I'd been managing with before, Pool Botty was an absolute dream and became my new best friend.

Now I unpacked my latest gadget, the water-flosser.

"What? You have never tried a water flosser before?" Karly had said the week before, amazed. "My dentist says they are the best thing since sliced bread."

I read the instructions folded up in the box. The type was so tiny I had to find a magnifying glass before I could even read it.

You do take water device and make a pleasing choice of brush.

Do I? Okay.

Being a water-flosser novice, I picked the smallest brush and fitted it successfully.

Put in water from your faucet until you meet Max.

I wondered who Max was but concluded I was supposed to fill the tank up to the line marked Maximum. Done.

Please do now push the On and move tip brush slowly over all of the tooths.

Nervously, I directed the nozzle into my mouth, and pressed the On button. A thin but powerful jet of water shot out. I was so surprised, I jerked it out and shot the wall behind me.

My second attempt nearly took out my eye, but I persevered. By the time I mastered it, the tank needed refilling and every corner of the bathroom had been shot at, but I wasn't deterred. However, I decided that my new flosser should be kept in the shower where it wouldn't matter if my aim wasn't perfect.

"Well, you've done a good job of keeping your teeth clean," said my dental hygienist when I attended my next check-up and polish.

Music to my ears. I love it when I get a new gadget that actually does its job, don't you? Unlike the elegant lemon squeezer with the long handles I bought online. One of the handles snapped off the first time I used it.

We very sorry, the sellers replied when I sent a complaint. *Our squezer lemon only good for squezing the dainty lemon.*

Pardon? *Dainty lemon?* I didn't even bother to reply and went back to the loyal lemon squeezer that had served me faithfully for twenty years.

Still no rain had fallen and Australia was parched. Severe bushfires were breaking out, particularly in the northern state of Queensland. On September 6th, strong winds worsened the bushfire conditions, leading to more than sixty serious fires burning across the state by the following day. As the rest of Australia watched helplessly, the situation continued to escalate.

Fires forced the closure of ten schools. People in several threatened towns were urged to leave immediately. Prisoners and staff at a women's correctional centre in the Numinbah Valley had to be evacuated when it was threatened by the fires.

Despite the efforts of hundreds of firefighters and several firefighting aircraft, many homes and other structures were destroyed in the extreme conditions. One particular fire, which broke out on September 9th, required over one hundred fire crews to bring it under control.

Our state of New South Wales held its breath, and we didn't have long to wait. Fires, mostly ignited by lightning setting fire to tinder-dry deadwood and leaf litter, began to break out. To begin with, nothing compared in size or ferocity with the fires burning in Queensland or South Australia, but our turn would come in the following month.

"So, have you found a flight yet?"

"No, but I've started to look. It's getting cold

here in the UK, and I just have to go to a couple more appointments, and then I'm free to leave."

"That's good news. It's boiling hot here and it isn't even summer yet. We still haven't had any rain at all. You should see the oval, it's baked hard and the grass is all brown and dead. And you must have heard about the bushfires in Queensland and South Australia?"

"Yes, no fires in New South Wales, though?"

"Well, yes. There are a few."

"Nothing near us though?"

"No, not yet, thank goodness, but it's worrying. Bushfire season doesn't officially start until October and there are fires burning all over the place already."

"Hard to imagine when it's so cold here in the UK. Anyway, I'll be home soon."

I was worried. I knew that if the fires came any closer, apart from the danger, our air quality would be compromised. And for somebody with Joe's condition, that could be extremely serious. His ragged lungs were already struggling, and I was sure that breathing in smoke would damage them further.

But I didn't voice my fears.

Not yet.

One day, I saw an advert for a local dog-walking group. Apparently, they met regularly and walked together along the lake edge, on the beaches and in the forests. For the sake of anonymity, I'll call it Paws United.

"What do you think, Lola? Fancy going on lots of long walks and making heaps of new doggy friends?"

The enthusiastic tail wag was definitely a Yes.

The Central Coast is a stunning area, blessed with more beautiful beaches than Lola could shake a stick at, lakes and lagoons, and great expanses of bushland. There are trails that cling to the coastline, clifftop tracks and easy, flat walks that follow the curves of the many lakes. The choice is enormous, but what fun it would be to share walks with new friends, both two-legged and four. I decided to join.

Our first walk was along the lake. Lola made friends with two pugs, a German shepherd, a labrador, two retrievers, Jack Russells and border collies. Big dogs, little dogs, dogs in prams, dogs wearing clothes, dogs that barked, hairy dogs, curly-coated dogs, they were all there.

Of course, their owners were all there, too, but

GADGETS

I noticed something curious. I quickly learned the dogs' names, but I found the humans' names much harder to remember. Maybe that is a senior problem.

There were beautiful dogs, stylish dogs, and also some rather, um, unusual-looking animals. Sometimes, during the walk, an old man joined us part of the way through, then disappeared before the end of the walk. He was accompanied by a tiny, overweight, brown, short-haired dog that waddled beside him. Judging by the dog's bandy back legs, long back and squashed face, I guessed it may be a mix of Shihtzu, dachshund, and possibly chihuahua.

After a few walks, I realised that the old man lived in a van parked half-hidden in the bush. I tried to strike up a conversation several times, to no avail. I know he heard me, but he refused to answer.

One day, I tried again.

"Hi! What breed is your dog?" I asked, trying to sound casual and friendly. There was a pause.

"He's a border collie," he said, and I had to laugh.

I never heard him speak again, and one day, the van, dog and man disappeared. I guess they moved on.

Lola and I enjoyed the walks and making new

friends, and there was always something new to discover, like a place I'd never been to before or a chance encounter with a wolf spider taking his dinner back to his lair.[2]

I wish I'd kept the recording going a little bit longer because when the spider reached his lair, he lost his grip on the orange moth. The moth flew several feet into the air, then unbelievably dropped down again, right into the spider's jaws. We can assume the spider feasted that night.

But I remember that very first Paws United walk very distinctly, not only because I made a lifelong friend but also because Lola fell in love.

---

2. Wolf spider carrying his live prey back to his lair. https://youtube.com/shorts/2WHssdfwOuU

SUPER-QUICK AIR FRYER HOT DOGS

Not only do air fryers toast buns perfectly, but they'll cook the hot dogs, too.

Ingredients

4 hot dog buns

4 hot dog sausages

Your choice of condiment: ketchup, mustard, relish, barbecue sauce, chilli jam or whatever you fancy.

Method

Place buns in a single layer on the air fryer shelf, or in the air fryer basket.

Cook at 180°C (350°F) until crisp, about 2 minutes.

Remove buns to a plate and set aside.

Place hot dogs in a single layer on the air fryer shelf, or in the air fryer basket and cook for 3 minutes.

Serve hot dogs in toasted buns topped with your choice of condiment.

22

DOGS, DOGS, DOGS

As we walked along the lakeside path, Lola and I fell in step with a lady holding the leashes of three little dogs, each one very different. We began to chat and I recognised her accent as being German.

"What breed are your dogs?" I asked.

"They are Bitsas."

"Bitsas?"

"Yes, bits of everything, we don't actually know," said Hildy, my new friend. "They are all rescue dogs."

"What are their names?"

"This is Benny," said Hildy, pointing at a beautiful brown and white dog with long, silky hair. "He has an overbite problem."

Benny's brown eyes gazed up at me, and I saw

that his bottom jaw was set back, giving him an endearing expression.

"He looks like he may have some Papillon in him," I said.

"Yes, we think so, too. And this is Gracie. She is definitely part chihuahua. She's the smallest and the only girl, but she's the boss. Don't be fooled by her delicate looks, she's as hard as nails."

Gracie was an extremely pretty dog, with silver, almost blue, short hair, and big, liquid eyes.

"And this is Sylvester."

It was then that I noticed that Lola was behaving in a very odd fashion. She was focused on only one dog in the entire walking group: Sylvester. She sniffed him, circled him with wagging tail, and wouldn't leave him alone. I can find only one word to describe it.

Lola was *flirting*.

Never mind the handsome black labrador, or the feisty kelpie. Forget the border collie and don't even bother with the golden retrievers. Lola had fallen in love with little Sylvester, who was about a third of her size.

Sylvester was a little, brown, happy-go-lucky chap with a big smile and curly tail. He probably had some fox terrier in his DNA, and who knows what else. He wasn't the most handsome of dogs, but he was definitely the happiest and most relaxed.

Sylvester good-naturedly ignored Lola's attentions, turning his head away when she tried to kiss him. He was much too busy enjoying life and certainly didn't need a girlfriend.

Hildy and I immediately connected and have remained great friends ever since that first meet-up. Hildy is clever, kind, generous and funny and I can't begin to thank her for all the times she's helped me out in different ways.

It didn't take long for me to realise that Hildy has one overwhelming passion in life.

Dogs.

Dogs in general, her own three dogs in particular, and dog health and nutrition as her specialist subject. She researches every pack, box or tin before allowing her dogs to eat, closely examining the ingredient list and checking the country of origin. She is a member of like-minded Facebook groups where views on various dog foods are hotly discussed. Kibble is a dirty word.

Lucky Gracie, Benny and Sylvester! No mundane meals for them! Despite the fact that Hildy never cooks for herself, she devotes hours to dog food preparation. I have seen her serve the most delicious meals to her gang, fit for the royal corgis, if not royalty itself.

Zoom forward to the time of writing this chapter. I was searching for a photo to demonstrate an example of the gangs' gourmet feasts, so I texted Hildy.

> Hildy, please may I use one of your doggy-dinner photos? I'm just writing about the fabulous meals you always prepare for the gang.

> Of course! No problem! I'll see what I can find.

> Thanks!

> How about this one?

> Ooooh, perfect! What is Benny eating here?

Shredded chicken, dehydrated chicken breast, a free-range locally laid quail egg and sardines in spring water.

> Wow, all fit for human consumption.

Yes, of course. On second thoughts, it wasn't really a balanced meal, and I think it might get criticism from your readers.

> Haha, I doubt it! Bet the gang didn't complain either!

Every meal is a healthy work of art, often topped by a sprinkle of probiotic seaweed supplements. No wonder the little dogs' coats shine and their eyes sparkle.

Hildy provides toys and puzzles to enrich their lives. They go to Agility every weekend, which they love, and have regular visits to the salon for pampering sessions. On birthdays, each dog is given lavish gifts and they all have a wardrobe of warm coats, raincoats and bathrobes.

When I die, I want to come back as one of Hildy's dogs.

It doesn't stop there. She knows the characteristics of every breed of dog, can judge a dog's health from its poo, and gives far more than she can afford to dog charities.

Exercising the gang is important, and Hildy walks miles in all weathers, the dogs happily trotting beside her. Judging by the spring in their steps, an observer would never guess that all three dogs were elderly. And the walks allow her to indulge in her other favourite pastime.

Photographing the dogs.

The first time we walked with Hildy and the gang, I was astounded. I admired the lake, the clouds' reflections in the water, and the cormorants diving for fish. But Hildy was not diverted by such trivia. She was looking for a photo opportunity, and she soon found one.

"Come on, guys," she said, swerving off the path towards a rustic bench.

Gracie, Benny and Sylvester knew exactly what to do. Lola and I watched as the three jumped onto the seat, then stood side by side on their hind legs, with their front paws resting on the backrest of the bench, posing. With the gleaming lake and sky as the backdrop, it was a perfect picture. Hildy knelt and took the photo. Another one to add to her vast collection.

Each little dog was rewarded with a treat and we carried on walking until the next photo opportunity arose. Sometimes it was a fallen log, or a boulder, or a tree stump. The gang posed. *Click, click,* and another masterpiece was created to be sent to Hildy's Instagram page.

Benny, Sylvester and Gracie

"Come, let's see if Lola will join them," suggested Hildy. "Lola, up!"

Jumping up on a bench or a boulder was no problem for Lola, but she didn't grasp the standing still and posing part. She'd much rather cover Sylvester's face with kisses, bark, then jump off. On the rare occasion when she sat still and behaved herself, the resulting picture made her look like a giant.

There came a time when I wanted to visit the family in Sydney and I happened to mention to Hildy that I needed to organise somebody to look after Lola. She didn't hesitate.

"Lola can come and stay with us," she said. "No problem."

"Are you sure?"

"Yes, of course! Let's have a trial sleepover and if it goes well, she can come any time."

I couldn't believe Hildy's kindness.

We set up a date, and I arrived with Lola. I knocked on the door and the gang barked furiously from within. Hildy opened the front door, and the three dogs, led by the boss, chihuahua Gracie, burst out and barked in Lola's face for a full thirty seconds. I imagine they were telling her the house rules and what she could and couldn't do.

Lola has always practised good dog etiquette and knows when to back away and be submissive. Today, she stood her ground, but she listened intently and didn't argue with them.

After the thirty-second lecture, the resident dogs relaxed and fell silent. They allowed her to come inside and largely ignored her from then on. She had been completely accepted. From that moment onwards, the gang looked upon Lola as a visitor. If she stepped out of line, Gracie would immediately scold her, but it was rarely necessary.

Lola adored Hildy and loved the sleepovers. When I parked the car outside Hildy's house, she always knew exactly where she was and what was happening and barked excitedly. When I opened the car door and unclipped her safety harness, she cannoned out and raced to the front door, hurling herself at it until Hildy opened the door. Gourmet meals, long walks, and quality time with Hildy and Sylvester were her idea of the perfect holiday. Poor Sylvester. He treated Lola like an annoying little sister, but he never lost his temper with her.

At night, Lola was allowed to sleep on Hildy's bed with the gang. Snuggled up to her beloved Sylvester (if he let her), it was the end of a perfect day.

Hildy sent me photos, so I knew what they were all doing. On hot days she provided a paddling pool, and on cooler days she took them all on long walks by the lake.

By now, my family had settled well into their new home. Bandsaw and Burgers, the two cats, enjoyed exploring their new garden. And LJ was having adventures of his own.

Cam was the first to meet one of the neighbours, the man who lived in the huge house backing onto their garden.

"Hi! Welcome to the neighbourhood," called the man. "My name's Pete. Hope you're settling in okay?"

"Thanks, mate, I'm Cam. Yes, it's all going great. The kids love it. I must introduce you to my wife, Karly, she'd love to meet you."

The pair shook hands and chatted easily. Pete told Cam that he had recently fallen off a ladder and injured his back but that he was resting it, and it was healing.

That evening, Karly met Pete when they were both pulling their garbage bins up the shared lane to the main road for collection.

"Ah, you must be Karly!"

"Yes, and you must be Pete! Cam told me he'd met you."

"I hope you haven't been worried about your dog today," said Pete.

"Worried about LJ?" asked Karly, surprised. "No, why? Should I be worried about him?"

"Well, I was lying on my bed resting my back

this afternoon and LJ walks into my bedroom. He had a good look at me, then jumped on the bed and lay down beside me."

Karly's mouth dropped open. "You are kidding! I didn't even know he had gone missing!"

"Yes, I must have left the back door open and he walked in to have a look around."

"Did you chase him away?"

"No, we both fell asleep on the bed. When we woke up, he was spooning me, so I think we both slept pretty well. I didn't want to give him any food in case that might encourage him to keep coming back, so I gave him a drink of milk. I was going to bring him home but then we both heard you call him, and so I let him out. I guess he went home."

"I'm so sorry. I didn't know he'd gone visiting! When I called him, I thought he was just in the front garden. Although, come to think of it, he did take a couple of minutes to arrive."

"No worries, he's a really cool dog."

No harm seemed to have been done, but the family made sure to keep the gate properly closed in future. Not everybody would react so calmly to a big dog like LJ suddenly appearing in their bedroom and sharing their bed.

And we're still not really sure why Pete offered LJ a bowl of milk, but nobody liked to ask.

As the month of September unfolded, the news on the TV was dominated by bushfire updates. Every household in Australia was instructed to prepare bushfire escape plans. *Be safe and leave early*, we were urged. But so far, no fires had been reported anywhere near us so I held my tongue when Joe rang. I didn't share my fears. I guess I was hoping all the fires would be put out before October when he was hoping to come home.

Hildy and I spent a lot of time walking the dogs along the lake path, stopping only for coffee. I photographed the scenery, the black swans, the pelicans and the strange Aussie plants and flowers that never fail to fascinate me. Hildy took dozens of snaps of the dogs.

We laughed a lot. One day, we were so deep in conversation that I tripped over my own feet. Off balance, I did a ridiculous stomping sideways dance and lost my hold on Lola's leash at the same time.

Lola's recall is excellent 99% of the time. However, if she is giving chase, or has stolen a sock, she is deaf to my calls. Unfortunately, she had spied a flock of seagulls wading at the lake's edge. Irresistible.

"Lola!" I shouted but she was already a golden streak, intent on chasing them.

The seagulls screeched and scattered and took to the air, but Lola didn't stop. Into the mud she galloped, until the seagulls wheeled away into the distance.

"Lola!" I shouted again but my voice had absolutely no effect on her.

Some may suggest she couldn't hear me because her ears were full of mud and she was too far away. But I know better. She *chose* not to hear me.

Mud! The blacker and stickier the better. I watched in horror as Lola dropped down and lay in it. Next came the commando crawl for several yards until she stood up and shook herself. My golden dog was now two-tone; a stripe of gold along her backbone but with a black chin, legs, underside and tail.

"Lola!"

I was trying to reach her, but there was a marshy, squelchy strip I had to navigate across.

"Quick, hold the leads," said Hildy, thrusting the gangs' leashes into my hand.

Good old Hildy, she's nearly thirty years

younger than I am and far more athletic. Hildy would save the day.

Hildy sprinted towards Lola across the marsh, her shoes squelching into the mud. *Not a moment too soon*, I thought, as my now black and gold dog happily sniffed something white lying on the ground.

"Lola, no!" I shrieked, and Hildy's three little dogs jumped.

Too late. I saw what Lola was so engrossed with.

And I knew what was going to happen next.

The white object on the mud was the rotting carcass of a seagull. And Lola was happily rolling in it. She was in heaven.

And what had happened to Hildy, my saviour? There she was, crouched down, laughing, taking photo after photo, making absolutely no attempt to stop Lola's disgusting behaviour.

Neither Hildy nor Lola were repentant. I took my black, maggoty, feathered, stinking dog home via the auto dog-wash at the petrol station.

Hildy and I often laughed when we recalled that day, but occasionally our doggy adventures weren't amusing at all.

HOMEMADE GRAIN-FREE DOGGY DINNER

A healthy, nutritious meal for your dog that can be frozen in airtight containers. It contains vitamins, minerals, essential fatty acids and protein.

Ingredients

4 medium carrots, peeled and chopped

2 apples - peeled, cored, and chopped (make sure pips are removed as they are harmful to dogs)

¼ cup water

6 eggs

1.5kg (3lb) chicken mince

175g (6oz) chicken livers, chopped

3 tablespoons olive or sunflower seed oil

4 cups baby spinach leaves

Method

Preheat the oven to 175°C (350°F).

Place carrots, apples, and water into a pot. Bring to a boil, then cover, reduce the heat to low, and simmer until soft, 10 to 15 minutes.

Meanwhile, crack eggs into a bowl and set aside. Place eggshells onto a baking sheet.

Bake eggshells in the preheated oven until dry, 5 to 7 minutes.

Remove eggshells from the oven and crush using a mortar and pestle.

Combine the chicken mince, chicken livers, eggs, ground eggshells, and oil in a large skillet.

Heat over medium heat, mixing occasionally, until chicken is browned and crumbly and livers are no longer pink, 5 to 7 minutes.

Place spinach on top of meat mixture, then cover with a lid and steam until soft, about 5 minutes.

Mash softened carrots and apples in a bowl with a potato masher and add to meat mixture.

Mix until well combined.

23

FIRE

Lola's sleepovers at Hildy's became a regular occurrence. I was so grateful to her for looking after Lola and I knew Lola absolutely loved her stays at Hildy's 5-Star Doggy Hotel.

Their day was divided into different activities, including play sessions, delicious meals, naps and walks. As Hildy doesn't drive, the walks were usually by the lake and that was where she and the four dogs were heading one particular day.

There was nothing different about this day until Hildy saw and heard movement. She looked around. Out of nowhere, charging towards them, came a huge dog, snarling and bearing down on them.

Hildy may be shy, quietly-spoken and gentle,

but beware anybody or any creature that threatens her gang. Instantly she turns into a ferocious mama bear as she defends her babies without a thought for her own safety.

It wasn't the first time they'd been attacked by loose dogs. All small dogs, in particular Benny, with his long, fluffy coat, seemed to trigger the attacking dog's prey drive. This time, Hildy had four dogs to protect from the snarling brute's advance.

She let go of the leashes, and Benny, Gracie, Sylvester and Lola streaked, terrified, across the main road, somehow avoiding being run over by passing cars.

At the same time, Hildy yelled, lashed out and hurled a missile at the attacker, which hit the mark.

"What did you throw?" I asked when she was relating the story later.

"My phone! That's all I had."

The dog paused in surprise, just long enough for Hildy to lunge forward and grab its collar. To her relief, the bully turned into a whimpering coward. While it cringed, she scrabbled in her bag for the spare leash she always carried, and secured the bully to a nearby picnic bench.

Shaking with shock, she retrieved her phone and found the number of the council ranger.

FIRE

"What happened with the gang and Lola?" I asked.

"Luckily, people heard me shout, and all four of them were caught really quickly on the other side of the road. The ranger said he couldn't come straight away, so I didn't know what to do. So I took photos of the dog and put them on local groups on Facebook while we waited. It was lucky that it had a collar on or I'd never have caught it, but it didn't have a tag."

"Did the ranger come?"

"Yes, eventually, but the owner turned up first. Somebody must have recognised the dog and told her."

"Was she sorry?"

"Not really. She said it must have got out somehow, and that it had never happened before. Yeah, right."

"I know, they always say that."

"And when the ranger asked why it didn't have a tag on, she said it must have fallen off. Yeah, right."

"I'm so sorry this happened to you, Hildy, especially when you had Lola to look after as well as your three."

"Oh well, luckily nobody was harmed. But you know what really bothered me?"

"What?"

"The horrible reaction on Facebook. People waded in and attacked me for tying it up to the picnic bench. What was I supposed to do? And they said I should have put it in the car and taken it to a vet or the pound. Even if I could drive and had a car, how was I supposed to put all four dogs and their attacker in a car together?"

"That's ridiculous. You did the right thing. Don't worry about it."

"And the sad thing is, that dog will get out again and probably actually kill a small dog next time."

I agreed with her, but there was nothing we could do.

This incident was serious, but most of Hildy's stories made me laugh. Like when she described what happens during a simple call of nature during a walk. There are several public toilet blocks dotted along the lake path. Hildy's love of coffee means she regularly feels the need to pop into one.

The problem is, that the three little dogs don't like being left by themselves tethered to something, so Hildy has no option but to take them in with her. Each cubicle is divided from the next by a wall that doesn't reach the floor, leaving a gap of about nine inches.

"I can only imagine what a fright somebody

must get when they use the cubicle next to mine," laughed Hildy. "Three curious little faces peering under the screen, watching everything the poor person is doing!"

Hildy and her husband celebrated their tenth wedding anniversary recently.

"You know what?" she said. "Jason reckons he is only still alive because he has always made sure I never run out of coffee. Well, I reckon *I* am only still alive because I don't show him all the bills for the dogs."

The sun continued to scorch Australia day after day, and inevitably, my state of New South Wales also began to burn.

The heat created shimmering waves on the pavements. Wildfires flared up without warning. Some were ignited by lightning strikes, discarded cigarettes, or, worse still, malicious arsonists. Nobody knew where the next fire would break out, but we all kept our TVs and radios tuned in to local channels for advance warning of any emergency.

Everybody downloaded a new app called Fires Near Me, which showed where fires were burning and whether they were classified as 'planned burn', 'under control', 'watch and act' or 'emergency', out of control'.

To be honest, the details of the following months have become a bit of a blur to me as each tragic event followed the last. Forests burst into flame and bushland burned.

I know that on the 26th of October, 2019, a powerful electrical storm swept through Wollemi National Park. Apparently, a single lightning strike set a tree ablaze near Gospers Mountain, leading to the massive bushfire that burned for the next 79 days. This terrifying blaze became known as the Gospers Mountain Mega-Fire and grew to enormous proportions, stretching over one hundred kilometres. Before it was finally extinguished in the following year, it threatened the outskirts of Sydney.

Even Joe, watching the daily news in the UK, was beginning to get an idea of how massive the problem was without me having to spell it out to him. I knew he shouldn't come home until the danger had passed, but I didn't want to say the words. After all, no fires had broken out *very* close to us. Yet.

One windy day, I smelled burning, and the air was grey and thick. I walked down to the pool and saw countless ash pieces floating on the surface and black debris littering the ground. I checked the Fires Near Me app, sure that there must be a fire nearby. The app informed me that the nearest fire was a hundred kilometres away, and that's when I knew I couldn't hold back any longer. Smoke and debris were being driven great distances, and the terrible resulting air quality would be life-threatening to Joe with his already failing lungs.

I had to face the truth and tell him.

When he phoned that evening I was tense and unhappy, and he picked up on it right away.

"Everything okay with you and Lola?"

"Yes. Well, no, not everything."

"What's the matter?"

And so I blurted it out, aware that I was telling him exactly what he didn't want to hear. I knew he was homesick and desperate to come back to us in Australia, but to return now would be foolish, even deadly.

"The sky has been dark grey all day today, even though the sun is shining and there aren't any clouds. And everything smells of smoke. The pool and garden are covered in bits of charred wood and leaves."

"There's a fire near you?"

"No. It was on the news today that the wind has carried them from Port Stephens, that's a hundred kilometres away! There's a big fire there at the moment, and the Gospers Mountain fire to the west of us is still spreading."

"You are kidding!"

"No. And they said that the air is so bad, hospitals are filling up with patients who are struggling to breathe, and that simple Ventolin supplies are running low in pharmacies. They said we should keep windows and doors closed, and anybody with breathing problems should stay at home unless told to evacuate."

A small silence, then, "So, are you saying I shouldn't book my flight home?"

"Yes. I'm so sorry."

Another small silence, and a sigh. "I guess it can't be helped. I'll wait."

I was desperately sad, but unbelievably relieved that he understood. It just wasn't worth the risk. He told me later that he knew he'd be crazy to come home while bushfires raged, but he was hoping against hope that all the fires would be put out quickly. The truth was that many of the fires burned uncontrollably. Some took weeks, and others took months to extinguish.

On November 8th, seventeen separate fires broke out, all classified as Emergency, the highest alert level. With so many fires raging, they sometimes merged to form enormous, uncontrollable 'mega-fires'. Another addition to our growing bushfire vocabulary. Along with 'ember attack' and 'defendable space'.

I now understand the danger of an 'ember attack'. Pieces of charred wood or leaves, still alight and borne by the wind, can drop anywhere. And Australia was so dry and parched that any stray spark could set off yet another mega-fire.

The 11th of November marks Remembrance Day, but on this day, parts of New South Wales were issued with an unprecedented, terrifying warning. Starting from midnight, a vast area, including where we lived, was declared under a Catastrophic Alert, a status that had never been announced before. The New South Wales government was declaring a State of Emergency.

I was familiar with the roadside signs displaying an arrow pointing at the current danger rating, but it was shocking to see that the arrow was resting on a new category: Catastrophic.

The ratings were explained in local newspapers like the Blue Mountains Gazette.

LOW-MODERATE: Fires can be easily controlled and may spread up to 250 metres an hour.
HIGH: Fires can be controlled but still present a threat. Embers may be blown ahead of the fire and around homes, causing other fires to occur close to the main fire. Rates of spread up to 500 metres an hour are possible.
VERY HIGH: Fires can be difficult to control and present a very real threat. There may be ember attacks up to two kilometres from the fire front and rates of spread up to 1km an hour.
SEVERE: Fires will likely be uncontrollable, unpredictable and fast-moving with flames that may be higher than rooftops. There may be ember attacks up to 4km from the fire front and rates of overspread up to 1.5km an hour. Leaving early is the safest option for your survival. Well prepared homes that are actively defended can provide safety but only stay if you are physically and mentally prepared to defend in these conditions. If you're not prepared, leave early in the day.
EXTREME: Fires can be uncontrollable, unpredictable and fast-moving, with flames in tree tops and higher than rooftops. Thousands of

embers will be blown up to 6km from the fire front, causing other fires to start and spread quickly ahead of the main fire. Rates of spread can be up to 2km an hour. Leaving early is the safest option for your survival.

CATASTROPHIC: Fires will likely be uncontrollable, unpredictable and very fast-moving, with highly aggressive flames extending high above tree tops and buildings. Thousands of embers will be blown violently into and around homes, causing other fires to start and spread quickly up to 10km ahead of the main fire with rates of spread up to 5km an hour. Ensure your survival is the primary consideration in any decision. The safest option is for you and your family to leave in the early morning of any day declared Catastrophic, even the day before, as soon as the rating is issued. Under no circumstances will it be safe to stay and defend.

"Pack your possessions," said the grim spokesman on the TV news, "and be prepared to move fast if ordered to do so. Head for your nearest shopping mall where emergency refuges will be set up."

We were urged to have an escape plan, and to prepare our emergency kits to grab if needed.

. . .

Standby Emergency Kit
Drinking water to last at least three days per person
Portable battery-operated AM/FM radio with spare batteries
Waterproof torch
First aid kit
Woollen blanket
Emergency contact numbers

What to pack on the day of evacuation
Wallet, keys and phone with charger
Change of clothes
Towels
Specific requirements for your family members, including pets
Medications
Toiletries
Important documents and valuables

Cam, as an experienced voluntary fireman, was kept busy. These brave volunteers were needed to back-burn, trying to redirect or suppress existing fires. Cam agreed with the spokesman's words.

"Nobody should even think about staying and trying to defend their homes," he said. "Chances are that the water pressure will be very low, and you'll have no way to fight unless you have a pump set up to syphon water from a pool. And don't expect a wall of fire to be the main danger. It's far more likely that you'll be under an ember attack, in which case there will be dozens of small fires flaring up so fast that you won't be able to control them."

The skies were a strange colour—leaden grey but orange. When Hildy and I walked along the lake, we couldn't see to the other side. Some days, I couldn't see the bush or hills from our windows because of the smoke haze. Some nights, I saw tiny live embers floating in the air like a multitude of deadly fireflies.

None of us knew what the next days would bring.

A total fire ban was in place for all of us: no bonfires, candles or barbecues were permitted until further notice. Even Bunnings' charity sausage sizzles ceased.

Sydney was in danger. In their new penthouse apartment, Shealan and Daria lost sight of the city and harbour shrouded in smoke below them. Traffic speed dropped to a crawl on the freeways because visibility was so poor.

I was worried about Karly, Cam, and the kids, who lived in a wooden house on the edge of dense bushland in the suburbs of Sydney. Cam's parents lived only minutes away and were also in danger.

Following the state of emergency announcement, Karly had a serious word with her daughters.

"Now, girls, you both understand that there are big bushfires happening, don't you?"

Both girls gazed at her with big eyes and nodded.

"We're not in any danger at the moment, but we must be prepared to move fast if the fires start coming in our direction."

More nods.

"Daddy is helping with the fires, isn't he?"

"Yes."

"Like Paw Patrol?"

"Yes. Now listen carefully, I need you to do something really important."

FIERY RED PEPPER POTATOES

This is a traditional and uniquely-flavoured Korean side dish.

Ingredients

1½ tablespoons soy sauce

1 pinch cayenne pepper, or to taste

1½ tablespoons vegetable oil

3 potatoes, cut into bite sized pieces

4 green onions, chopped

1 large red bell pepper (capsicum), chopped

2 teaspoons sesame seeds

Method

Whisk the soy sauce and cayenne pepper in a small bowl until the cayenne pepper is dissolved; set aside.

Heat the vegetable oil in a large skillet over medium-high heat.

Cook the potatoes in the hot oil until golden brown, about 5 minutes.

Stir in the onions, bell pepper, and sesame seeds and cook for a further minute.

Pour the soy sauce mixture over the potatoes.

Cook and stir until the liquid is completely absorbed, 1 to 2 minutes.

24

THREE TO TEN DAYS

"Right, these are for you," said Karly, thrusting bags into my granddaughters' hands.

Both little girls' eyes grew bigger and rounder.

"I need you to go to your bedrooms," ordered my daughter. "Then look around and think hard. Imagine there is a fire coming, and you can put in your bag whatever you really, really want to save."

"What about the cats?"

"And LJ?"

"And the hermit crabs?"

"And the chickens?"

"Well, of course, we'll save them. These bags are just for *you* to pack your most precious and essential possessions. We can't save everything, there won't be space in the car, so choose carefully."

Indy (age seven) and Winter (age three) clattered up the stairs to carry out their mission.

"Choose carefully!" Karly called after them.

But the girls were too busy to reply.

By November 12th, an area twice the size of Spain had already been burnt.

I opened the shutters that morning, aware of an unusual stillness. The sky was a flat, orange colour although the sun had risen hours ago. I felt a sense of foreboding.

I switched on the news which only added to my unease. More fires, more stories of heroics, more photos of devastation and more warnings.

The Gospers Mountain fire was thriving and gathering in strength despite the efforts of our firefighters and teams from the Canadians, US and Europe, who were arriving daily to help. The fire was unstoppable, consuming homes and entire farms, wiping out all their crops and livestock. The flames moved as fast as galloping horses.

They say the sound of an approaching bushfire

is like the roaring of jet engines, and I prayed none of us would ever hear it.

Fires throwing up plumes of smoke rose into the atmosphere and bumped up temperatures in the lower stratosphere over Australia by 3°C. More than two thousand kilometres away, New Zealanders reported smoke and ash reaching them. White glaciers turned brown.

And the searing heat and flames were creating their own weather. Collisions of particles in strange black clouds resulted in a build-up of electrical charges like colossal sparks. In other words, lightning.

A man who witnessed this extraordinary phenomenon in the state of Victoria, where megafires raged, said, "Even before you see the fire, you can hear it roaring like jumbo jets landing. We sat silent, waiting for the sun to rise, which it never did. And then there were explosions like atom bombs, with dirty, great, black columns of smoke like Hiroshima, powering upwards and billowing out like massive mushrooms. And then lightning of all colours, white, yellow, red, shot into the sky."

TV newsreaders recommended that people in rural areas stay near their homes unless told to evacuate. The heat was predicted to rise throughout the day, with the biggest threat beginning at midday, when 90 kph winds were expected to carry live embers far and wide.

My phone rang. It was Hildy.

"Hi! I have to go to an interview today. Would you mind listening out for fire updates, and collecting the gang if necessary?"

"Of course I will!"

The heat was oppressive. The sky stayed that sickly orange-grey colour, and the air was thick and sticky. I couldn't see the distant hills through the smoke haze.

At 11:30, the winds began. Signs began flapping. Anything not fixed to the ground, including cafe furniture, hurtled along the pavements. Litter flew through the air. I could smell and taste the smoke.

Darkness came two hours early that day as smoke blotted out the sun. Blackened leaves, charred twigs and bark rained from the sky as night fell. There was nothing more to do but try to sleep and keep checking the app, which I did every hour.

Fires Near Me told me that a fire had sprung up dangerously close to Karly and Cam's home. I held my breath, but thank goodness, this one was swiftly dealt with by the heroic Rural Fire Service.

It was a long night.

THREE TO TEN DAYS

"It's the waiting that's the worst thing," somebody on the TV said. "You know the fire is there, blazing away, but you don't know when it'll arrive. Or whether you've done enough to protect yourself. Or whether it'll come fast or slow. The waiting is agony."

My ears pricked up when the news presenter spoke, mentioning a name that was familiar to me.

"The Australian Walkabout Wildlife Sanctuary in Calga has sent out an urgent emergency call for bags, boxes, and containers of all sizes. Trailers, drivers, and volunteers are needed to help evacuate hundreds of animals from the path of the advancing fires."

I was filled with horror. How on earth could the wonderful people at the sanctuary hope to evacuate all those animals? Koalas, kangaroos, wombats, Tasmanian devils, flying foxes, parrots, emus ... Surely it was impossible?

It wasn't until years later that I heard more of the story from Tassin, the sanctuary's owner, and her sister, Sally. We arranged a meeting so that they could tell me the whole story as it had unfolded and I could take notes.

"It all started with a phone call from the RFS[1]," Tassin said. "They said that the Gospers Mountain fire was heading in our direction and would be on us within three to ten days. They said they couldn't stop it. They said they didn't know what we could do with that information; all they could do was tell us that the fires were coming."

"Oh, no," I whispered.

"We couldn't wait, we had 250 animals depending on us. It would take days to move them all safely. We had to start evacuating immediately. I crawled into bed after midnight after hours of preparation. We couldn't do it on

---

1. Rural Fire Service

our own. As I lay in the dark with my eyes wide open, I put out a Facebook post asking for help."

"I remember that."

Tassin took a deep breath. "The next morning," she said in wonder, her eyes wide, "the cavalry arrived."

She stopped, reliving that moment and I think all of us felt goosebumps. Tears welled in my eyes, and I wasn't the only one.

"It was the most *incredible* surge of spontaneous response. People from the Central Coast to Newcastle came forward, not only giving us what we needed, but giving us what we didn't even *know* we needed yet. They brought boxes, horse trailers, blankets… They brought tools, rope, water carriers. I remember one message from a lady who said, 'I'm afraid of animals so I can't help, and I run my own business and I can't take time off. But I'm a caterer and I will help feed your team.' Somebody else said she had a car, and the pair of them kept us fed."

"And people offered homes to our animals. Qualified people who we could trust to keep our animals safe. Rescuers from WIRES[2] and Wildlife ARC.[3] They were *fantastic*."

"I can't imagine how you would even start such an enormous task," I said, shaking my head.

"I realised quickly that this was not going to be a 'normal' evacuation. We needed a plan."

"I dropped everything and came to help," said Sally. "While Tassin was focused on saving animals, I helped to pack up her personal possessions. Clothes, paperwork, photographs. Then began the task of responding to the flood of Facebook messages and offers of help. It was a full-time job."

"So many things to think about," said Tassin. "We had to decide which animals would go first. Did we have a place for them to go to? How hard would it be to catch them? How could we transport them? Did they need sedation? How would they respond to the stress of being caught, transported, and being away from their home? The farmyard animals with Waffles, our pig, were the safest to transport. So they went first."

"And the fire was still approaching?"

"Every day when we woke up, we were

---

2. WIRES: NSW Wildlife Information Rescue and Education Service
3. Wildlife ARC: Wildlife Animal Rescue & Care Society

advised that the fires were still three to ten days away. Then, two weeks in, we had an afternoon of dry lightning strikes, and we watched as these ignited eight new fires in the valley next to us. Now the fires could reach us in one day. That was the day the Three Mile Fire and the Gospers Mountain fire joined, and the mega-fire was created."

I couldn't speak.

"Every day, I had to revisit the plan depending on what the fire was doing, to do the most that we could in the safest way possible in the remaining time. It should have been exhausting, but I never felt it. I was very clear on what we needed to do. It's fascinating how fear affects you when you can't fight the danger, and you can't run away."

"I guess the adrenaline kicks in."

"Yes! I was running on about an hour and a half of sleep per night, that's all. And I couldn't eat. After two weeks, one of our new friends, a volunteer, insisted I tell her what I would eat if I was hungry. I said roast potatoes, but that the idea of food made me feel ill. She made me a teeny plate of roast dinner. I remember, it was exactly what I needed."

"What Tassin did was just incredible," said Sally. "I think I need to explain. I'm thinking of that last day, Tassin, when the RFS said the fire would arrive the next day. That video of the team catching the emus, and the rangers in tears, crying with exhaustion."

Tassin nodded.

"You see, Tassin has a lot of animals in enclosures, but there are hundreds and hundreds that live in the bush. They are not in enclosures, and not used to being handled. But there was this commitment from Tassin, and the rangers, and the volunteers, that they were not going to leave a single animal to die in the flames. What Tassin and her team went through, both physically and mentally…"

Sally paused, but we understood what she was trying to express. "Tassin, do you remember that possum baby?"

"Oh yes!" exclaimed her sister, her face lighting up. "People were out in the bush, night after night, looking for animals to rescue. We caught Mumma Poss. She was a brush-tailed possum mum who lived in the Visitors' Centre roof, but she was wild. We could see she had a milk-producing teat, but we couldn't find her joey. Mumma Poss went to a wildlife carer and we went out every night looking for her joey. Four days later, we found a joey, but we didn't know if it was Mumma Poss's baby or not. We took it to the carer and set it down. And there was this *wonderful* moment when Mumma Poss just grabbed the baby and began to feed it."

"And they were fine. When the fire threat was all over, Mumma Poss and her joey moved back into our Visitors' Centre roof."

"That was the level of things happening. There were people working in the day, people staying in our bunkhouse and working through the night. Nobody slept much. And locals brought in trays of sandwiches every day to feed everyone."

"So you decided to evacuate all the animals?" I asked.

"Well, no, not at first. Initially, I decided we should protect the kangaroos and emus on site. They don't handle stress well. To catch and transport them would be too dangerous for them."

I nodded. I believe kangaroos are closely related to deer, and I remember in England, deer often died of shock when hit by a car, even if they were uninjured.

"I decided we could contain all the kangaroos and emus," Tassin continued, "and protect them onsite, if need be. We had got them all into a holding area. We had a plan with the RFS. They would defend them from outside the sanctuary fence, and we would defend them from inside, with a water wagon and fire hoses. But the fire surprised everyone by running inland and then advancing on us from two sides."

I held my breath.

"At two o'clock in the morning, I saw the flashing lights of a fire truck outside our gate. The firefighter said, 'The fire will be here tomorrow, around three o'clock in the afternoon. Our crews are all defending the town up the road. We can't be here to protect the animals. All we will be able to do is send a fire crew to cut the fence so they can run from the flames.'"

"Oh," Sally gasped, "I'd forgotten that!"

"It was at that moment that I realised I'd made a *terrible* mistake. I'd miscalculated. There were about fifty kangaroos and ten emus in the holding area facing certain death. We didn't have time to move them. And that was the first time I cried."

Nobody spoke as Tassin paused, reliving the helplessness.

"That night I put out the news on Facebook. I didn't ask for help. I didn't think anyone could help. There wasn't enough time. I just said that I'd made the wrong decision and didn't know what to do. There was *no way* we could move those animals."

"I'd blocked all this out," Sally exclaimed.

"At 3 am I got a phone call from one of the volunteers, a new and very special friend who had previously organised a helicopter to fly our wombats to safety. She said, 'Tassin, if I had a magic wand and could give you *anything* you wanted, what would it be?' Well, of course, I started thinking of the most ridiculous things."

Sally smiled, knowing what was coming next.

"I said, a luxury horse trailer, air-conditioned, with stainless steel hooks on the walls, cushioned and padded so the hanging kangaroos don't get hurt as they swing around…"

"Hanging kangaroos?"

"Yes. You transport kangaroos in pouches. It doesn't matter how big they are; you just have to have a very big pouch for a 40kg kangaroo. They feel safe, like they are back in their mother's pouch. But we were just being silly, it was a fantasy that could never happen."

Both Tassin and Sally were smiling now.

"At about 11 o'clock that morning, a shiny, black horse trailer drove up! We opened the back doors and it had stainless steel hooks, padded walls, and air-conditioning! That friend is a fairy godmother. The guy driving it looked absolutely stunned. He said, 'I told the lady who phoned me very firmly that I was on my way to pick up some very expensive racehorses from Sydney, so I couldn't help'. He didn't understand how it happened, but somehow he was persuaded to turn around and come to us instead. He looked completely shellshocked."

We were all laughing, picturing the scene. It was like a scene out of Cinderella, complete with the magic stagecoach.

"We caught up and bagged our biggest kangaroos and hung them from the shiny stainless steel hooks, and off he drove to Newcastle. Volunteers helped us with the rest, and at 12.30 that afternoon, the last animal was evacuated. Yes, it was a miracle."

"How close did the fire get?" I asked.

"Four kilometres. There were days when the firefront advanced more than 30 kilometres in a few hours. Can you imagine? Everything depended on the wind direction. In the end, we were lucky. The fire never reached us."

We all fell silent, thinking.

Sally and Tassin looked at each other.

"It's hard to explain," said Sally, "to put in words just how incredible it all was. I'm so proud of my sister. I don't think we've ever revisited that time before. I hadn't realised just how raw some of those memories would turn out to be. And yet we had never really talked it through. Thank you, Victoria, for the therapy!"

"It's my pleasure," I said, smiling. "I can't thank you enough for your time and the stories. I hope I can help spread the word about the fantastic job you all do at the sanctuary." [4]

Back in Sydney, some time later, when the immediate fire danger had passed, Karly checked her daughters' carefully packed emergency bags. She opened Indy's first.

Indy had packed countless pairs of shoes (even outgrown ones), the fruit bowl, eye makeup, and a ziplock bag containing her dead bug collection.

"Do you really need all those shoes?" asked her mother.

"But they hold so many memories!" said the seven-year-old.

And what about three-year-old Winter's bag?

Winter had packed her favourite book. Was it a classic? Grimms Fairytales or perhaps a book by Enid Blyton?

No. I'm sorry to say it was her beloved *Farts Around the World*.

There hadn't been much to smile about as the bushfires continued to rage. Strong winds were still fanning the flames and carrying smoke and

---

4. A gift to my readers from the Walkabout Park See Page 286

live embers hundreds of miles. Lives had been lost, homes burned, and wildlife devastated.

But just for a moment, the contents of my granddaughters' emergency bags brought smiles to all our faces.

FIRE-ROASTED CHERRY TOMATO SALSA

Ever wondered what to do with that glut of cherry tomatoes that appear every year? Here's a delicious suggestion.

Ingredients

2 teaspoons olive oil

1 pint cherry tomatoes, or more to taste

1 yellow onion, roughly chopped

8 cloves garlic, unpeeled

3 jalapeño peppers, sliced, or to taste

⅓ cup firmly-packed fresh coriander (cilantro) leaves

1 lime, juiced

¼ teaspoon ground cumin

1 pinch cayenne pepper, or to taste

1 pinch dried oregano

salt and ground black pepper to taste

Method

Line a baking sheet with aluminum foil and brush with olive oil.

Spread tomatoes, onion, garlic, and jalapeño peppers onto prepared baking sheet.

Cook under a grill for about 5 minutes. Turn the sheet and continue grilling until the vegetables are slightly charred.

Allow to cool for a few minutes.

Peel the garlic and discard skins.

Blend tomatoes, onion, peeled garlic, jalapeños, any accumulated juices from the baking sheet, coriander leaves, lime juice, cumin, cayenne pepper, and oregano in a blender until salsa is smooth.

Transfer to a bowl, cover with plastic wrap, and refrigerate until flavours blend, at least 2 hours.

Season with salt and black pepper.

25

RAINDROPS AND SPIDERS

The wildfires burned their way through December. On the 15th, a back-burning operation went terribly wrong in the Blue Mountains, west of Sydney, and grew out of control. It was a well-meaning attempt to contain the ever-growing Gospers Mountain mega-fire but it proved utterly disastrous.

The main road that climbs up the Blue Mountains has the strange name of Bells Line of Road. All traffic passes through the little town of Bilpin, where small businesses line the road and invite visitors to sample their wares. It's known as the 'land of the mountain apple,' and apple and stone fruit orchards abound. My family knows it well, and we usually stopped in Bilpin to sample the local cider or enjoy a cream tea with homemade jam and scones. Often we bought delicious apple pies to take home.

"You remember Bilpin?" I asked Joe later that week, and tears ran down my cheek.

"Yes, the place with all the apples for sale that we go through on our way to Cam and Karly's friends' farm?"

"That's it."

"What about it?"

"There's hardly anything left of it. The Rural Fire Service was trying to divert the Gospers Mountain fire, which has been burning for nearly two months, and it escaped. It destroyed twenty homes and masses of orchards. I couldn't believe the pictures they showed on the TV. You know we always stop at the Fruit Bowl? They lost 5500 apple trees and 500 fig trees. And the Tutti Frutti shop? It went up in a red fireball, a huge ball of flame. The outhouses are just heaps of black smoking rubble, and any tractors and vehicles that didn't get away are all burnt out."

"That's terrible."

"I know. Do you know why the Blue Mountains are called that?"

"Yes, because of the blue haze they have sometimes?"

"Yes, I researched it. Apparently, the oil

droplets of certain eucalyptus trees combine with dust and water vapour and appear blue in certain lights. That's what creates the blue haze. Anyway, the fires have destroyed the ancient Blue Gum Forest."

"That's terrible," said Joe again, and this time he didn't ask if it was safe to come home.

It's hard enough to see the destruction of strangers' lives, their homes and livelihoods destroyed as they gaze at what is left: a pile of smoking ruins. But when you recognise the familiar landmarks and remember the locals' faces, it's so much harder.

That December we celebrated Nana's 88th birthday. I remember a wonderful day orchestrated by Cam's mum, a birthday party with a Chinese theme. All the great-grandchildren, including Indy and Winter merged to become a dancing, writhing Chinese dragon, complete with a dragon's head, and processed around the garden. Nana loved it, and so did we all.

If you've followed the Old Fools series, you may remember Alice, from Two Old Fools in Turmoil, Book 5. She was the lovely lady who traced me through the Salvation Army and revealed a family secret that took my family's breath away.

That same December, Alice, in the town of Bath in the UK, celebrated her 101st birthday.

Christmas came, but I have few memories of it. I worried about the bushfires. Would they ever end? I worried about Joe, marooned and homesick in the UK without me to look after him.

The iconic Sydney Harbour New Year fireworks display was cancelled, as were fireworks displays all over the state. For many, 2019 ended in thick, black smoke. According to Wikipedia now, the air quality was eleven times the hazardous level on some days, making it even worse than New Delhi's, where it was also compared to "smoking 32 cigarettes" by Associate Professor Brian Oliver, a respiratory diseases scientist at the University of Technology, Sydney.

And there were more terrifying incidents to come in our state of New South Wales.

As the ABC news channel reported:

"In the lakeside village of Conjola Park, residents relive memories of houses seemingly spontaneously combusting, birds dropping from a black sky, a roaring wind and taps with no water, as a firestorm enveloped them on New Year's Eve."

The fire bore down on the helpless village. There was no escape. Firemen, tourists, and residents were trapped by towering flames on three sides. They had no choice; they stampeded into the lake.

Some took to boats, some waded in, and others drove their cars into the water. Even kangaroos and other creatures sought sanctuary in the lake. People hugged and sobbed as the power went out and telecommunication towers tumbled. There was no road access and no water in any taps to fight the fire.

One in three homes would be destroyed. Three men would lose their lives. One died defending his home, and the other two men died in their burnt-out cars as they tried to escape.

I believe thirty-four lives were lost directly to the Black Summer New South Wales bushfires. An air tanker and two helicopters crashed during operations, killing three crew members. Two fire trucks were caught in fatal accidents, killing three firefighters. Air quality dropped to hazardous levels, killing an estimated four hundred Australians with pre-existing breathing problems.

Around three thousand homes were lost, and

roughly five thousand outbuildings in New South Wales alone.

Ecologists from The University of Sydney estimated that 480 million mammals (later updated to one billion), birds, and reptiles had been lost since September, with concerns that entire species of plants and animals may have been completely wiped out.

It was now midsummer in Australia. Some welcome rain fell in January, assisting the firefighters in extinguishing more fires, but the fear of further fires still remained. The Gospers Mountain fire was not declared contained until January 12th.

"So are the fires all out now?" Joe asked, and I could hear the hope in his voice. "Am I safe to book a flight back?"

"No, not yet. Just wait a little longer. It's crazy-hot here and we've been warned that wildfires will flare up again. Complete fire bans are still in place. That means still no barbecues, bonfires, or flames of any kind. Even dirtbike riding is banned in case a spark lights another fire."

"I bet Cam isn't happy about that."

"No, he's not, and now we're being warned about something else!"

"Oh? What's that?"

"The most dangerous venomous spider in the world."

"Not the funnel-web?"

"Yep, that's the one."

The ABC news channel warned that the current hot, humid conditions were absolutely perfect for funnel-web spiders. They were now on the move, looking for partners and mating furiously. The males were leaving the safety of their underground lairs and wandering around in search of lady funnel-webs.

I was shocked to learn that there are 36 different species of funnel-web spiders found in eastern Australia, many of them equipped with highly toxic, fast-acting venom. But the most dangerous is *atrax robustus*, better known as the Sydney Funnel-Web.

And we lived in its preferred location.

Funnel-web spiders utilise an existing hole in rotting tree stumps, leaf litter, or in the ground, and line it with silk. They disguise the entrance with pieces of bark and set up clever trip-lines. Unsuspecting prey, like beetles, lizards or tree frogs, trigger the trip-lines, alerting the hidden spider sitting just inside the entrance with its front legs resting on the trip-lines. The spider dashes out and sinks its fangs into the hapless creature, injecting a huge dose of lethal venom.

Wandering love-sick males often tumble into backyard swimming pools. They can't swim, but the hairs on their abdomens can trap air bubbles, which will keep them alive for at least thirty hours. They'll float around the pool for a while, but eventually, they become waterlogged and start to sink.

A spokesman from the Australian Museum warned:

It should not be assumed that a non-moving spider at the bottom of a pool is dead as they often recover.

This sent pool owners scurrying to buy pool cleaning robots that would vacuum the floor of their pools, scooping up any submerged spiders.

Luckily, the Australian Reptile Park near Gosford, NSW, has a venom-milking program. Thanks to this anti-venom, which is held at major city and regional hospitals, no lives have been lost to funnel-web spider attacks since the 1980s.

Not only were we warned to beware of funnel-web spiders on the move, we were also requested to catch them, if we could, and donate them to the venom-milking program.

But how does one catch a lethal spider, assuming one is brave enough to try? (If I encountered one, you wouldn't see me for dust.)

Luckily, they can't jump, but they can lunge surprisingly quickly if feeling threatened. The secret is to encourage them to enter a smooth-sided plastic or glass container which they can't climb out of.

Yeah, right.

In this video, keeper Jake Meney from the Australian Reptile Park demonstrates how this is safely done.[1]

Fascinating and extremely worthy, but still not an activity I'll ever participate in.

"And you know what?" I added. "The newsreader said that they rarely come into a house. But if they do, one of their favourite places to hide is in a shoe. Imagine!"

"So you're not going to be volunteering any

---

1. How to catch a funnel-web spider: https://youtu.be/Fs1h-etI-sU?feature=shared

spider-catching services, then?" said Joe, chuckling.

"Nopetty-nope-nope."

APPLE SNACK CAKE

This apple snack cake is easy to make, moist, light and so delicious. It will disappear in no time! Fabulous hot or cold.

From https://www.carolinescooking.com/apple-snack-cake/#recipe

Ingredients

113g or 4oz unsalted butter room temperature, cut in small pieces

200 g sugar (1 cup)

2 eggs

5 ml or 1 teaspoon vanilla extract

185g plain flour (1⅓ cup all-purpose flour)

1 teaspoon baking powder

½ teaspoon baking soda (bicarbonate of soda)

¼ teaspoon salt

½ teaspoon cinnamon

⅛ teaspoon ginger

⅛ teaspoon cloves or allspice

300g (2 cups) apples, peeled and diced small, approx 2 apples (peeled and cored weight/vol)

55g (⅓ cup) chopped dates

For the maple frosting (optional)

60 ml confectioners sugar, (¼ cup is 4tbsp) icing sugar

1 tablespoon maple syrup

Method

Preheat oven to 175°C/ 350°F. Line a 23x23 cm (9x9 inch) cake pan with parchment.

Cream together the butter and sugar until well combined (you can use either a stand or hand mixer). Add the eggs one at a time along with the vanilla and mix in well.

In a separate bowl, mix together the flour, baking powder, baking soda, salt, cinnamon, ginger and cloves. Add this to the butter mixture - I suggest folding in with a spatula rather than beating (you can add part at a time, if easier). The mixture will be relatively stiff.

Add the diced apples and dates, mix them through then tip into the lined prepared pan. Smooth the top then bake for approximately 35 minutes until a medium brown color and a skewer inserted in the middle comes out clean.

You can enjoy the cake warm or cool, but if you want to add frosting, it will need to be cooled first.

If adding frosting, sift the icing sugar then stir in the maple syrup. Mix until smooth. Drizzle or spread over the cake once it has cooled then cut and serve. It will keep approx 3-4 days at cool room temp in a sealed box.

26

CHRISTMAS BEETLES AND COWS

More beautiful rain fell from the skies in early 2020 and Australia sighed with relief. TV news snippets now brightened our days by showing us hilarious, joyous clips of farmers and their families dancing in the rain.[1] The drought was over.

Then came the longed-for day when the Gospers Mountain fire was declared under control and contained. Karly and Cam's friends, who owned a hobby farm in the Blue Mountains, invited them to come and use the farm for the weekend, as they had plans to be elsewhere.

---

1. Farmers dancing in the rain: https://www.youtube.com/shorts/Cmptd75QmB4

CHRISTMAS BEETLES AND COWS

"Would you like to come, Mum?" asked Karly. "There's space for you if you want to."

"Oh, I'd love to! I'll just check that Hildy can have Lola."

Of course, Hildy welcomed Lola with open arms. (Thank you, Hildy.) And Lola was beyond excited to be dropped off at her boyfriend's house. Sylvester greeted her cheerfully, good-naturedly ducking away from Lola's passionate kisses. Benny pretty much ignored her, and Gracie looked down her nose, exuding disapproval at Lola's exuberance.

On the Friday evening, we drove into the Blue Mountains, higher and higher along the twisting road. It didn't take long before stark, blackened tree trunks replaced the healthy forest on both sides of the road. With no foliage, the setting sun flashed through the trees like hectic strobe lighting, blinding us. Lumps of black, misshapen metal sat where there used to be cars, trucks or farm machinery. Roadsigns were bent, sooty and unreadable.

The little town of Bilpin was almost unrecognisable. Burnt-out buildings and blackened rubble marked where there used to be shops and stalls selling fresh produce, jams and cider. Here and there, a building stood untouched, a random winner of the bushfire lottery, somehow having escaped the flames.

None of us spoke as we passed through. I was thankful that the failing light prevented us from seeing the full extent of the horrors.

Night was falling as we reached the farm. We were relieved to see the farm building was intact, but it had been a close shave. Flames had licked around the edges of our friends' land and had consumed some of their woodland, but they were lucky. As we began to unload the cars, a cow mooed in the distance.

"Oh good, Mark asked us to check on the cows," said Karly.

"Oh, I didn't know they had cows."

"Yes, they have four. They are free-range, pretty much. They're retired and wander around as they please, but they come back every evening for a hay feed. We'll go for a walk in the morning and check them out."

Just then, a small, hard missile hit my face. Then another. I was also aware of a whirring sound.

"Mummy!" yelled Indy. "Something just flew at me."

"And me!"

"And me!"

"What are they?"

CHRISTMAS BEETLES AND COWS

I switched on the torch on my phone to see what on earth was happening. The beam of light caught the culprits. The air was filled with hard, round, whirring missiles that appeared to have no navigation skills, their clumsy flights causing them to crash into whatever was in their flight path. Including us.

"Aussie Cam, what's going on?"

"Christmas beetles!" said Cam, laughing. "We've arrived on the day the adults emerge from the soil. Now they'll start feeding on foliage, find a wife, mate, and she'll start the cycle again by laying eggs."

"But why do they keep flying at me?" wailed Indy.

"They don't mean to, they're just excited to be free, and they don't steer very well. They won't hurt you. As soon as they've mated and the females have laid eggs, they'll die."

"Oh, poor things."

I'll never forget that night of the Christmas beetles. The air was thick with hundreds and thousands of them blundering around. Swooping, diving, zig-zagging, dropping, crash-landing. They were everywhere. One landed on my lapel and stayed there like a brooch. I named him Peter.

Karly had brought LJ's bed and put it on the

porch. Within seconds it was plastered with Christmas beetles.

It wasn't much better inside the house. A swarm of beetles followed us in to join their friends and relatives who had already made their way inside. Spiders of all sizes crept out of unseen crevices and were feasting. Beetles crawled up the walls, crunched underfoot and flew at us. They even fell into our wine.

The next morning, with a coffee warming my hands, I sat on the little wooden deck. Having swept away the Christmas beetle corpses from the chairs and floor, I settled and watched the new day arrive.

The scenery was stunning. The mountain was shrouded in a silvery mist, and every blade of grass was decorated with dewy diamonds.

"We'll take a look around this morning," said Karly, joining me. "Check those cows are okay. Have you seen or heard them?"

"No, I haven't."

It occurred to me then that I hadn't heard a bird dawn chorus, either.

A little later, we ventured into the burnt forest

in search of the cows. The last time I visited the farm, tall trees reached for the sky and the dense undergrowth teemed with life. Now charred tree trunks stood like solemn sentinels, their blackened branches pointing ragged fingers at the grey sky. A carpet of ash and debris muffled our footfalls on the forest floor. The eerie silence was a stark contrast to the lively symphony of nature that once filled this forest.

We saw wombat dens, now exposed where the fire had burned away the undergrowth, but we saw no wombats. I hoped they stayed safe and cool underground as the flames raged overhead. No birds chirped in the trees. The only sign of life I saw were delicate spiders' webs glistening with crystal-clear dew drops. As the gentle breeze swayed the webs, the diamonds sparkled against the coal-black backdrop of charred tree stumps.

I took one photo that made my heart sing. It shows a burnt, blackened tree trunk, but it already sprouted fresh, green baby green leaves. In such a short time, new life was beginning, and not every ruined, blackened tree stump was dead. It is still one of my favourite photos of all time. [See it in the free Fair Dinkum photo album https://bit.ly/Free--Stuff]

"Can anyone see the cows?"

"No!"

"Nope!"

We searched for the missing cows all weekend but never caught a glimpse of them. We heard no more distant moos, and they never returned to eat their hay. Karly was really worried.

"I can't believe we've lost four cows!" she kept saying. "Mark asked us to do ONE thing: check on the cows. And what happens? We lose them. All four of them!"

"Hey Siri," I asked, "do cows come home on their own?"

Siri's reply didn't help much. "Cows are notoriously languid creatures and make their own way home at their own unhurried pace," she said.

Despite the absent cows, we enjoyed ourselves and the time to leave arrived too fast. But we had planned a stop-off on the journey home.

Do you remember how the hashtag *#metoo* went viral on social media? To a much lesser extent, so did *#bringanemptyesky* in Australia that weekend.

The residents of Bilpin were proud. They didn't want charity. They just wanted a chance to sell their wares and get back on their feet. Visitors were urged to come to the stricken, burnt village of Bilpin and to stop at the shops and stalls and buy the produce that the vendors could still offer.

That Sunday, we left the farm after one last

search for the cows and drove down the mountain heading for Bilpin. We were prepared. Our cars were packed with empty eskies.

As we neared Bilpin, we spotted huge homemade signs tied to railings, trees and fences. Painted in huge letters on sheets or tablecloths were thank-you messages to the brave firefighters who had done their best to protect the community.

Car parks were full, and vehicles lined the roadside. Like us, hundreds of other visitors arrived with empty eskies, and we were delighted to see long queues at every shop and cafe counter. It warmed my heart.

I will never forget the atmosphere in the little ruined town of Bilpin that day. Supportive, cheerful strangers descending on a stricken community. I admit to becoming quite teary and loving the Australian spirit even more than I already did.

We filled our eskies with honey, jam, homemade cakes, apple crumbles, bottles of cider and assorted Bilpin produce. It was a pleasure to hear the cash registers ringing and see the grateful faces of the locals, many of whom had lost so much.

The owner of the Bilpin Fruit Bowl, Margaret Tadrosse, said later, "I can't begin to thank people enough for the support we've been getting since the fires. On Sunday, the oven could not keep up. People were waiting twenty minutes for their apple pies. The oven was pumping them out all day."

Oh, and the cows? They came home that Tuesday. Trees had fallen across the boundary fence and the cows had gone walkabout. They came home unharmed and hungry.

Finally, in February 2020, the very last wildfire was put out with the help of torrential rain. To everybody's astonishment, the rain was heavy and continuous, lasting five full days. The ground, baked by drought, then burnt by flames, was unable to soak up the deluge.

Unbelievably, the east coast of Australia now

had another problem: extensive flooding. Ironically, areas like Conjola, only just emerging from a bushfire catastrophe, were now severely flooded.

"Torrential rain?" asked Joe. "Really?"

"Yes, the lake here is flooded, too. I'm glad our house is on high ground."

"But there are no more fires?" repeated Joe.

"All the fires are out," I confirmed, grinning. "There are no more fires burning. The extreme heat is over and the air quality is good."

For once, I welcomed the question I knew was coming next.

"Can I book a flight home now?"

"Yes! You can come home."

LATTICE APPLE PIE

Utterly delicious, golden brown apple pie with that traditional taste, from https://vjcooks.com/lattice-apple-pie/

Ingredients

5 large apples, peeled & diced

45g (1½oz) butter

½ cup brown sugar

¼ cup white sugar

½ tsp vanilla

2 tbsp flour

½ tsp cinnamon

¼ tsp nutmeg

800g (28oz) shortcrust pastry

1 egg, whisked

Method

- Add apples, butter, brown and white sugar to a saucepan and bring to the boil.
- Cook for 10 minutes or until the apples start to soften.
- Add the vanilla, sifted flour and spices, stir until thickened, remove from the heat to cool.
- Grease a 23cm (9inch) pie dish and preheat oven to 200°C fan-assisted, 180°C, (390°F).
- Roll out half the pastry to line the pie dish, add the apple filling.
- Roll out the remaining pastry and cut into strips. Create a lattice top by weaving the strips together.
- Egg wash the top and sprinkle with white sugar, place towards the bottom of the oven and bake for 30-40 minutes.
- Remove and allow the pie to cool before slicing.
- Serve warm or cold with fresh cream or ice cream.

27

SHEEP

The post-bushfire flooding turned out to be severe, creating flash floods that took everybody by surprise and washed houses and vehicles away. Beaches were closed because of the king tides, and warnings were issued. Anyone attempting to swim, surf, or fish risked their lives.

Our pool overflowed. A power-line fell on Cam and Karly's house. Luckily, nobody was hurt, and the damage wasn't serious.

Apparently, larrikins were jetskiing on our local MacDonald's car park. (I admit to not knowing what a larrikin was and had to look up the definition. I was amused to read that it's an Australian term for 'a boisterous, often badly-behaved young man'.)

SHEEP

Understandably, water restrictions were lifted, but now there were other worries. After the drought and bushfires, local dams had almost run dry. But although 81% full from the new rain now, there were fears about the quality of the water. Bushfire ash and debris rendered it undrinkable.

Was there ever an end to extraordinary weather events in Australia? It seems not. On February 18th, an incredible storm plucked massive trees from the ground and threw them aside. In Sydney, garden furniture flew through the air. One thousand homes lost power. And a freak accident killed a man hit by a barbecue gas bottle picked up by the wind from a balcony.

Our damage was minimal, but I stayed awake all night, convinced that the wind would rip off our roof.

"Good news, I've booked a flight for the 3rd March. I've been in touch with my specialist and he's going to give me a 'fit to fly' letter to carry for the airline, and I'll take the portable oxygen concentrator with me on the journey, in case I need it."

"That's good."

"All you need to do is contact the shuttle service, please, so they can pick me up from Sydney Airport."

"Too easy," I said, showing off my latest Australian slang.

"I can't wait to see you both. It's been such a long time." There was a tremor in his voice.

"I know, such a long time! Lola will be beside herself when she sees you. I'll be counting the sleeps until you get here. But never forget, being overseas during the bushfires probably saved your life."

"I know."

Exhausted by the Black Summer fires, sometimes described as hell on earth, one would think it would be difficult for people to find any positives. But Australians are a wonderfully cheerful, resilient people. Some heartwarming stories came to light in the wake of the bushfires.

For instance, there are fifteen species of wallaby in Australia, and most of them are endangered. So it warmed my heart to hear that New South Wales officials arranged a rather unusual airdrop. They gathered together four thousand pounds of vegetables, including sweet potatoes and carrots, and dropped them from helicopters at known habitats of the critically endangered brush-tailed rock wallabies.

And I learned that the Wollemi National Park, which is where the Gospers Mountain mega-fire raged, has a secret. It holds the world's only known cluster of Wollemi pine trees, which are known as 'dinosaur trees' because they date back to prehistoric times. Indeed, they were thought to be extinct already until scientists discovered this group in the early 1990s.

Aware of the importance of these trees growing in an isolated gorge, huge efforts were made to save them from the mega-fire. A combination of methods was used. Helicopters water-bombed the trees, and fire-retardant and irrigation systems were deployed, resulting in a successful outcome. The trees were saved. Their precise location remains a secret in an attempt to protect them.

Imagine the excitement when wildfires uncovered an ancient aboriginal aquaculture system, even older than the Egyptian pyramids, in southwest Australia. This 6,600-year-old landscape is lined by stones to form pools to manipulate water flow for the purpose of hunting eels. The system was created by the Gunditjmara people, an indigenous group with a rich heritage in Australia.

I don't know of an equivalent in the UK, but in Australia, 'Men's Sheds' are popular. They began in the 1980s to address the problem of loneliness. Men's Sheds are fantastic spaces where retired men hang out, chat, and work on projects. The shed usually houses tools and equipment for woodworking and other activities. I was delighted to hear that dozens of Men's Sheds had taken on the project of making possum hutches on poles to tempt the possums back to their desolated forests.

There was even a little post-bushfire black humour. (Excuse the pun.)

"Karly and Cam have a friend whose house was damaged in the bushfires. Not seriously, but enough for them to move out while the work is being done," I told Joe.

"Were they insured?"

"Yes, no problem there. There was another problem, though."

"What was that?"

"Well, the insurance company paid for them to rent a house temporarily while waiting for their house to be fixed. What they didn't know was the home they were allocated had recently been rented by a pair of prostitutes."

"It was a brothel?"

"Yes! Men kept knocking on the door asking if there was any chance of a $15 dollar quickie!"

"Oh dear!"

"I know! The wife doesn't answer the door herself anymore; she makes her husband do it, wearing a long blonde wig. He says they get a real fright when he opens the door, especially as he has a beard."

"Haha! I bet they never come back!"

Joe was due home in less than a month, and I planned to get everything spick and span before that date. I didn't want him to worry about anything. We'd often talked about replacing the rusty railings that surrounded the pool with glass fencing but hadn't done anything about it. I arranged for the job to be done and was delighted that it would all be finished in time for Joe's return.

Two burly glass specialists arrived to start the job and began by dismantling the old railings, leaving open access to the pool for a while. Of course, Lola took full advantage of the situation, expecting Mike and Harry to constantly throw her ball into the pool for her to retrieve.

"I'm so sorry," I said. "I'll take her inside, out of your way."

"No, leave her," said Harry, "she's okay. We're both dog lovers."

Every time I looked out of the window, either Harry or Mike was throwing the ball for her, followed by an almighty splash as she jumped in after it. I'm sure my fencing job took twice as long as it should have.

Another reason the job took so long was that Harry had so many stories to tell. When he began a story, his partner, Mike, would smile and shake his head, but I noticed his work would slow down, and he was listening intently. Some people have that gift for storytelling, and Harry had it in abundance. Even Lola lay down at his feet for a while and listened.

"Have you always lived in this area?" I asked Harry.

"No," he said, "I was born and raised way out west. Our parents had a bit of a farm. We couldn't grow much because the soil wasn't great, and it was hilly, but grass grew, and most of the farmers raised sheep. It was red-hot and dusty in summer and bitter cold in winter. Our mum used to give us hot baked potatoes to carry to school to keep our hands warm on the four-mile walk."

"Much better than woolly gloves, I expect," I said, setting down a tray of mugs of tea and biscuits.

"Sure was," he replied.

Harry's weatherbeaten face crinkled, and his eyes sparkled with mischief. I had already come to recognise that expression. It meant that he had a story to tell.

"You mentioning woolly gloves reminded me of something that happened to a mate from my home town," he started and sat down in a garden chair.

Mike followed suit, knowing a story was about to be spun. Lola lay down with her chin on her paws.

"I had this mate, Greg, who was a truck driver and he used to carry all kinds of cargo. The time I'm thinking of, he was transporting sheep. The lorry he was driving had two layers, sheep on the top storey and more sheep below. You know the kind I mean?"

Mike and I nodded.

"So Greg reaches a town and he's surprised how super-friendly everybody is. People are turning and waving at him like he's some kind of old friend, or celebrity or something.

"When he reaches the town centre, he stops at the traffic lights. It was then that he smells burning and realised he was enveloped in black smoke.

"Somebody bangs on the cab and yells, "Your truck is on fire!"

"Then it's pandemonium. People are jumping out of their cars and scarpering. Traffic is at a standstill and the sheep are baa-ing fit to bust. Greg's in shock but he knows he has to act fast to save the sheep. So he leaps out of the cab, runs round to the back and unlocks and lowers the ramps and sets the sheep free.

"The sheep stream out, and the main street is now awash with sheep, baa-ing and running hither and thither. They run between cars, into open shop doorways, up side-roads and into driveways. Some found the children's playground and were grazing happily there.

"Oy! Stop eating my stock," shouts the florist as she shoos a bunch of sheep out of her shop.

"I've got one!" somebody shouts. "I'll see if I can catch some more and I'll keep them in my garden."

"I've got two in my storeroom," says the lady from the Post Office.

"And so it went on. The fire truck didn't take

long to arrive. They soon put out the fire, but by then, the sheep were thoroughly dispersed."

Harry shook his head, chuckling at the memory. He sipped his coffee, chewed on another biscuit, and carried on.

"My mate Greg summoned a replacement truck but it didn't arrive until nearly two days later. When it turned up, the word was passed around to all those who had given temporary homes to the sheep, asking them to bring them back. Some were herded down the road; others arrived in trailers. A few were wearing dog collars and leashes and were led along the street. It was a bit of a miracle, but by the end of the day, only three were missing."

Harry replaced his mug on the tray and stretched. "Better do some work, I guess! This fence won't put itself up. Shame, I've just remembered another sheep story from back home."

"Oh, tell it when I bring out your next cuppa," I said. "I'll look forward to that!"

That afternoon, I admired the glass fence panels completed so far.

"That looks amazing," I said. "So much better than the old railings." I set down the mugs of tea and snacks. "Now, what was that other sheep story you were going to tell us?"

"Ah," said Harry, warming up, "there were a lot of real characters in those days where I came from. Of course, most of the farms have been sold now, and roads and houses have been built where sheep used to graze.

"But I remember there were these three old sheep farmers who used to live in the same area. Every few months, they liked to meet up and have a few beers and something to eat. You know how it is in Aus, although they were technically next-door neighbours, they lived about forty kilometres apart.

"It's your turn to bring something to eat next time we meet up," said one farmer to his closest neighbour, Jed. "We'll have a barbecue at my place, so bring some meat."

"When the day came, Jed drove up the long track to Tom's farmstead and arrived with a live sheep in the back of his ute.

"What? We have to kill it before we get any supper, do we?" asked Tom, laughing.

"It's a good sheep," said Jed.

"I'll do it," said Ray, "We don't want to go hungry." He approached the ute and lifted the unlucky sheep out. "Hold on a minute," he said, staring at the tag in the sheep's ear. "Tom, that's your tag, isn't it?"

"Tom examined the tag. "Dead right it is! he

said. "This here is one of my sheep!"

"Jed?" asked Ray. "How come you brought one of Tom's own sheep to his barbecue?"

"Well, I don't know how that happened," answered the old rogue, not quite making eye contact. "Us being neighbours, I guess it must have jumped over the fence onto my land."

"No way," protested Tom. "We live forty kilometres apart! You just grabbed one of my sheep on your way here, didn't you?"

Both Mike and I were laughing by now because Harry was reenacting the scene like a seasoned actor, using different voices and expressions and much finger-pointing.

"That old Jed just shook his head and hotly denied it, but nobody ever believed him."

"Were they still friends after that?" I asked.

"Yes, I think so. Ray and Tom were used to Jed's shenanigans and I reckon they had been known to pull similar pranks themselves.

The bushfires were all out, every single one of them. The air quality was good. There was no more torrential rain, no flooding, no king tides, nor storms. Our house was spotless and ready, and the pool fencing was finished and looking fabulous.

"Yes, I think we are completely ready for him to come home now," I said to Lola, and her tail wagged. "And I'm certainly not worried about that awful pneumonia bug or whatever it is they are talking about in China."

SLOW-COOKED ROAST LEG OF LAMB

This is just the best and easiest recipe! **Top Tip**: Roughly chop up a few potatoes and onions and sit the lamb on them to cook. No liquid needed.

Ingredients

1 (1½ kilos or 3lb) bone-in leg of lamb

½ cup red wine

1 lemon, juiced

2 tablespoons honey

3 cloves garlic, minced

1 tablespoon apple cider vinegar

1 tablespoon dried rosemary

1 teaspoon dried thyme

1 teaspoon sea salt

½ teaspoon fresh cracked pepper

Sprigs of rosemary (optional)

Method

Pour wine into a slow cooker.

Mix lemon juice, honey, garlic, vinegar, rosemary, thyme, sea salt, and pepper in a medium bowl until a thick paste forms. Massage paste into lamb using your hands; gently place into the slow cooker.

Cook on Low for 6-8 hours. That's it!

28

PLAGUES

"Hi Karly, how are you doing? Everything okay?"

"Well, yes, it is now, but today didn't start well."

"Why not? Let me guess, another accident with Winter again?"

"Nope, not that for a change."

And then she told me what had happened that morning.

I'm sure we all remember what life was like when we had little ones who needed to be up and dressed, breakfasted, and ready for school, not forgetting their homework, PE kit, packed lunch, reading book, latest project, and goodness knows what else. For Karly, it was a particularly stressful morning because Indy had Elementary

Strings before school. That meant they had to remember her violin, too, and be at the school extra early.

Karly had to work, and time was tight. It was pouring with rain, and the girls were being uncooperative.

"Indy! Hurry up! Don't just sit there, find your shoes and put them on. Where's your violin? Winter, eat up, we've got to go."

"But I don't want to go!" wailed her youngest.

"Oh, for goodness sake! Indy, where are you?"

"I can't find my sock."

"I don't want my toast!"

"Okay, leave it! You'll be hungry later. We've got to go."

At 7:20 am, she succeeded in getting both girls and their paraphernalia into the car.

"Have you got your seatbelts on?"

"Not yet."

"Yes, but I don't want to go!" Winter kicked the back of the driver's seat in temper.

Karly couldn't take it any more.

"This is ridiculous! If you two can't behave and get ready for school without a fuss every morning, it's the last time we have a pizza and movie night! I mean it! And you won't be going to Mila's party on Saturday."

Realising they'd probably pushed it too far

today, the whining ceased. Winter stopped kicking the seat. Indy put on her seatbelt.

As she had done countless times before, Karly began reversing the car from under the carport.

You know how you catch sight of something and think, *hold on, that shouldn't be there*? Well, Karly suddenly had one of those moments. She stopped the car and focused.

Standing on the dashboard of the car, looking back at her with all of its eight eyes, was the biggest huntsman spider she had ever seen. Full-grown huntsman spiders' bodies are about an inch long, and their leg span is five inches. That's quite a bit bigger than the palm of my hand.

Just for a second, Karly froze. The huntsman started advancing. Karly slammed the brakes on and threw herself out of the car.

"Aaaaagh!" she screamed.

The girls sat up straight, wide-eyed. Oh no! Had they gone too far this morning? Had they driven Mum completely crazy?

Karly has always tried really hard not to pass her own fear of spiders on to her daughters but has never succeeded, just as I probably passed my own fear on to Karly and Shealan when they were young.

"H-h-h-huntsman!" yelled Karly and pointed with a trembling finger.

"Aaaaagh!" yelled Indy and leapt out of the car.

"I can't get my seatbelt off!" howled Winter.

I know what you are thinking: huntsmen spiders are harmless. They have no venom and are not aggressive. They are just *massive* spiders. But if one has arachnophobia, one doesn't listen to reason.

Karly's mind was racing. What now? They were already late. Cam was at work. It was pouring with rain.

"Quick! Open all the doors."

"Shall I prod it with my umbrella?" asked Indy.

"No! It might run and hide in the car!"

"I CAN'T UNDO MY SEATBELT!" yelled Winter, close to hysteria.

The spider stood still.

Karly was formulating a plan.

Cam and Karly's home was built on what Australians call a battle axe block. In real estate, a battle axe block is a block of land situated behind another, with access to the street through a narrow driveway shared by both properties.

Karly figured she had two options. She could either run up the driveway to the main road and flag down a passing car. Or, if she ran further down the lane, she might get help from Pete, their neighbour. He was the man who had shared his bed with LJ and had given him a drink of milk.

"I can't get out!" screamed Winter, and Karly made her decision.

"Indy, I'm going to ask for help from Pete down the lane. I need you to get your sister out of the car, and at the same time, you need to watch that spider! I mean it! You need to know where it is at ALL TIMES! We can't lose it in the car! Do you understand?"

"Yes, but…"

"No buts! I mean it! Watch that spider!"

Indy nodded.

Without shame, Karly grabbed Indy's umbrella and pelted down the lane, leaving her daughter in the rain. She hammered on Pete's door. The door opened to reveal Pete's surprised face.

"Pete! Can you help? Cam's at work, and we have a spider situation!"

"Right! Funnel-web?"

"Um, no. It's a huntsman."

Pete relaxed visibly. "You know they are harmless?"

"Yes, I know! But it's a really big one…"

Maybe Pete understood that Karly was beyond reasoning because he reacted with just the ghost of an eyebrow twitch.

"Right, where is it?"

"In the car, I've left the girls watching it."

"Okay, let's go," said Pete, grabbing a cloth on his way out.

They ran back through the rain to find Winter had exited the car. Both girls were now huddled under Winter's little umbrella, watching the spider from a safe distance.

The huntsman had made himself comfortable. He was settled nicely in the dry, cosy car and was mocking the humans getting drenched.

"Stand back," said Pete, taking charge. "I'm going in."

He lunged forward and dropped the cloth over the spider. Nobody breathed. But he wasn't quick enough. The spider ran along the dashboard.

Simultaneously, Karly, Indy and Winter squeaked and jumped back.

Quickly, Pete tried again, but the huntsman had disappeared.

"Did you get it?" asked Karly.

"I don't know! Did anyone see where it went?"

Nobody had.

"Well, maybe I've got it," said Pete and picked up the cloth, loosely bunched.

Walking backwards, he backed down the drive and shook the cloth near the grass verge. Karly said later that it was at that point that she realised it wasn't just a cloth that Pete was using. It was a pair of his underpants. A rather snazzy pair of boxer shorts.

Even from a safe distance, Karly and the girls heard the soft thud as the huntsman fell out of the underwear and landed on the ground, making all the females squeak again.

"We got the little bugger," said Pete proudly.

"Thank you so much, Pete," said Karly. "You saved the day."

"My pleasure," said Pete, and turned away to head home. "And it's stopped raining."

"Wait! It's coming back!" yelled Indy, pointing.

Karly, Indy and Winter stared, poised for flight. The spider collected itself together and, instead of running into the grassy verge, began to run towards them.

"Aaaaagh!" yelled all three and scarpered.

I don't know if spiders have ears and it heard the shout. Whatever, it suddenly changed direction and began to run down the lane towards Pete's house.

"That's okay," called Pete, as he followed it. "He's welcome to eat all the flies and cockroaches at my place."

The day resumed. Indy was late for Elementary Strings, but it couldn't be helped.

"Well," I said as Karly reached the end of her story. "That's Australia for you. There's an adventure around every corner."

"That's true. I could have done without that huntsman adventure though."

"I'll bet. Thank goodness there was just one. Imagine if there was a plague of them."

"Pardon?"

"Oh, I was just thinking aloud," I said. "You know, we had the drought, then the bushfires, then the floods, and now we have plagues of mice…"

"Mice? Do we?"

"Well, not us, but parts of Australia. They are predicting that mouse numbers always rocket following exceptional rain, particularly after a drought."

"Oh yuk. Poor farmers."

"I know," I said, "and have you been watching the news?"

"Not really, evenings are always pandemonium here getting the girls fed, bathed and put to bed, but I've heard bits on the car radio. You mean about that Chinese virus?"

"Yes, they are calling it Covid-19 now," I said.

"Are you worried about it?"

"No, not really. I'm sure they'll contain it and stop it spreading further."

"I agree. It'll never get into Australia."

"Oh, Mum, I nearly forgot the reason I called you. What date is Grumps home from the UK?"

"On the 3rd March."

"Oh right. We can't wait to see him! It's been such a long time!"

"I know."

"Let me look at the calender. Yes, I thought so. We have a free weekend that week. Doesn't happen often what with kids' parties and stuff! Shall we plan a caravan trip somewhere not too far and meet up?"

"Great idea! I'll get my caravanning book out and find a nice, quiet, scenic caravan park that'll be easy for us both to get to."

"Brilliant! Can't wait!"

I whiled away the hours before Joe would arrive home by searching for a suitable destination for all the family to meet. I found a caravan site at a place called Vineyard, which I guessed would be a lovely rural area for us to explore, and maybe even do some wine tasting.

I suggested it to Karly.

"There's a caravan park at Vineyard. They've

got a jumping pillow for the kids and a pool. I think it'll be easy for you to get to as it'll be after school for you, and it's pretty direct for us, too."

"You got me at the name Vineyard. Book it!"

"Will do. Sounds lovely, doesn't it?"

I wasted no time booking two caravan plots side by side. Then, I began preparing for the holiday, packing Sheila and making sure we had fresh bedding, insect repellant, sunscreen, and all the paraphernalia necessary for a weekend in the countryside.

I couldn't wait! Joe was finally coming back, and we were going to spend a fabulous rural weekend together as a family. All I could think about was Joe's return and our trip.

As planned, on the 3rd of March 2020, Joe's plane landed at Sydney Airport. As soon as he had collected his luggage and passed through Customs, he called me.

"I've arrived."

Lola pricked up her ears and wagged her tail. She recognised his voice, even on the phone.

"Great! How was the journey?"

"That long-haul trip is hard for me, but I'm home now. I'm so looking forward to seeing you."

"Not long now!"

"I'm very tired. I'll need a good long rest. And don't let Lola out of the front door, will you? You know how she catapults out like a bat out of hell, and it's very embarrasi... Wait, there's my driver! I recognise his Hawaiian shirt. Speak later, see you very soon."

And the line went dead.

To be honest, I was a tiny bit worried. I hadn't told Joe about the planned caravan trip to Vineyard in three days. Would he be too tired? And I certainly wasn't going to tell him about the conversation I'd just had with my Aussie friend, Debbie.

"Vineyard? You know there aren't any vineyards there, don't you?"

"Aren't there?"

"No. It's just a suburb. Western Sydney, not really a tourist hotspot."

"Oh."

She was right, of course. I looked it up and discovered that, indeed, there once were vineyards in Vineyard, planted in the 1860s, but the land had long been given over to housing. The nearest vineyards nowadays were a good thirty-minute drive from the suburb.

Never mind.

All worries were banished when I saw the familiar airport shuttle bus round the corner and pull up outside our house.

"Here we are, mate," said the driver.

"Thank you," said Joe, getting out. He looked frail. "Maybe my wife will keep our dog in this time. If she doesn't, I'll bet the bloomin' dog will shoot out like greased lightning."

"He's here!" I squeaked and threw open the front door.

Lola streaked up the drive to the bus and hurled herself at Joe, nearly knocking him over. The driver in his bright Hawaiian shirt roared with laughter, and the bus windows framed the chuckling faces of Joe's fellow passengers.

"No change there then," said the driver, his shoulders shaking with mirth.

"Get down, Lola, for goodness sake! Vicky, I *told* you to keep her in!"

And then I was in his arms.

We both forgot that we had an audience, and that our dog was dancing on her hind legs, barking her head off. Memories of the time apart, the drought, the bushfires and the floods melted away.

Joe was back home.

We didn't hear or see the bus drive away.

SPOOKY SPIDER DEVILLED EGGS

Great for kids as a fun snack and perfect finger food at Halloween.

Ingredients

6 hard-boiled eggs

2 tablespoons mayonnaise

1 teaspoon white sugar, or to taste

1 teaspoon white vinegar

1 teaspoon prepared mustard

½ teaspoon salt, or to taste

A pinch of paprika, or to taste

15-20 black olives

Method

Hard boil the eggs and cut them in half lengthways.

Scoop out the yolks into a bowl and set the whites aside.

Add the mayonnaise, sugar, vinegar, mustard and salt, then mash until smooth.

Spoon the mixture into a small plastic bag and snip off a corner.

Squeeze the yolk mix into the egg white halves.

Sprinkle a small amount of paprika over the top.

Use half an olive for the spider bodies, and thin olive slices for the spider legs.

29

EPILOGUE

After so many months away in the UK, Joe was more than ready to settle back into life in Australia.

"I thought those bushfires would never end," he said. "It was lovely to catch up with everybody there, but I couldn't wait to get back."

We resumed all our usual daily routines: morning coffee on the verandah and a glass of wine in the evening while watching the sunset paint the sky in shades of orange and pink.

"It's been tough for everybody," I said. "Thank goodness it's all over. You're home now and we can forget all about disasters."

We didn't know then that Joe had arrived back in Australia in the nick of time. We didn't know that if he had delayed his return by just a few days, he would have been forced to stay in the UK until further notice.

Unknowingly, he had taken advantage of a two-week window of opportunity after the bushfires to travel before flights were grounded and airports shut down worldwide.

We talked for hours, catching up and filling in all the gaps as we swapped news.

"Are you looking forward to our trip to Vineyard?" I asked. I had confessed that I may have made a mistake with my hasty booking, and that Vineyard may not be the rustic destination I had expected it to be.

"I'll be honest. I'm really looking forward to seeing Cam, Karly and the girls, and I don't really mind what Vineyard is like. But I am worried that I won't be able to cope."

"You'll be fine," I said.

But I had noticed that he seemed thinner, more tired and frail than he had been before his UK visit.

"Are you sure it's just for the weekend? Judging by the amount of stuff you've been carrying backwards and forwards to stash in Sheila, we'll be away for weeks."

"Nope, just the weekend."

Life was back to normal, I thought, as my

EPILOGUE

heart beat with excitement at the thought of the adventures ahead. Joe was home, and I would make sure he ate properly and grew stronger. We were exploring Australia together, just as we had always wanted.

As for the nasty virus that seemed to be spreading from China, well I was quite sure that would be promptly nipped in the bud.

No, there was no way Covid-19 would affect our lives in any way at all.

A REQUEST ...

If you've reached this page, you've probably read the whole of *Fair Dinkum*. I so appreciate your patience in waiting five long years since the last Old Fools release.

And, if you've read *Fair Dinkum*, chances are you've already read all the other six books in the Old Fools series, plus the two prequels. Some of you may even have read *Dear Fran, Love Dulcie*.

Thank you so much! I couldn't be more grateful!

We authors absolutely rely on our readers' reviews. We love them even more than a glass of chilled wine on a summer's night beneath the stars.

Even more than chocolate.

If you enjoyed this book, I'd be so grateful if

you left a review on Amazon, or wherever you bought the book, even if it's simply one sentence.

Amazon link: https://bit.ly/OldFools-Fair-Dinkum

A GIFT TO MY READERS ...

Would you like 10% off entry tickets to my favourite wildlife sanctuary, the Australia Walkabout Wildlife Park?

As a result of mentioning the Walkabout Wildlife Park in this book, I was delighted to be made a partner with a page just for me on the Walkabout website.

https://bit.ly/Walkabout-Park-Victorias-page

Visit it, and you'll get 10% off entry tickets for an absolutely fabulous day out for all ages, getting up close and personal with Australian animals of all kinds.

Be a ranger for the day, sleep in the sanctuary with the animals. Play tug-of-war with Tasmanian devils. Cuddle Happy Feet the emu who thinks he's human. Explore the bush tracks, visit aboriginal sites. So much to do and see!

Walkabout Wildlife Sanctuary
1 Darkinjung Road
cnr Peats Ridge Road
Calga, NSW 2250
Australia

Tel: (02) 4375 1100 Australia
Email: info@walkaboutpark.com.au

SO WHAT HAPPENED NEXT?
TWO OLD FOOLS FIND THEIR TRIBE

An excerpt from the next book in the Old Fools series,
Book 8: Two Old Fools Find Their Tribe

"Did you bring toilet rolls?"

"Yes, of course I did."

It wasn't an idle question. To our astonishment, the world was going crazy and shoppers were buying toilet rolls as fast as the shelves could be stocked. Fights over toilet rolls broke out in supermarkets.

"It was the same in the UK," Joe remarked. He had arrived back in Australia from the UK just a few days before. "It's ridiculous. As far as I know, catching this Covid-19 thing doesn't even mean you will need stacks of toilet paper. It doesn't make sense."

"No sense at all," I agreed.

Our destination was a place named Vineyard, where we planned to meet my daughter Karly, son-in-law Cam and the two grandchildren. They hadn't seen Joe for months because he had been forced to stay in the UK while the bushfires raged in Australia. His lungs couldn't have handled the smoke-laden air.

"I think we're almost there," I said, consulting Google Maps. "And the caravan park is on our right, in about a kilometre."

I had hoped to discover a small village nestled in the heart of rolling hills, exuding timeless charm. I pictured a winding dirt road revealing acres of lush vineyards, their green foliage glistening under the warm sun.

Sadly, that was not the case. Vineyard, in spite of its misleading name, turned out to be a western suburb of Sydney, its streets lined with houses and huge areas of land given over to urbanisation. I remember seeing a few trees dotted about, but there were definitely no acres of vines. It wasn't bad, but it certainly wasn't a rural retreat.

"So this is Vineyard," said Joe.

"Never mind," I said. "We're here to spend time with the family, not gallivant around the countryside. I wonder if they are here yet."

"I'm past gallivanting," said Joe, yawning. "We've arrived. Let's get set up."

He steered us through the caravan site entrance and parked outside the Reception building. I hopped out, but the shutters were down, the door was locked, and nobody was about.

I walked around the car to speak to Joe through the driver's window.

"It's all locked up," I said, "but that's okay. They sent me a plan of the park with our plot marked. And I know the number we have to key in to lift the boom gate. Just follow me slowly."

Joe nodded and I began to walk in front. Dark clouds were gathering in the sky and I hoped it wouldn't rain.

When I reached the yellow box on a pole in front of the boom gate, I checked the sequence again and carefully pressed the string of numbers. When I pressed 'OK', the long, horizontal arm juddered slightly and began to lift.

Joe drove slowly forward just as another car came towards us, exiting the park, using the other boom gate provided for out-going traffic. Maybe this passing car distracted Joe, because he slowed his speed even more, and swerved a little to politely give the oncoming car as much space as possible.

It suddenly dawned on me. Joe had forgotten he was towing Sheila, our caravan.

I looked up, and to my horror, I saw the boom judder above us and begin to descend. Joe had driven the car through safely, but the caravan had not yet passed under the arm.

"No!" I gasped, but there was nothing I could do.

The arm swung down to its horizontal position, narrowly missing the back of the car. Neither did it hit the caravan, ending in a shuddering halt somewhere between.

But we were in big trouble.

When Joe had swerved, he'd sent the caravan's course far too close to the yellow metal box on the pole that housed the numeric keypad.

"Stop," I yelled, but it was too late.

Joe was still driving forward and I heard a sickening crunch.

The yellow box was embedded in Sheila's side window, and the boom was a barrier dividing the car from the caravan.

Joe stuck his head out of the window and looked back. The dying sun caught the shards of broken glass lying on the ground.

"Oh dear," he said. "That wasn't supposed to happen."

This sorry tale continues in the next Old Fools adventure, *Two Old Fools Find Their Tribe*.

If you'd like to keep up with Old Fools' adventures, and be notified when the next book comes out, please join me on Facebook.

And if you are not subscribed already or have fallen off my mailing list, do subscribe to my newsletter on my website. You'll get an email reply from me (with a free book), which you must click to complete the process. I send a newsletter out every few months, and it typically contains news, stories, competitions, photos, free books, book recommendations and a recipe.

Victoria Twead, 2025

THE OLD FOOLS MEMOIRS SERIES

Book #1 **Chickens, Mules and Two Old Fools**
If Joe and Vicky had known what relocating to a tiny Spanish mountain village would REALLY be like, they might have hesitated...

Book #2 **Two Old Fools - Olé!**
Vicky and Joe have finished fixing up their house and look forward to peaceful days enjoying their retirement. Then the fish van arrives, and instead of delivering fresh fish, disgorges the Ufarte family.

Book #3 **Two Old Fools on a Camel**
Reluctantly, Vicky and Joe leave Spain to work for a year in the Middle East. Incredibly, the Arab revolution erupted, throwing them into violent events that made world headlines.

Book #4 **Two Old Fools in Spain Again**
Life refuses to stand still in tiny El Hoyo. Lola Ufarte's behaviour surprises nobody, but when a millionaire becomes a neighbour, the village turns into a battleground.

Book #5 **Two Old Fools in Turmoil**
When dark, sinister clouds loom, Victoria and Joe find themselves facing life-changing decisions. Happily, silver linings also abound. A fresh new face joins the cast of well-known characters but the return of a bad penny may be more than some can handle.

Book #6 **Two Old Fools Down Under**
When Vicky and Joe wave goodbye to their beloved Spanish village, they face their future in Australia with some trepidation. Now they must build a new life amongst strangers, snakes and spiders the size of saucers. Accompanied by their enthusiastic new puppy, Lola, adventures abound, both heartwarming and terrifying.

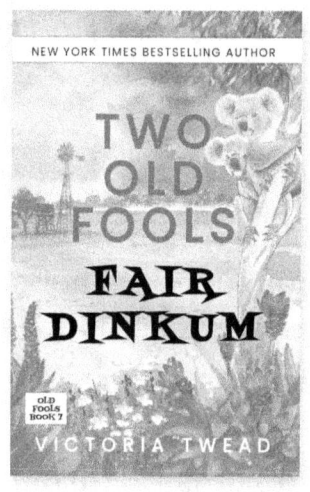

Book #7 **Two Old Fools Fair Dinkum**
Life is good. The grandchildren are thriving despite swallowing magnets and sticking crayons up their noses.
Meanwhile, farmers anxiously watch their fields turn brown as a terrible drought grips Australia. Even worse, bushfire season arrives early, and flames rage across the land.

Will love and laughter be enough to keep the Two Old Fools and their family safe from harm?

One Young Fool in Dorset (PREQUEL)
This light and charming story is the delightful prequel to Victoria Twead's Old Fools series. Her childhood memories are vividly portrayed, leaving the reader chuckling and enjoying a warm sense of comfortable nostalgia.

One Young Fool in South Africa (PREQUEL)
Who is Joe Twead? What happened before Joe met Victoria and they moved to a crazy Spanish mountain village? Joe vividly paints his childhood memories despite constant heckling from Victoria at his elbow.

Introducing The Mrs Arden series for 2 to 5 year olds.

Read-aloud rhyming picture books, packed with animals, laughter, and surprise twists. With bold, cheerful illustrations and playful storylines, these books are perfect for giggles at storytime, bedtime, or anytime.

If you prefer to read paperbacks, and would like to pay lower prices by buying direct, do visit Victoria's own cut-price bookstore.
Books.by/Victoria-Twead

DEAR FRAN, LOVE DULCIE

Life and Death in the Hills and Hollows of Bygone Australia

Dear Fran, Love Dulcie is a true story, a rollercoaster read, with *an unguessable, astonishing ending*. It will inform you, surprise you, reduce you to tears and haunt you forever. I've never quite been the same since Dulcie's life touched mine.

I'm deeply humbled to have been asked to put the story together for the world to enjoy.

"Shocking, yet heart-warming. Overwhelmingly gripping." Beth Haslam, author of the Fat Dogs and French Estates series.

"Wow! Goosebumps." Elizabeth Moore, author of the Someday Travels series and Top 1000 Amazon reviewer.

"A truly remarkable young woman and a unique record of Australian life." Valerie Poore, author of Watery Ways.

"There are no words that can do this book justice." Julie Haigh, Top 1000 Amazon reviewer.

THE SIXPENNY CROSS SERIES
SHORT FICTION, INSPIRED BY LIFE

A is for Abigail
Abigail Martin has everything: beauty, money, a loving husband, and a fabulous house in the village of Sixpenny Cross. But Abigail is denied the one thing she craves... A baby.

B is for Bella
When two babies are born within weeks of each other in the village of Sixpenny Cross, one would expect the pair to become friends as they grow up. But nothing could be further from the truth.

C is for the Captain

Everyone knows ageing bachelors, the Captain and Sixpence, are inseparable. But when new barmaid, Babs, begins work at the Dew Drop Inn, will she enhance their twilight years, or will the consequences be catastrophic?

Subscribe to the Old Fools Updates for advance news, free books and recipes. https://www.victoriatwead.com/free-stuff/

THE STILLWATER MURDERS BY VICTORIA TWEAD
DEAD OF NIGHT SERIES BOOK 1

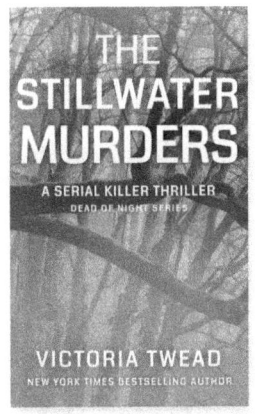

THE STILLWATER MURDERS

Stillwater Cove is a town built on quiet.

When a string of unexplained deaths shatters the calm of Stillwater Cove, detective Lara Lennox is sent from Sydney to investigate. Each victim is found carefully posed, a small paper star left behind.

The Stillwater Murders (Chapter 1)

This is my time.
I am calm, but ready, prepared.
The dead of night, when the world exhales and falls utterly still. When darkness gathers like a velvet tide, drawn quietly over the earth. The sky becomes an ink-

deep ocean without horizon or seam. A place where the stars seem to hesitate before shining. Even the gulls tuck their heads beneath their wings and stay quiet, surrendering to the dark.

There is a moment just before dawn, when the world forgets to breathe. The sea holds still. The reeds stop whispering.

I wait for that moment.

It is the best time a person can cross from this life to the next without struggle. Without fear. Without the burden of the weight of the world pressing in behind their ribs.

The old woman couldn't sleep. She sits on her veranda swing, wrapped in a faded, knitted shawl.

Her eyes are closed, her hair silvered by the moon.

I've been watching her. She didn't see me. I heard her trying to hum a tune she no longer remembered.

Her voice trembled.

Her hands trembled.

Her soul trembled.

But not now.

Now she is still. Perfectly still. Her heart no longer beats.

Now she is beautiful in her quietness.

I kneel beside her, careful not to disturb the blanket tucked around her knees. A faint night breeze lifts a strand of hair from her cheek, and I smooth it gently back into place.

Warm. Soft.

She earned this.

She carried her burden for so long that the weight bent her shoulders. No one noticed how tired she had become.

But I noticed.

I always notice.

There is no fear in her face. Only the softness and peace that comes when the world finally releases you, lets you go.

I take the small, red paper star from my pocket.

It is imperfect. Torn by my fingers. A little crooked at the edges. The first star I ever made was for her, the woman who taught me how to say goodbye.

I place it gently under the old woman's hand, letting it rest on the shawl.

I breathe in.

A new beginning always starts with a quiet ending.

I stay with her until the light begins to rise behind the drowned forest.

Until the world remembers to breathe again.

Then I stand.

Gently close her eyes.

And leave her to her peace.

No one should die alone.

Amazon Link: https://bit.ly/Stillwater-Murders

REVIEWS

"I'm going: 'Nooooo! Don't go out, lock your door, don't let anyone in!' If this was TV I would be shouting at the screen."

"Totally wowed with it!"

"A brilliant edge-of-your-seat read."

"Totally and utterly gripping. I got nothing done while reading this."

THE BONE GARDEN BY VICTORIA TWEAD
DEAD OF NIGHT SERIES BOOK 2

THE BONE GARDEN

Some patterns should never be completed.

Bodies are turning up, posed with impossible care, surrounded by spirals built from bleached bones.

Detective Senior Constable Lara Lennox expects a straightforward hunt. Instead, she finds a killer who seems to know her team's next move before they do.

The Bone Garden (Chapter 1)

The bucket of bones stood waiting. He inhaled, controlling his excitement. Allowed his hand to dip in. Eager, trembling fingers gripped the first bone. He drew it out.

Not too long, not too short. Good. Almost silky to the touch.

He fumbled and it slipped from his fingers and disappeared into the dark soil.

He hissed with annoyance, crouching to find it again by touch, feeling for its smooth curve. The lantern at his feet threw a shallow circle of light, not quite reaching the treeline. Beyond that, the night pressed in: a black wall of trunks and wet leaves and insect sound.

"Focus," he murmured.

His breath ghosted white in the cool air. He found the bone at last, pinched it between thumb and forefinger, and set it in place.

Now he worked steadily, almost oblivious to the night sounds and the woman's motionless body.

The last bone completed the curve of the spiral, almost perfect now. He studied it critically, head tilted, then nudged one of the vertebrae a fraction to the left.

Much better.

The line flowed again.

The woman in the centre of the pattern didn't move. She would never move again. Never breathe, blink, smile or speak.

He kept an eye on her anyway. The lantern's light softened the harshness of her features, turned them almost peaceful. Straw-coloured hair spilled across the flattened grass like fluid, poured. One of her hands lay palm-up beside her head, dead fingers curled. He tried to uncurl them, arrange them more neatly.

He stepped back, heels sinking slightly into the mulch. His boots made no sound. The small clearing was quiet now.

"This one is important," he told the corpse on the ground. "The first impression matters. You understand."

She did not answer, of course. They never did, not at this stage. That was all right. He wasn't really speaking to her anyway.

He moved around the spiral, placing the last few bones from the bucket. They were small ones, birdlike, scavenged months ago and saved for this. He had cleaned them himself, boiled and bleached and dried, his kitchen thick with the smell for days.

The last bone fell into place with a tiny, satisfying click against its neighbours. The spiral was complete. A pale, graceful swirl encircling the woman's body, curling inward as if to claim her.

He stepped back until his shoulder brushed the rough bark of a tree. From this distance, the whole design came together. The body was the centre point, the axis. The spiral drew the eye straight to her pale, dead face.

He felt a thrill rise, sharp as cold water. It was so… Right.

Better than the practice layouts in his cottage, better than the chalk mock-ups on the concrete floor. Better than the rehearsals in dense bushland where human feet rarely trod.

Those had been exercises.

This was the *real thing*.

ABOUT THE AUTHOR

Victoria Twead is the New York Times bestselling author of *Chickens, Mules and Two Old Fools* and the subsequent books in the Old Fools series. She is also the founder of Ant Press and the popular Facebook group, We Love Memoirs.

After living in a remote mountain village in Spain for twelve years, and owning probably the most dangerous cockerel in Europe, Victoria and Joe retired to Australia to watch their new grandchildren thrive amongst kangaroos and koalas.

For photographs and additional unpublished material to accompany this book, download the Free Photo Book from www.victoriatwead.com/free-stuff

CONTACTS AND LINKS
CONNECT WITH VICTORIA

Email: TopHen@VictoriaTwead.com (emails welcome)
Website: www.VictoriaTwead.com
Old Fools' Updates Signup: www.VictoriaTwead.com
This includes the latest Old Fools' news, free books, book recommendations, and recipe. Guaranteed spam-free and sent out every few months.
Free Stuff: http://www.victoriatwead.com/Free-Stuff/
Facebook: https://www.facebook.com/VictoriaTwead (friend requests welcome)
Instagram: @victoria.twead
Twitter: @VictoriaTwead
Publish with Ant Press: www.antpress.org
Victoria's Cut-Price Paperback Bookstore: Books.by/Victoria-Twead

We Love Memoirs

Join me and other memoir authors and readers in the We Love Memoirs Facebook group, the friendliest group on Facebook.

www.facebook.com/groups/welovememoirs/

VICTORIA'S BOOKSTORE

If you prefer to read paperbacks, and would like to pay lower prices by buying direct, do visit Victoria's own cut-price bookstore.

Bookstore Link: Books.by/Victoria-Twead

MORE ANT PRESS MEMOIRS
AWESOME AUTHORS
~ AWESOME BOOKS

If you enjoyed this book, you may also enjoy these other Ant Press memoir authors. All titles are available in ebook, paperback, hardback and large print editions from **Amazon**.

These two booksellers offer FREE delivery worldwide.
Blackwells.co.uk and Wordery.com
More Stores
Waterstones (Europe delivery), Booktopia (Australia), Barnes & Noble (USA), and all good bookstores.

VICTORIA TWEAD
New York Times bestselling author
The Old Fools series

1. Chickens, Mules and Two Old Fools
2. Two Old Fools ~ Olé!
3. Two Old Fools on a Camel

4. Two Old Fools in Spain Again
5. Two Old Fools in Turmoil
6. Two Old Fools Down Under
7. Two Old Fools Fair Dinkum
8. Two Old Fools Find their Tribe
One Young Fool in Dorset (Prequel)
One Young Fool in South Africa (Prequel)

Dear Fran, Love Dulcie: Life and Death in the Hills and Hollows of Bygone Australia

BETH HASLAM
The Fat Dogs series

Fat Dogs and French Estates ~ Part I
Fat Dogs and French Estates ~ Part II
Fat Dogs and French Estates ~ Part III
Fat Dogs and French Estates ~ Part IV
Fat Dogs and French Estates ~ Part V
Fat Dogs and French Estates ~ Part VI
Fat Dogs and Welsh Estates ~ The Prequel

DIANE ELLIOTT
Lady Goatherder series

Butting Heads in Spain: Lady Goatherder 1
El Maestro: Lady Goatherder 2

EJ BAUER
The Someday Travels series

1. From Moulin Rouge to Gaudi's City
2. From Gaudi's City to Granada's Red Palace's City to Granada's Red Palace
3. From an Umbrian Farmhouse to Como's Quiet Shores

For more information about stockists, Ant Press titles or how to publish with Ant Press, please visit our website or contact us by email.

WEBSITE: www.antpress.org

EMAIL: admin@antpress.org

FACEBOOK: https://www.facebook.com/AntPress/

INSTAGRAM: https://instagram.com/publishwithantpress

www.ingramcontent.com/pod-product-compliance
Lightning Source LLC
Chambersburg PA
CBHW070455120526
44590CB00013B/653